**FOURTH EDITION**

# The ID CaseBook

## Case Studies in Instructional Design

**Peggy A. Ertmer**
Purdue University

**James A. Quinn**
Oakland University

**Krista D. Glazewski**
Indiana University

## PEARSON

Boston  Columbus  Indianapolis  New York  San Francisco  Upper Saddle River
Amsterdam  Cape Town  Dubai  London  Madrid  Milan  Munich  Paris  Montreal  Toronto
Delhi  Mexico City  São Paulo  Sydney  Hong Kong  Seoul  Singapore  Taipei  Tokyo

**Vice President, Editorial Director:** Jeffery W. Johnston
**Executive Editor:** Linda Ashe Bishop
**Senior Marketing Manager:** Darcy Betts
**Project Manager:** Maggie Brobeck
**Manager, Central Design:** Jayne Conte
**Cover Designer:** Suzanne Behnke

**Cover Art:** Abstractus Designus/Fotolia
**Full-Service Project Management
and Composition:** Munesh Kumar, Aptara®, Inc.
**Printer/Binder:** Courier/Westford
**Cover Printer:** Courier/Westford
**Text Font:** 10/12 Times LT Std

**Library of Congress Cataloging-in-Publication Data**

Ertmer, Peggy A.
    The ID casebook : case studies in instructional design / Peggy A. Ertmer, Purdue University, James A. Quinn, Oakland University, Krista D. Glazewski, Indiana University.—Fourth edition.
        pages cm
    ISBN-13: 978-0-13-325825-7
    ISBN-10: 0-13-325825-4
    1. Instructional systems—Design—Case studies.   I. Quinn, James A.   II. Glazewski, Krista D.
III.  Title.
    LB1028.38.E78 2014
    371.3—dc23
                                                                    2013004232

10 9 8 7 6 5 4 3 2 1

**PEARSON**

ISBN 10:  0-13-325825-4
ISBN 13:  978-0-13-325825-7

To Dave: This one's for you!
PE

To MJJ: Thanks for driving the getaway car.
JQ

To CM, NM, and RM, all my best fellas.
KG

And a collective acknowledgement to David Jonassen,
whose legacy is imprinted in this text.
PE, JQ, and KG

# Contents

## Case Studies
## Section 2: Post-secondary Audience/Context 81

# Foreword

I doubt that many instructional design and technology faculty would argue with the notion that the preparation of instructional design (ID) professionals is no easy task. The skill set required to be successful at ID is extensive and complex, mandating not only conceptual knowledge of the design process, but also procedural knowledge of how to go about executing the process in a variety of contexts and for an endless array of clientele. Designers must demonstrate analytical skills to determine the learning and/or performance need and understand how to select and develop an intervention to address that need in a way that is culturally and contextually appropriate. The skills needed for this level of analysis and subsequent solution planning and creation cannot be developed simply from learning about the principles of instructional design. To truly learn the ID process and be able to apply the conceptual, procedural, and analytical skills in an effective way necessitates learner engagement in authentic practice with appropriate feedback. Although these ideas are reflective of the basic principles of ID, they are not so easy to carry out in the context of the typical ID course. Within the constraints of the semester, students may have the good fortune to work on a single project for a real client, but to gain the kinds of problem-solving skills and design competencies needed for broad application, such limited experience is not adequate. In this fourth edition of the *ID CaseBook*, Ertmer, Quinn, and Glazewski provide an important contribution toward the preparation of ID professionals, because their work supports this significant need for learners to apply newly learned skills and knowledge to solve real-world ID problems. One of the aspects of the *ID CaseBook* that I find most impressive is the comprehensive manner in which it serves its various stakeholders—students, instructors, and the instructional design and technology (ID&T) community.

For the learner, the *ID CaseBook* offers the chance to apply what seems in early, introductory classroom experiences to be a straightforward and logical process to the sometimes messy and ill-structured challenge of addressing instructional needs. As noted in the text, the practice of ID is a problem-solving process, filled with decisions that are best informed by what we know about how people learn. Also, as learners begin to delve into the ID process, they benefit by encountering the many logistical issues posed by developing solutions for the targeted learning environment, as well as the wide variety of learner groups with differing characteristics, prior knowledge, experiences, and belief systems whom they seek to assist. Learners of ID would also be well served by confronting the project management process that underpins the development of ID solutions, and all of the details and often-unpredictable stumbling blocks that can throw a wrench in even the best project plans. By engaging in the ID process within the scenarios included in the *ID CaseBook*, students are placed at the center of all of these issues, supporting the development of their own expertise in a way that will transfer more readily to the workplace, no matter the context.

For the instructor, the *ID CaseBook* provides an ID teaching framework that promotes a deeper level of learning than is possible with a more didactic approach. Although the cases included in the fourth edition are sufficiently open-ended to encourage multiple solutions, the guidance provided on using cases for learning is helpful to the instructor (as well as the student) who may be new to using this approach. The use of cases and all of their inherent dilemmas can seem daunting from a teaching perspective; however, the authors have done a terrific job, providing specific strategies for how to incorporate the use of cases into the context of the ID course. In addition, the compendium included in the ID *CaseBook* exemplifies a great breadth of learning outcomes, content types, intended audiences, and targeted environments that will enhance the instructor's ability to provide a pragmatic and comprehensive learning experience. Instructors will also appreciate the discussion questions provided with each case, as they can help center the discussion around key issues. Through the organization of the text and the thoughtful ancillary materials, the authors have created an effective "performance support system" for instructors who wish to utilize the case-based approach to teaching ID.

For the instructional design and technology community, the *ID CaseBook* serves as an exemplar of empirically grounded, student-centered learning. The power of case-based instruction has been demonstrated through extensive research, as is also reflected in the prior and current work of these authors. Ertmer, Quinn, and Glazewski have produced another significant contribution toward the advancement of the ID&T profession, one that is based on sound theory and long-standing evidence of effective instructional design. We are fortunate to be able to benefit from their ongoing work in this area and thank them for helping us prepare the next generation of instructional designers.

Barbara B. Lockee
*Past President, Association for Educational Communications and Technology*
*Professor and Associate Director, School of Education, Virginia Tech*

# Preface

Education within the professions isn't always as effective as we would like. Within a number of professions, including instructional design (ID), educators often report that their graduates are unable to apply what they've learned in school to the solution of authentic problems in practice. The consistent theme in these reports is the "inert knowledge problem" (Bransford, 1993, p. 174, paraphrasing Whitehead), which refers to graduates who have acquired domain knowledge but who are not adept at applying their knowledge to the solution of common problems in the discipline (Stepich & Ertmer, 2010).

Instructional design educators have recognized this problem for a long time and have worked to integrate the development of practical skills with conceptual knowledge in a variety of ways. For example, Quinn (1994) and Woolf and Quinn (2009) reported on an approach to learning and teaching ID in which small teams of students worked under the supervision of an instructor to design instruction for a real client. Rowland, Parra, and Basnet (1995) created a "design studio" (p. 231) in which students worked collaboratively to solve ID problems that gradually increased in complexity. Jonassen and Hernandez-Serrano (2002) provided students with stories that had been elicited from experienced instructional designers as a way to help them gain "conditionalized" knowledge (Bransford et al., 2000, p. 43).

In each of these examples, students were asked to apply their emerging knowledge of instructional design within the context of "real-world" situations, with their inherent messiness left intact. This allowed students to develop their technical skills while working on realistic, complex problems.

Similar to these examples, the case teaching approach used in this book enables ID educators to contextualize their students' mastery of ID skills by conveying the complexity and ill-structured nature of ID. In addition to the technical skills and knowledge needed to solve these problems of practice, students also gain the skillfulness needed to operate creatively and effectively in ambiguous, uncertain, and open-ended contexts. Case-based teaching and learning encourages students to focus on issues in addition to specific ID tasks and allows them to explore, in depth, the range of problems occurring within a given situation. In addition, case-based learning enables students to experience multiple, varied problem situations to a much greater extent than would be possible through a single internship or practicum experience. This, then, allows students to continually reflect on their emerging knowledge as they examine ID issues within a broad range of settings.

## What Is a Case Study?

Wasserman described a case study as a "darn good story" (1994, p. 44). According to Barnes, Christensen, and Hansen (1994), a case study presents students with a "partial, historical, clinical study of a situation which has confronted a practicing administrator or managerial group" (p. 44) and asks them to provide solutions to the problems presented in the situation through analysis, reflection, and discussion. In this text, we use an approach to case studies that is based on the business school model—that is, case studies are problem-centered descriptions of design situations, developed from the actual experiences of instructional designers.

The cases in this book are designed to be dilemma oriented: each case ends before the solution is clear. Students are expected to evaluate the available evidence, to make reasonable assumptions as necessary, to judge alternative interpretations and actions, and, in doing so, to experience the uncertainty that commonly accompanies design decisions. In particular, we hope that by analyzing the cases presented in this book, students will learn how to identify ID problems and subproblems; to recognize the importance of context in resolving such problems; and to develop, justify, and test alternative plans for resolving ID problems.

## Organization

*The ID CaseBook* is divided into two parts. In Part I, "The Case-Learning Process: Strategies and Reflections," we provide students with suggestions and strategies for how to approach learning from case studies. Although students are typically excited about using cases in their ID courses, they often are apprehensive as well, probably because they are unfamiliar with this approach. We have found that providing helpful suggestions up front can considerably lessen students' initial concerns.

Part II includes 30 case studies situated in a variety of educational and business contexts. Case titles are categorized by audience/context. In addition, the matrix (included at the end of this preface) allows readers to see, at a glance, the variety of content areas addressed by the cases. This matrix helps instructors, particularly, select cases that are most appropriate to their students' needs. (Note: The Instructor's Resource Manual provides additional information about the issues and subissues addressed in each case.)

## New to This Edition

- The fourth edition of *The ID CaseBook* consists of 30 instructional design case studies, including 10 new cases as well as 20 of your favorite cases from the previous editions.
- In general, the new cases in the book are longer and more complex than many of the earlier cases, and include more case details, artifacts, and dialogue.
- Together, the new and "returning" cases provide students with wonderful opportunities to examine a variety of demanding situations involving a wide range of contents, contexts, and audiences.
- Several new cases are situated in international contexts and deal with diverse audiences (e.g., nursing students, English language learners, health care workers, and teenage driver education students).
- We have also increased the number of cases dealing with issues related to game-based learning, Web 2.0 tools, and the design and evaluation of online instruction.

As in the previous three editions, each case consists of a case narrative and a set of questions designed to invoke ID practice. The *case narrative* includes relevant background information for the case, such as the problem context, key players, available resources, and existing constraints. In addition, each case includes *relevant data* presented in a variety of forms and formats. There are two sets of discussion questions at the end of each case to stimulate students' thinking and to provide a focus for class discussion. The first set of questions—*Preliminary Analysis Questions*—asks students to identify and discuss issues from the case, to consider the issues from multiple perspectives, to develop a plan of action to resolve problems, and/or to specify possible consequences resulting from their recommended plans. The second set of questions—*Implications for ID Practice*—requires students to think more broadly about the issues presented in the case from the point of view of ID theory and practice.

As was true for the third edition, we've made it easy for instructors to identify and select relevant cases for their students. For example, each case title includes a subtitle that reflects the content of the case or the context in which it occurs. Sometimes these subtitles also provide information about the specific issues in the cases without giving away any of the more subtle details.

Perhaps even more helpful to instructors than the addition of case subtitles, however, is the organization of the text. Cases are combined into sections, with each section representing the specific context in which that group of cases occurs. For example, the first section of the text contains 7 cases that are situated in K–12 environments, followed by a section containing 11 post-secondary cases. The final section includes 12 cases situated in a corporate or manufacturing environment. This organization helps instructors identify which cases are most relevant to their needs. As noted earlier, a matrix pulls all of this information together, making it easy for instructors to determine which cases are appropriate for their students. Finally, we have expanded Part I, "The Case-Learning Process: Strategies and Reflections," to introduce readers to learning from cases using case-based reasoning and to provide guidance on selecting strategies for completing case analyses.

Instructors will be pleased to know that all cases, including those that appeared in the previous edition but are no longer included in the fourth edition, can be accessed through Pearson's Custom Library. This site enables instructors (and students) to order only the specific cases they would like to use in their courses. This will be particularly helpful to those who use a limited number of cases and don't typically require their students to purchase the book.

# Ancillaries

The *Instructor's Resource Manual* for this book is available in a downloadable, digital format at the Instructor's Resource Center (IRC) at www.pearsonhigher.com. If you have any questions regarding access the IRC, please contact your local Pearson sales representative.

The *Instructor's Resource Manual* includes learning objectives, background information, and additional references for each case. Specifically, the IRM presents:

- *Case Matrix:* A summary matrix, similar to that located at the end of the preface, but with two additional columns that allow instructors to see, at a glance, the particular issues and subissues of each case

- *Teaching Suggestions:* Ideas for instructors regarding the different ways the cases can be used with different levels of students
- *Case Overview:* A brief description of the case, including the "big idea" students should glean from the case
- *Case Objectives:* The specific focus of the case (the supporting concepts/principles learners should use in analyzing the case issues); the knowledge, skills, and/or attitudes students should gain from their case analyses and discussions
- *Debriefing Guidelines:* Suggestions from the case authors regarding how to think about the case

It is our hope that the combined features of *The ID CaseBook* and the Instructor's Resource Manual provide both students and instructors with a challenging and rewarding learning experience. If you or your students have suggestions for future editions, we'd love to hear from you! Our e-mail addresses are pertmer@purdue.edu, quinn@oakland.edu, and glaze@indiana.edu.

# Acknowledgments

Throughout this endeavor we have benefited from the support, advice, and encouragement of a number of individuals, including the contributing authors, supportive colleagues, patient family members, insightful students, two supportive editors, and thoughtful reviewers. Without the contributions of all of these people, this book would not have been possible.

First, we thank all the authors who contributed to this volume. We have enjoyed working with all of them, for they have made our work interesting and enjoyable. We firmly believe that each author has added something unique to the text and sincerely appreciate the time they all gave to develop and revise their cases. For your information, we have provided a brief biography of each author in the "About the Authors" section.

Our current and past students continue to be influential in shaping many of the details of the text, particularly in making suggestions for how to think about the case-learning process. We are also grateful to our colleagues who were willing to pilot the cases in their courses and to provide valuable formative feedback that improved numerous aspects of the cases.

In addition, we thank our editors, Kelly Villella Canton and Linda Bishop, and the production staff at Pearson and Aptara®, Inc. Kelly and Linda and their teams have enthusiastically supported us in our efforts to produce what we hope will be an excellent and useful fourth edition. We were also assisted in the design and development process by the insights and suggestions from a number of reviewers, including Christine Fleming, Regis University; Feng-Qi Lai, Indiana State University, Bayh College of Education; Molly M. Lane, Cappella University; Richard D. Phillips, Delaware State University; and Consuelo Waight, University of Houston.

# References

Barnes, L. B., Christensen, C. R., & Hansen, A. J. (1994). *Teaching and the case method: Text, cases, and readings*. Boston: Harvard Business School Press.

Bransford, J. D. (1993). Who ya gonna call? Thoughts about teaching problem solving. In P. Hallingen, K. Leithwood, & J. Murphy (Eds.), *Cognitive perspectives on educational leadership* (pp. 171–191). New York: Teachers College Press.

Bransford, J. D., Brown, A. L., & Cocking, R. R. (Eds.) (2000). *How people learn: Brain, mind, experience, and school*. Washington, DC: National Academies Press.

Jonassen, D. H., & Hernandez-Serrano, J. (2002). Case-based reasoning and instructional design: Using stories to support problem solving. *Educational Technology Research and Development, 50*(2), 65–77.

Quinn, J. (1994). Connecting education and practice in an instructional design graduate program. *Educational Technology Research and Development, 42*(3), 71–82.

Rowland, G., Parra, M. L., & Basnet, K. (1995). Educating instructional designers: Different methods for different outcomes. In B. B. Seels (Ed.), *Instructional design fundamentals: A reconsideration* (pp. 223–236). Englewood Cliffs, NJ: Educational Technology Publications.

Stepich, D. A., & Ertmer, P. A. (2010). "Teaching" instructional design expertise: Strategies to support students' problem-finding skills. *Technology, Instruction, Cognition, and Learning, 7*, 147–170.

Wasserman, S. 1994. *Introduction to case method teaching: A guide to the galaxy*. New York: Teachers College Press.

Woolf, N., & Quinn, J. (2009). Learners' perceptions of instructional design practice in a situated learning activity. *Educational Technology Research and Development, 57*(1), 25–43.

# Case Matrix

## K–12 CONTEXT

| Title | Subtitle | Content | Audience/Context |
|---|---|---|---|
| 1. Scott Allen | Designing Learning Objects for Primary Learners | Constructivist and simulated learning environments | K–12 Australian learners |
| 2. Michael Bishop | Implementing Gaming Technologies in Traditional K–12 Contexts | Middle School Science (genetics) | K–12 teachers |
| 3. Denny Clifford | Designing Learning Experiences for Middle School Science Teachers | Science teaching | Middle school teachers |
| 4. Paul Lindley | Developing a Video Game for History Education | Internment of Japanese-Americans during World War II | Alternative high school students |
| 5. Sandra Sanchez and Vincent Peters | Helping a School Prepare for a New Mandate | Common Core Standards | K–12 teachers |
| 6. Tina Sears | Evaluating the Impact of a K–12 Laptop Program | Technology integration and impact | Fifth-grade teachers |
| 7. Maya Thomas | Implementing New Instructional Approaches in a K–12 Setting | Pre-algebra for at-risk students | Seventh-grade learners |
| 8. Jackie Adams | Evaluating a Federally Funded Faculty Training Program | Faculty development for technical educators | University and high school teachers |
| 9. Jennie Davenport and Pedro Lopez | Converting a Powerful Workshop to an Online Format | HIV/AIDS prevention | Adult gay and bisexual men |
| 10. John Falkin | Designing an Online Graduate Seminar | Graduate social work education | Social work faculty |
| 11. Malcolm Gibson | Designing Authentic Online Experiences for Adult Learners | Computer science | Professional certification |
| 12. Helen Ginn | Evaluating a New Driver Training Program for Teenagers | Converting content from face-to-face to online settings | Drivers' training for high school students |
| 13. Lindsey Jenkins | Piloting Case-based Learning in a Blended Learning Nursing Curriculum | Undergraduate nursing courses | Nursing school faculty |
| 14. Mark Jones and Sue Gulick | Meeting Challenges in the Design and Delivery of a University-wide First-year Experience Course | First-year experience program | First-year university students |
| 15. Pat Kelsoe and Jean Fallon | Implementing Innovation within an Established Curriculum | Pediatrics education | Medical school |
| 16. Beth Owens | Addressing Multiple Perspectives and Constraints in ID Practice | Culinary arts program | Professional education |

**K–12 CONTEXT** (*Continued*)

| Title | Subtitle | Content | Audience/Context |
| --- | --- | --- | --- |
| 17. Camille Suarez | Redesigning Curriculum for Hybrid Training in a Public Health Setting | Elder home safety | Outreach social workers Elder citizens public health setting |
| 18. Frank Tawl and Semra Senbetto | Designing Curriculum for Southeast Asian Trainers | ID training | Asian Training Institute ID consulting |
| 19. Abby Carlin | Documenting Processes in a Manufacturing Setting | Equipment operation | Manufacturing |
| 20. Iris Daniels | Cross-Cultural Challenges in Designing Instruction | CBT for manufacturing management software | International corporate consortium |
| 21. Lynn Dixon | Designing an Interactive Kiosk to Celebrate World Wetlands Day | Wetlands | Visitors to aquarium |
| 22. Craig Gregersen | Balancing a Range of Stakeholder Interests When Designing Instruction | Product liability training | Corporate ID consulting |
| 23. Scott Hunter | Developing Online Assessment in an International Setting | Sales consultant certification | Automobile industry |
| 24. Margaret Janson | Developing Learning Objects for Adult Learners | Incorporating interactivity into learning objects | Oil exploration industry |
| 25. David Jimenez | Performance Improvement of Engineers | Oil drilling software | Natural gas industry ID consulting |
| 26. Davey Jones | Designing an Electronic Performance Support System | Retail support tool | Retail |
| 27. Diane King | Rapid Design Approach to Designing Instruction | Team leader training | Corporate ID consulting |
| 28. Natalie Morales | Managing Training in a Manufacturing Setting | On-the-job training and certification | Manufacturing |
| 29. Andrew Stewart | Managing Consulting Activities in an Evaluation Context | Transportation training | Corporate ID consulting |
| 30. Jack Waterkamp | Managing Scope Change in an Instructional Design Project | Software development training | System administrators, software trainers |

# About the Authors

*Peggy A. Ertmer* is Professor of Learning Design and Technology at Purdue University. She continues to love teaching with case studies and is finding more and more connections between case-based learning and the development of ID expertise. Peg actively mentors both students and peers, including pre- and in-service teachers, in the use of case-based and problem-based learning (PBL) pedagogy, online teaching and learning, and self-regulated learning skills.

*James A. Quinn* is Associate Professor of Education at Oakland University, where he teaches courses in instructional design. He continues to enjoy teaching with cases and grappling with the considerable challenges of doing so. Jim is very happy that the *ID CaseBook* has reached its 15-year milestone and hopes that it continues to be a resource for ID students and instructors for many more years.

*Krista D. Glazewski* is Associate Professor of Instructional Systems Technology at Indiana University. Her research interests include supporting complex problem solving in problem-based learning. She works most predominantly with K–12 teachers, supporting them as they transition their instructional approaches and their students to more open-ended environments.

## Contributors

*Sue Bennett* is Associate Professor in the University of Wollongong's Faculty of Education with 20 years of experience designing technology-based projects for school and university education and for industry training. Sue's research investigates how people engage with technology in their everyday lives and in educational settings, and she has a particular interest in design thinking.

*M. J. Bishop* is Associate Professor in Lehigh University's Teaching, Learning, and Technology Program. Her teaching and research interests include examining how various instructional media and delivery systems might be designed and used more effectively to improve learning. She has also explored ways that instructional technologies might be employed to facilitate students' academic and social transition from high school to college.

*Laurie Brantley-Dias* is Associate Professor of Learning Technologies at Georgia State University. Her current scholarship and teaching focuses on examining teachers' knowledge for technology integration, designing web-enhanced instruction for K–12 audiences, and using video-based reflection for teachers' professional development. She has worked as an instructional designer, trainer, and/ or consultant for K–12, corporate, and higher education clients.

*Katherine S. Cennamo* is Professor of Learning Sciences and Technologies at Virginia Tech. With over 30 years of experience in designing instructional products, her work focuses on the nature of design practice and how to best prepare instructional designers for professional practice. She is co-author of the textbooks *Real World Instructional Design* and *Technology Integration for Meaningful Classroom Use*.

*Theresa A. Cullen* is Associate Professor in Instructional Psychology and Technology at the University of Oklahoma, where she coordinates the undergraduate technology integration courses. Her research interests include girls' interest in STEM careers and how pre-service teachers use social networks to prepare for their future classrooms.

*Melissa J. Dark* is a Professor in Computer and Information Technology. Dr. Dark has worked on several science, math, engineering, and technology curriculum and instruction projects with business and industry, government, and higher education. She has extensive experience in needs assessment, instructional design, development, and evaluation of STEM education programs and initiatives.

*Walter Dick* is Professor Emeritus of Instructional Systems at Florida State University. His major interests are instructional design and evaluation. He is the co-author of the widely used text *The Systematic Design of Instruction*. Walter lives with his wife in Pennsylvania and Alabama.

*Aaron Doering* is Associate Professor and Co-Director of the Learning Technologies Media Lab at the University of Minnesota where he designs, develops, and researches numerous forms of technology that support teaching and learning.

*Stephen Dundis* is Associate Professor Emeritus in the Human Resource Development Program at Northeastern Illinois University. He has taught courses in instructional design, needs assessment, and computer-based instruction at both the graduate and undergraduate level. His research interests include design issues in online learning/support, virtual collaboration and problem-solving, and case- and apprenticeship-based instructional strategies.

*Joanna C. Dunlap* is Associate Professor and Assistant Director for Teaching Effectiveness at the University of Colorado Denver. Joni's interests focus on the use of sociocultural approaches to enhance learners' development and experience in postsecondary settings. Recently, her work has revolved around online education, specifically social presence, student engagement, and social media and networking tools to support learning.

*Gary Elsbernd* lives in Topeka, Kansas, with his wife and three children. With more than 20 years of experience in the field of performance technology, Gary holds a patent on methods around electronic performance support systems. Gary is the lead web and mobile user experience architect for a leading insurance company in Kansas City, Missouri.

*Xun Ge* is Associate Professor in the Department of Educational Psychology, College of Education at the University of Oklahoma. Her primary research involves designing effective instructional scaffolds, tools, and open learning environments to support students' reasoning, ill-structured problem-solving, and self-regulated learning. She has collaborated extensively in research projects with faculty from various domains, including health sciences and engineering.

*Michael M. Grant* is Associate Professor in the Instructional Design and Technology program at the University of Memphis. His research considers how to best help K–12 teachers and university faculty integrate technology, as well as how students represent their learning with technology. Most recently, his research, service, and consulting has focused on teaching and learning with mobile computing devices.

*Allison Gulati* is Associate Dean of Students and Director of Strategic Initiatives at Lehigh University. In her role, she works with student life departments including First Year Experience, Residence Life, Leadership Development, Student Activities, and Community Service. Her areas of interest include organizational leadership development and planning and developing new co-curricular strategies for advancing college student learning.

*Barry Harper* is the University of Wollongong Program Dean in Malaysia. He was previously the Dean of the Faculty of Education, Director of the Educational Media Laboratory, and leader of the Intelligent Environments research group for the Smart Internet Technology Centre. His research focuses on the theory, design, development, implementation, and evaluation of technology-supported learning environments.

*Ronni Hendel-Giller* is a seasoned learning and development professional, who currently serves as Vice President of Client Services for Maritz Learning. She has extensive experience in the design, development, and delivery of training and organizational development initiatives across multiple industries. She holds a master's degree in instructional and performance technology from Boise State University.

*Shanna M. Hicks* has over 15 years' experience supporting human performance in human resource management and development and currently works for Eclipse Aviation. But this just gives her the opportunity to do what she loves most: teach yoga.

*Janette R. Hill,* Professor in the College of Education at the University of Georgia, has over 17 years of experience in the areas of instructional design, particularly in online learning environments. Dr. Hill has an extensive publication record and has served as PI or co-PI on several grant projects funded by leading foundations such as NSF and the Wallace Foundation.

*Simon Hooper* is an Associate Professor at Pennylvania State University, where he studies, designs, and develops technology to support teaching and learning.

*Kun Huang* is an instructional designer at the University of North Texas Health Science Center. Over the past few years, she has been working with health science faculty to design and develop technology-supported constructivist learning environments. Her research focuses on scaffolding students' metacognition, knowledge transfer, complex problem-solving, and conceptual change in science.

*Julie Jabaley* is co-founder and principal of Leverage Points Consulting, which supports public health entities striving to amplify effectiveness and outcomes through instructional and project management solutions. She has created curricula and delivered training in K–12, higher education, and public health environments. Julie most recently worked on developing a hybrid curriculum for a parenting intervention at Georgia State University.

*Carol S. Kamin* is Associate Professor in the Department of Medical Education at University of Illinois in Chicago, College of Medicine. In addition to teaching in the medical school, she also teaches a master's degree in health professions education online and in person in an international program. Her research interests include greater understanding of the role of media in learning.

*Mable B. Kinzie* applies ID and new technology to support learning and development across disciplines and environments; her current work focuses on teaching quality to support early child development. With more than 50 interactive/instructional products and 50 publications, she has been recognized as a Harrison Outstanding Faculty Member at the University of Virginia and received national awards for scholarship and instructional development. So far, she's found it's impossible to have too much fun.

*Molly M. Lane* is core faculty in the Instructional Design for Online Learning specialization at Capella University, where she teaches online courses in instructional design and mentors doctoral learners. She has over a decade of experience as an independent consultant and has completed instructional design projects for nonprofit and corporate clients. Molly earned her PhD in Educational Technology from Purdue University.

*Valerie A. Larsen* is Director of the Arts & Sciences Center for Instructional Technologies at the University of Virginia. Her current professional interests focus on emerging technologies relevant to instruction and collaborative research, second language acquisition, mobile learning strategies, e-learning and blended learning, faculty development, and associated assessment methodologies.

*Lori Lockyer* is Professor of Educational Technology in the Faculty of Education at the University of Wollongong. Over the past 15 years she has designed, developed, implemented, and researched technology-supported learning environments within a range of educational settings.

*Deborah L. Lowther* received her PhD from Arizona State. She is a professor of Instructional Design and Technology and Department Chair of Instruction and Curriculum Leadership at the University of Memphis. Her work includes nationally recognized research initiatives focused on the impact of technology integration in K–12 environments.

*Martha Mann* specializes in the design of classroom and online course materials and consults on best practices for technology integration in learning environments. She has had the pleasure of teaching a variety of subjects in self-contained classrooms and in higher education, including technology integration, multimedia design and development, web design, and usability.

*Gary R. Morrison* serves as Professor in the instructional design program at Old Dominion University. He is co-author of *Designing Effective Instruction* and *Integrating Computer Technology into the Classroom.* He is author of more than 25 book chapters, more than 40 articles, and more than 100 conference presentations on topics in instructional technology, and he is the editor of the *Journal of Computing in Higher Education.*

*Christie Nelson* has a master's degree in educational technology from Purdue University. She has worked in a variety of instructional design roles for large consulting firms and boutique e-learning companies in both America and Australia. After becoming a mom in 2009, Christie started her own photography business (www.christienelsonphotography.com.au). Her goal is to design online training modules to help parents take better photos of their kids.

*Chandra Orrill* is Assistant Professor in STEM Education at the University of Massachusetts, Dartmouth. Her research focuses on how teachers in grades 4–8 understand mathematics; how that understanding affects their practice; and the role of professional development in changing understanding. She has over a decade of experience designing and implementing professional development for mathematics teachers.

*Susan Pedersen* is Associate Professor of Educational Technology at Texas A&M University. Her research focuses on the design and implementation of virtual environments and games as a means to engage K–12 students in scientific inquiry. She has worked on several STEM-related projects, including as the director of the VELscience project, aimed at creating innovative educational materials for science.

*Thomas Michael Power* is Associate Professor in Educational Technology at the Faculty of Education, Laval University in Quebec City, Canada. He is a member of the Experts Committee for IFADEM and Deputy Director of the GeoEduc3D project, as well as researcher with CRIRES, ITIS, and CIRTA. He is author of *A Designer's Log: Case Studies in Instructional Design*, published by Athabasca University Press (www.aupress.ca/index.php/books/120161).

*Steven M. Ross* received his doctorate in educational psychology from Pennsylvania State University. He is currently a senior research scientist and professor at the Center for Research and Reform in Education at Johns Hopkins University. Dr. Ross is the author of six textbooks and more than 125 journal articles in the areas of educational technology, at-risk learners, educational reform, extended learning time programs, and research and evaluation.

*Sheila Rulison* received her PhD in Instructional Leadership and Academic Curriculum from the University of Oklahoma. A National Board Certified teacher, she has been a secondary school English teacher for 20 years, with the last 11 years as an Advanced Placement English teacher at the junior and senior levels. She recently left the classroom to become the English Content Coordinator for Laying the Foundation, a partner of the National Math and Science Initiative, in Dallas, Texas.

*Rod Sims* is a design consultant, specialising in e-learning within the higher education sector. Rod has over 30 years experience in technology and education, and his research interests focus on design models that maximize learner engagement and communication.

*David L. Solomon* has spent most of his vocational life working in the field of learning and performance improvement. Currently, he is Managing Partner for International Caregiver Network, a "think tank" driven by a mission to empower family caregivers, to humanize professional caregiving communities, and to enlighten business leaders about the abundance everyone can enjoy when caregivers are celebrated.

*Timothy W. Spannaus* is coordinator of the Instructional Technology program and Senior Lecturer at Wayne State University in Detroit. He teaches and conducts research in multimedia for learning, message design, and scholarship of teaching and learning. Recent publications include a book, *Creating Video for Teachers and Trainers*, and papers on teaching and learning in higher education.

*Donald A. Stepich* is Associate Professor in the Instructional and Performance Technology Department at Boise State University, where he teaches online instructional design courses. He has been working and teaching in the instructional design field for more than 20 years. His interests include the use of analogies and the development of professional expertise.

*Toni Stokes Jones* is a professor in the Educational Media and Technology program area of the Department of Teacher Education at Eastern Michigan University. Dr. Jones received her PhD in instructional technology from Wayne State University and has an MEd in instructional technology and a BS in business education–secondary.

*Monica W. Tracey* is Associate Professor of Instructional Technology, College of Education, Wayne State University. Her teaching and research focuses on theory and research of interdisciplinary design, including design thinking, designer reflection, and designer decision making. She has more than 30 publications on her research and practice of instructional design, including a co-authored book, book chapters, and refereed journal articles.

*Naomi Waldron* is an instructional designer with over 10 years experience designing for a wide range of projects and clients, mainly blended learning and e-learning in corporate and government sectors. Naomi has designed ID training for clients such as the Australian Army and Rio Tinto. Her special interests are Serious Games and the use of social media for learning.

*William R. Watson* is Assistant Professor of Learning Design and Technology at Purdue University and director of the Purdue Center for Serious Games and Learning in Virtual Environments. His research focuses on the critical, systemic change of education to realize a learner-centered paradigm, including using video games and learning management software to support customized and personalized learning environments.

*Shahron Williams van Rooij* is Assistant Professor in the Learning Technologies Division of the College of Education and Human Development at George Mason University. A certified Project Management Professional (PMP) with more than 10 years of experience in the software development industry, her research interests include open source software for education/training, instructional design project management, and workplace learning and development.

*Brent G. Wilson* is Professor of Information and Learning Technologies at the University of Colorado Denver, where he teaches classes on instructional design and learning technologies. His research focuses on instructional design practice (as opposed to formal theories and models). Active in several professional organizations, he served as program co-chair for the Ed-Media 2012 conference held in Denver, Colorado.

*Michael L. Wray* is Professor of Restaurant Management at the Metropolitan State University of Denver. Michael is a highly credentialed hospitality educator. He is a Certified Sommelier, Culinary Instructor, and holds the Master Certified Food Service Executive credential. Before receiving his PhD in education, he obtained a BS in nutrition and foods from Virginia Tech and an MBA from Salisbury University.

# PART I

# The Case-Learning Process: Strategies and Reflections

by Peggy A. Ertmer, James A. Quinn, and Krista D. Glazewski

Collecting stories from experienced practitioners will provide relevant information that can be used for interpreting and understanding problem-solving tasks in order to design instruction. In addition to providing potential case problems for solving, that information will also yield an abundance of conceptual and strategic knowledge that can be included in the instruction (Jonassen & Hernandez-Serrano, 2002, p. 71).

Storytelling has been part of the human experience since people learned to communicate with symbols and words and continues to be a regular part of our lives today. We tell stories to gain attention, elicit emotion, illustrate our position, humanize a situation, explain the complexity of something, make distinctions, build commonalties, and create meaning (Bruner, 1986, 1990; Jonassen & Hernandez-Serrano, 2002; Kolodner, 1992). But perhaps a more meaningful idea to consider is what you, as the learner, have to gain from the stories of others, and more specifically, what you have to gain from the experiences and stories of other instructional designers. As Jonassen and Hernandez-Serrano noted, problem solving from within the stories of others may yield an abundance of conceptual and strategic knowledge.

Instructional design (ID) represents an ill-defined skill that is largely dependent on the context in which it is practiced and occurs within a series of iterative decision-making cycles as designers consider both constraints and resources (Jonassen, 2008). In other words, there is no single set of principles and procedures that can be applied in the same way in every situation. Although there is no formula for good design (Cates, 2001), there is evidence to suggest that the more we know about ID, and the more we practice solving ID problems, the more "expert" we become (Atherton, 2003; Bransford, Brown, & Cocking, 2000; Ertmer & Stepich, 2005; Hardré, Ge, & Thomas, 2005).

It is our hope that the cases in this text provide you with the kind of opportunities you need to initiate the development of your instructional design expertise. The case studies are purposefully complex and, by design, do not lend themselves to simple, "right" answers. The goal of the case method is not to help you find answers to every possible design issue but rather to increase your understanding of the types of complex problems professional designers encounter in their everyday practice. We expect that by analyzing and reflecting on a variety of complex design situations you will be better prepared to solve similar problems in your own instructional design practice. This assumption is based on our understanding of a practice known as case-based reasoning.

## Case-Based Reasoning

Imagine a designer asked to develop instruction to train teachers and administrators on a new student information management system for a K–12 school district. The project manager suggests to the ID professional that she may want to develop three separate trainings to target three levels of personnel: elementary, middle, and high school. The designer has never worked for a public school system before, but she has extensive experience designing instruction on information management systems for universities and community colleges. Her prior experience informs her that instructors, administrators, and staff will use the information system for different purposes. Instructors will use the system primarily for organizing assignment information, inputting grades, and communicating with students. Administrators will use the system largely for tracking sites and programs when it comes to matters of compliance and reporting. However, she is not sure how staff at the schools may use the system, because she has limited knowledge of their role, which she imagines to be much different from the role of a staff member at a university. In fact, she remembers a former graduate school classmate who worked as an assistant principal at an elementary school. Her classmate regularly referred to the staff as being the "central nervous system" of any school, signifying that their role involved interacting with and providing information to parents, students, administrators, teachers, public officials, and visitors. The instructional designer reasons that she should leverage her limited, but relevant, knowledge as a starting point for the initial needs analysis. She concludes that there may, indeed, be a need for three separate trainings, but rather than dividing them by associated school level (elementary, middle, and high), she decides to explore dividing them by role (teacher, administrator, and staff).

In comparing her prior experiences in higher education settings to the K–12 setting, the designer is able to consider some of the similarities and differences between these settings. Her prior involvement with universities and community colleges gives her related experience. For example, she recognizes there are at least three target audience groups who will use the system for distinct purposes, but that these audiences are most likely determined by their roles in the district, not the school level or building in which they work. Furthermore, her interactions with her former classmate provide her with direct insight into the role of the staff. Thus, although neither situation is exactly the same as the current one, both of her prior experiences represent case examples that she can use in initiating the analysis. This type of reasoning, from direct and indirect past experience, is known as case-based reasoning (CBR).

Formally defined, case-based reasoning involves "using old experiences to understand and solve new problems" (Kolodner, 1992, p. 3). However, the process of case-based reasoning may be easier to define than to carry out. First of all, the individual must have prior knowledge and understanding that will inform the current situation. Furthermore, this knowledge must be readily usable. For these reasons, Kolodner, Owensby, and Guzdial (2004) argue that it is not enough to have extensive experience; this experience must be reflected on and interpreted for meaning, relevance, and lessons learned. Only then can the individual use it as a relevant case to reason from in future applications. In other words, each meaningfully interpreted experience is stored in an individual's memory as a case, and it is helpful to think of this collection of cases as a metaphorical *case library*. From our earlier example, you know that the ID professional applied reasoning from two separate cases in her case library—her prior experience developing similar trainings for higher education professionals and her related interactions with an assistant principal.

The second step in the CBR process involves *indexing* the cases (Kolodner et al., 2004); if we continue with the library metaphor, we know that a resource can be located efficiently within a collection only if the indexing itself is logical and organized. In other words, the individual must recognize when a prior case has applicability. Meaningful transfer of this knowledge depends first on indexing the case for relevant aspects, features, and significance. Imagine again our ID professional—you can reasonably conclude that at some point in the past, she indexed conversations with a classmate (who also served as an assistant principal) as potentially relevant to K–12 settings. Similarly, it is just as easy to imagine someone else participating in the same conversations, but never reflecting on or creating meaning from them.

The final step of case-based reasoning involves *case retrieval and application* (Kolodner, 1997; Kolodner et al., 2004). At this stage, the individual must know when a case's stored lessons and meaning relate to the new problem. Furthermore, the individual must know which lessons can be leveraged to inform the current situation. Our ID professional knew when to apply relevant experiences from her past employment and when to apply relevant knowledge gained from conversations with a former classmate.

## The Case-Learning Experience

Although case methods have been used in business, law, and medicine for more than 100 years, it is likely that this will be one of your first experiences with the case approach. This may give rise to a wide range of feelings—excitement, nervousness, curiosity, intimidation. In addition, you will probably have a lot of questions: How do I analyze a case? How long should a case analysis be? How will I know if I've done it right? Where will I find the information and resources I need to solve the case problems? Although it is our experience that students are typically excited about using case studies in instruction, they often feel a little apprehensive as well, possibly because of their unfamiliarity with this approach. We have written this section, addressed to you specifically, because we have found that initial concerns can be lessened by describing, up front, the types of tasks you will be expected to complete, as well as some of the adjustments you may need to make in your current learning "mindsets." As one of our former students noted:

> In my opinion, if students were told up front that this style of learning (case-based instruction) feels slow and cumbersome at first, and that they should read and re-read the information in the case a couple of times, do what they need to visualize and better understand the scenarios—it might be easier to adjust to. I think case-based learning is a valuable and interactive method that just takes a different mindset than most students are used to.

We think this student makes two excellent suggestions: tell students what this approach *feels* like and tell them how to *do* it (i.e., analyze a case). Although we don't really believe that we can tell you exactly how it feels to learn from cases or how you must go about analyzing a case, we offer a few thoughts and suggestions related to these two elements of the case-learning experience. We begin with suggestions on how to adopt a reflective mindset and then provide strategies and procedures for analyzing a case.

# Developing a Reflective Mindset

One of the primary goals of professional education is to help novices "think like" members of the profession (Shulman, 1992). This entails being able to look back on practice as a way to understand experience (Schön, 1983), as well as engaging in an internal process of reflection and inquiry as a way to improve future practice. According to Hartog (2002), this type of skillful inquiry takes "time, commitment, and practice" (p. 237).

Kitchener and King (1990) described mature, reflective thinkers as being able to view situations from multiple perspectives, search for alternative explanations of events, and use evidence to support or evaluate a decision or position. These qualities form an essential part of the mindset that we believe facilitates learning from case studies. We provide additional guidelines here, gleaned from our own experiences and those of our students, as well as from the results of an exploratory research study conducted by one of the authors (Ertmer, Newby, & MacDougall, 1996).

- There is no one right answer. If you enter the case-learning experience with this idea firmly planted, you are less likely to be frustrated by the ambiguity inherent in the case-study approach. There are many answers to the issues in each case. The solutions you propose will depend as much on the perspective you take as on the issues you identify. Accept the fact that you will not know how to solve each case. Furthermore, if you have no clue where to begin, give yourself permission not to know. Then begin the analysis process by paying attention to how others analyze the case based on their personal experiences.

  After you have analyzed the case, you may think that it would be helpful to know how the designers in the cases "solved" the problems. However, this is not as helpful as you might think. Being frustrated by a lack of answers can actually be very motivating. If you're left hanging after reading a case, chances are you'll continue to ponder the issues for a long time to come.

- There is more than one way to look at things. One of the advantages to participating in case discussions is that you get the chance to hear how others analyzed the case and to consider multiple points of view, thus gaining a more complete examination and understanding of the issues involved. Not only will listening to others' ideas *allow* you to see the issues from different points of view; it will also *force* you to consider exactly where you stand. By paying close attention to what others have to say, you can evaluate how their views fit with your own. Thus, you learn more about who you are, where you are coming from, and what you stand for. Your views of others, as well as of yourself, may be broadened.

- Keep an open mind; suspend judgment until all ideas are considered. This suggestion builds on the previous one. It is important to come to the case discussion with an attitude of, "Let's see what develops." Begin by regarding your initial solutions as tentative. Listen respectfully to your peers; ask questions to clarify and gather additional information, not to pass judgment on ideas different from yours. As one of our students recommended, "Be flexible and open-minded. Remember that problems can be attacked from many different angles." Use the case discussion to gather additional data. In the end, your final recommendation should be informed by the collective wisdom of the whole class, yet reflect your own best judgment.

■ Be leery of assumptions and generalizations; avoid seeing things in extremes. If data are ambiguous or there is little evidence to support why case players behaved as they did, be cautious of the assumptions you make. Be especially careful to state your assumptions tentatively, suggesting uncertainty. Furthermore, be careful about making assumptions that allow you to propose easy solutions. Before going down any single solution path, ask yourself if the assumptions you are making are realistic based on the facts of the case.

Along these same lines, be careful not to generalize your observations beyond the data provided. Avoid using labels or slogans that lump people together. If you're inclined to see things in black and white, all or nothing, stand back and look at the words you use in your analysis. It is fairly safe to say that you should avoid words such as *always*, *never*, *everybody*, or *nobody*. Stick close to the facts when describing the issues, drawing conclusions, and making recommendations.

■ Expect to get better; focus on the analysis process. At the beginning of a case-based course, you may feel overwhelmed with the challenge of trying to solve case problems. It is important to recognize, first, that this is not uncommon. Many students initially feel overwhelmed and apprehensive. Second, it is equally important to recognize that, as with most skills, design skills and knowledge improve with practice. Furthermore, most students actually start to enjoy the challenge involved in analyzing problematic situations. If you maintain the mindset that you learn as much from the analysis process as you do from identifying a potential solution, then your case-learning experience will be less frustrating. The analytic process is at the heart of the case method. Pay attention to the progress you make in analyzing the cases. Judge your success not by comparing your answer to what the authors of the case did, but by your approach to the analysis process. Did you consider all of the issues? Did you look at issues from the varying perspectives of the key players? Have you based suggestions on available data? If your skills are improving in these areas, you're gaining in precisely the ways promoted by the case approach. And remember that learning is a lifelong process. You'll never know all there is to know about designing. Yet each experience with design situations should move you closer to thinking and acting like a professional designer.

■ Take time to reflect. According to Campoy (2005), "Good problem solvers review their efforts and the results to incorporate what they have learned for future reference" (p. 197). Reflection is a recurring theme in our discussion of how to approach a case study. Quite simply, that's because we believe that reflection enhances everything that happens in the case method. According to Shulman (1996), "We do not learn from experience; we learn by thinking about our experience" (p. 208). Reflection, as a form of metacognition, is a prerequisite for deep learning and is key to developing your case library for future retrieval in case-based reasoning (Kolodner et al., 2004).

It is true that a case analysis takes more time to complete than traditional course assignments. Yet there is little to be gained by trying to rush the process. Acting or responding impulsively decreases the chances that you will gather all the relevant information, examine all the potential courses of action, and consider the many possible ensuing consequences. Take time to think. Ask questions of yourself, your peers, and your instructor. Hills and Gibson (cited in Grimmett & Erickson, 1988) describe how reflective practitioners might go about their work. The development of this type of reflective mindset can begin with your work on these cases:

> As you go about your work responding to phenomena, identifying problems, diagnosing problems, making normative judgments, developing strategies, etc. think about your responses to situations and about what it is in the situation, and in yourself, that leads you to respond that way; think about the norms and values on which your judgments are based; think about the manner in which you frame problems, and think about "your conception of your role." "Surface" and criticize your implicit understandings. Construct and test your own theories. (p. 151)

■ Enjoy yourself. As indicated earlier, the case method may at first feel like a strange and difficult way to learn. Yet, even when students indicate that learning from case studies can be frustrating and "unnerving," they also admit that it is exciting and valuable. Being actively involved, working with stimulating case material, having a chance to express your ideas and hear those of others—these are all enjoyable aspects of case learning. We think one of our students summed it up wonderfully: "I like how cases challenge you and frustrate you. My advice is to relax. Let the ideas flow. Don't say, 'This isn't possible.' And, most of all, be confident that what you are doing now will pay off in the future."

## Strategies for Analyzing a Case

There are a variety of ways to effectively analyze a case study. We offer the following as one possibility:

1. Understand the context in which the case is being analyzed and discussed. If your instructor is using this text to supplement another, then the cases will probably be used to provide real-world examples of the content or design steps you've discussed. This context can help focus your attention on relevant issues, questions, and concerns related to your readings and other coursework. Also, each case includes a set of focusing questions at the end. You may want to read these questions first, as a way to "prime the pump." Reading case questions before you read the case may help you read more meaningfully and more effectively.

2. Read the case. Your first reading should probably be fairly quick, just to get a general sense of what the case is about—the key players, main issues, context, and so on.

3. Read the case again. Your second (and subsequent) reading(s) should be much slower: taking notes, considering multiple perspectives, thinking about alternative

solutions and consequences. The benefits you reap from your case analysis will relate to how much time you spend—not necessarily reading, but reflecting on what you have read.

4. Analyze the case. This is probably the "fuzziest" and thus most overwhelming step of the whole case-analysis process. Assuming that you have already identified the facts of the case, relevant information, key players, context, and resources and constraints, we recommend that you address the following questions/points during your analysis:

   a. Who are the key stakeholders in this case? How would each stakeholder describe the primary issue in the case?

   b. Given the stakeholders' various perspectives, what do *you* see as the primary design issue(s) in the case?

   c. List any assumptions you make about information that is missing from the case. As much as possible, support your assumptions with evidence from the case. Why are your assumptions reasonable?

   d. Generate a list of potential solutions related to each issue.

   e. Specify possible consequences (pros and cons) of each solution.

   f. After weighing the advantages and limitations to each solution, make a recommendation for action.

   g. Describe how your recommendations address the issues listed in points a and b. Reflect on the extent to which you think that the suggested solution will solve the primary issue(s).

5. Actively participate in class discussion. The case class is a learning community— together you, your instructor, and your peers are working to gain a more complete understanding of the case situation and possible solutions. It is important that you be an active participant as well as an active listener. You must listen carefully to what others are saying so that your questions and contributions can move the discussion along. Coming to class prepared is critical to your ability to participate in, and benefit from, the case-learning experience.

6. Reflect on the case-learning experience. Boud (2001) advocated the use of reflection at three different points during a learning experience: at the *start*, in a preparatory phase when you start to explore what is required of you, as you become aware of the demands of the situation and the resources you bring to bear; *during* the experience, as a way of dealing with the vast array of inputs and coping with the feelings generated; and *after* the experience, as you attempt to make sense of it and index it for future application.

   The case method provides fertile ground for facilitating a reflective approach to learning. Starting with the first step in the analysis process, as you consider the context in which you are studying a case, you are immersed (already engaging) in a reflective process. As you implement your analysis approach, you complete a variety of activities that are inherent in a reflective design approach; that is, you "test the waters" through a process in which you consider previous experiences, connect with your feelings, and draw upon your existing repertoire of images, metaphors, and theories (Smith, 2001).

Finally, at the end of a case analysis, reflection helps you make sense of your experiences, deepen your understanding of the case, and solidify the case example for future retrieval. By reflecting on both the products and the processes of your learning experiences, you gain insights essential to improving future performance. Reflection can link past and future actions by providing you with information about the strategies you used (learning process) and the outcomes you achieved (learning products). It allows you to take stock of what has happened and to prepare yourself for future action. As noted by one of our former students:

> I have enjoyed the opportunity to reflect upon my performance (on my case analyses) because I think that it encourages me to take stock of where I have been, where I am, and where I need to go on the road to expertise. Self-reflection may, at times, be painful, but the gains stimulate growth and improvement necessary to become the best instructional designer possible.

# Becoming an ID Professional: Reflecting on Your Case Experiences

It should be evident by now that one of our primary purposes for using case studies as an instructional approach is to facilitate your growing ability to think like an instructional design professional. As in all professions, learning to "think like a designer" does not happen overnight. Furthermore, reflection has been established as a valuable part of this process. As Weil and Frame (1992) stated, "Experience and action do not themselves guarantee learning. We learn by doing and through reflection on doing" (p. 63).

As you analyze the cases in this book, and particularly as you come to the end of using the book, we ask you to consider *how* you learned from the case studies, and then more broadly, as a beginning ID professional, how you might use cases in your own design work.

First of all, consider what it was like trying to learn from case studies. Use the following questions to stimulate your thinking about the case-learning experience:

- ✔ How interesting, valuable, and relevant was the case approach?
- ✔ How challenging and/or frustrating was it? What features contributed to the challenge level? Should these features be altered, and if so, how?
- ✔ How would you describe your attitude toward using case studies as a learning tool?
- ✔ What strategies did you use to analyze each case? Did you use a systematic approach, or was it more hit-and-miss?
- ✔ Did your approach change over the course of the semester, and if so, how?
- ✔ What did you do when you hit a "snag"? (Did you give up? Did you consult other resources? Did you talk to other students?)
- ✔ What advice would you give to other ID students who are just beginning a course/text like this?

Second, we ask you to put on a different hat, so to speak, and look at the use of case studies from the point of view of a designer rather than a student of design. Use the following questions to stimulate your thinking regarding the usefulness of the case method as a teaching strategy:

✔ What particular design situations might be amenable to the case approach?
✔ Are there situations where the case method would not be appropriate?
✔ Are there any specific types of learners who would or would not benefit from the case approach?
✔ What different purposes might cases serve (e.g., building interest and motivation, contextualizing learning, enhancing problem diagnosis and problem-solving skills) in the education of instructional designers?
✔ How might cases be used with novice learners, "advanced beginners," and so on? How might cases be used in professional development courses for practicing instructional design professionals?

We hope that reflecting on questions such as these will help you feel comfortable using the case approach when you begin designing and teaching your own courses and workshops. We believe that cases offer a powerful means for facilitating the development of instructional design expertise. At the end of this course/text, as you look back on your own experiences using the *ID CaseBook*, we certainly hope that this is true for you, and wish you well in confidently employing the case method in your future instructional design practice.

# References

Atherton, J. S. (2003). *Doceo: Competence, proficiency and beyond*. Retrieved January 28, 2013, from http://www.doceo.co.uk/background/expertise.htm

Boud, D. (2001). Using journal writing to enhance reflective practice. In L. M. English & M. A. Gillen (Eds.), *Promoting journal writing in adult education. New directions in adult and continuing education* (No. 90, pp. 9–18). San Francisco: Jossey-Bass.

Bransford, J. D., Brown, A. L., & Cocking, R. R. (Eds.). (2000). How experts differ from novices. Chapter 2 in *How people learn: Brain, mind, experience, and school* (pp. 31–50). Washington, DC: National Academies Press.

Bruner, J. (1986). *Actual minds, possible worlds*. Cambridge, MA: Harvard University Press.

Bruner, J. (1990). *Acts of meaning*. Cambridge, MA. Harvard University Press.

Campoy, R. (2005). *Case study analysis in the classroom: Becoming a reflective teacher*. Thousand Oaks, CA: Sage.

Cates, W. M. (2001). Introduction to the special issue. *Educational Technology, 41*(1), 5–6.

Ertmer, P. A., Newby, T. J., & MacDougall, M. (1996). Students' approaches to learning from case-based instruction: The role of reflective self-regulation. *American Educational Research Journal, 33*(3), 719–752.

Ertmer, P. A., & Stepich, D. A. (2005). Instructional design expertise: How will we know it when we see it? *Educational Technology, 45*(6), 38–43.

Grimmett, P. P., & Erickson, G. L. (1988). *Reflection in teacher education.* New York: Teachers College Press.

Hardré, P. L., Ge, X., & Thomas, M. K. (2005). Toward a model of development for instructional design expertise. *Educational Technology, 45*(1), 53–57.

Hartog, M. (2002). Becoming a reflective practitioner: A continuing professional development strategy through humanistic action research. *Business Ethics: A European Review, 11*, 233–243.

Jonassen, D. H. (2008). Instructional design as design problem solving: An iterative process. *Educational Technology, 48*(3), 21–26.

Jonassen, D. H., & Hernandez-Serrano, J. (2002). Case-based reasoning and instructional design: Using stories to support problem solving. *Educational Technology Research and Development, 50*(2), 65–77.

Kitchener, K. S., & King, P. M. (1990). The reflective judgment model: Ten years of research. In M. L. Commons, C. Arman, L. Kohlberg, F. A. Richards, T. A. Grotzer, & J. Sinnott (Eds.), *Adult development: Models and methods in the study of adolescent and adult thought* (Vol. 2, pp. 63–78). New York: Praeger.

Kolodner, J. (1997). Educational implications of analogy: A view from case-based reasoning. *American Psychologist, 52*(1), 57–66.

Kolodner, J. L. (1992). An introduction to case-based reasoning. *Artificial Intelligence Review, 6*, 3–34.

Kolodner, J. L., Owensby, J. N., & Guzdial, M. (2004). Case-based learning aids. In D. H. Jonassen (Ed.), *Handbook of research for educational communications and technology* (2nd ed., pp. 829–861). Mahwah, NJ: Erlbaum.

Schön, D. A. (1983). *The reflective practitioner: How professionals think in action.* New York: Basic Books.

Shulman, L. (1992). Toward a pedagogy of cases. In J. H. Shulman (Ed.), *Case methods in teacher education* (pp. 1–30). New York: Teachers College Press.

Shulman, L. S. (1996). Just in case: Reflections on learning from experience. In J. A. Colbert, P. Desberg, & K. Trimble (Eds.), *The case for education: Contemporary approaches for using case methods* (pp. 197–217). Boston: Allyn & Bacon.

Smith, M. K. (2001). Donald Schön: Learning, reflection and change. *The encyclopedia of informal education.* Retrieved January 28, 2013, from http://www.infed.org/thinkers/et-schon.htm.

Weil, S., & Frame, P. (1992). Capability through business and management education. In J. Stephenson & S. Weil (Eds.), *Quality in learning: A capability approach in higher education* (pp. 45–76). London: Kogan Page.

# PART II
# Case Studies

## Section 1: K–12 Audience/Context

# CASE STUDY 1

# Scott Allen

## Designing Learning Objects for Primary Learners

*by Sue Bennett, Lori Lockyer, and Barry Harper*

Scott Allen e-mailed the rest of his design team the good news—they had won a bid for a major project with *SchoolsOnline*, a national initiative to develop online resources for primary and secondary schools.

Scott was happy with the team he'd put together. All members, including himself, Jeff Parker, Penny Johnson, and Tracey Ward, were academics on the education faculty. Each was also an experienced instructional designer, and they had all worked together on previous projects. Jeff was well known in the field of multimedia design and, as director of the college's multimedia unit, had developed several innovative educational DVDs that had received a number of international awards. Penny and Tracey worked as professors in educational technology with an emphasis on multimedia design. They both had worked on a wide range of DVD and web-based projects for industry groups, higher education, and primary schools over the past 10 years. In addition to his design experience, Scott brought technical and management skills to the group. All of the group members were also currently involved in a research study investigating the use of learning objects in education. Scott hoped that by conducting this study his team would gain additional insight for the upcoming project.

Scott believed that this would be an interesting project for two reasons. First, he knew they would work primarily on the design specifications while collaborating with two other small teams: one that would be responsible for proposing and researching the content for design briefs and another that would do the development work. Second, they would be creating educational learning objects, as opposed to a full DVD or web-based project.

Later in the week, Scott attended an initial meeting organized by *SchoolsOnline*. A representative from each of the project teams was there, as well as subject matter and educational experts; the overall project manager, Gordon Anderson; and other representatives of *SchoolsOnline*.

# Understanding the Project

After he returned from the initial project meeting, Scott called the design team together. He began by explaining the requirements for the project and how the process would work. As he distributed copies of the project brief for *Our Nation and Society* (see Appendix 1–A on page 23), he said, "To start us off, let's read through the project brief. This is similar to the information we were given to prepare the proposal. As you can see it's still quite general, because it's trying to describe the principles driving the overall project, rather than the specific learning objects that will be developed as part of it."

The team members spent a few minutes reading through the project brief. When they finished, Scott highlighted some of the main points. "Basically, in terms of the learning objects, *SchoolsOnline* wants fairly small-scale resources that are flexible enough for a teacher to use with a whole class or for a student to work with independently. By small, they mean focused on only one or a few objectives and also small in file size. But, because the learning objects need to be substantial enough to use as the focus of a lesson or an activity, these learning objects may be much larger than what most people would normally think of for a learning object."

"And from the brief, it's clear they want a particular pedagogical approach to be taken," Tracey added.

"That's right," said Scott, "there was a lot of discussion about the learning objects not just presenting content but engaging learners in activities. And those activities should be more constructivist than prescriptive. Still, we do have a lot of flexibility in terms of adapting the content that they gave us." Scott went on to describe a learning object that was demonstrated at the meeting, which was designed to involve students in solving a crime. The learning object required students to collect evidence after a robbery by visiting the crime scene to interact with witnesses and collect forensic evidence. The program then required students to select certain pieces of evidence from a list of possibilities, and then compare these with information about suspects to identify who committed the crime. Scott explained that a teacher could extend the task by having students discuss the process in class or asking them to write a report of their findings.

Scott added, "The learning object used simple animation, text, and audio. *SchoolsOnline* wanted to avoid using full-color graphics and video because this would increase the file size. All of the learning objects will need to be developed in Flash™ for a particular set of end-user specifications. That way all of the learning objects will have consistent technical requirements. That's mainly a concern for the development team, but we need to consider how to keep the learning objects small while we are developing our design specifications."

"In addition to the file size issue," added Jeff, "my impression is that these ideas are quite different from some of the other conceptions of learning objects that appear in the literature, especially in terms of context. A lot of those sources emphasize the need for learning objects to be context free. However, the learning objects we develop for this project will not be context free."

"Yes, I was also wondering about this issue of context," added Penny.

**FIGURE 1–1**   The Organizational Structure of the *Our Nation and Society* Project.

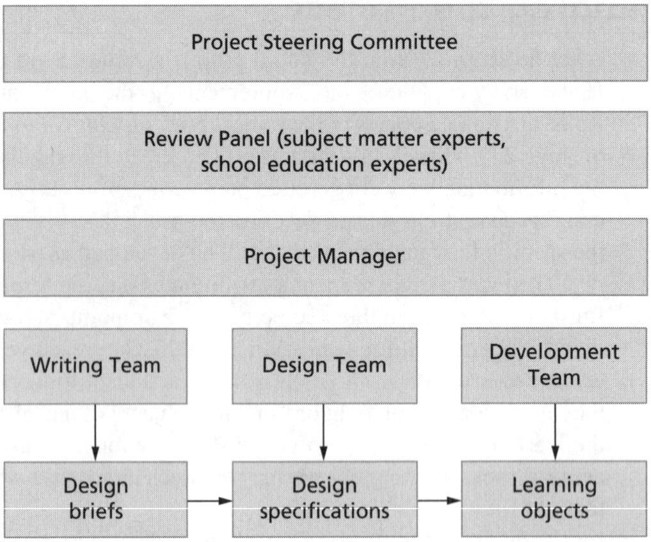

Jeff replied, "Obviously, these learning objects will be geared toward Australian K–12 students, designed to meet particular national curricular needs, which certainly enhances their reusability in the Australian context. But as a consequence, that will make them less usable in other national contexts."

Scott clarified, "Well, I think that the aim of the project is to make something for Australian students. So, I think the main point is that the objects should be reusable within the scope of *this* project, and that we need not be concerned with contexts outside of Australia."

"Let me tell you a little bit about how the project is going to work. I've photocopied a diagram from one of the handouts we got at the meeting and I'll take you through it," Scott said as he passed a sheet of paper to each of the other team members (see Figure 1–1).

Scott continued, "In this diagram they've represented the process and the organizational structure. We're the design team, and there are two other teams with whom we'll work. There are three people on the writing team, who have been busy generating design briefs based on suggestions from the subject matter experts on the steering committee. The members of the writing team have experience in technical and creative writing, but don't have backgrounds in education. So, the role of the writers was to capture the ideas produced by the steering committee, document these, and research additional content, as required. The learning outcomes and intended pedagogical approaches originated from the steering committee, as did decisions about what content each learning object should focus on."

Scott went on to explain that the writers had prepared 32 draft briefs, each of which was a couple of pages long and pretty rough. The design team must now choose the best 15 of these ideas to be developed further, and then the writing team would revise the briefs and prepare the content needed.

Scott explained, "The entire process actually involves a fair bit of consultation, so it's not as linear as it looks. And there are reviews and sign-off points between each of the stages. For example," Scott continued, "after the writing team prepares the content for the briefs we have chosen for further development, the briefs come back to us and we develop the full design specifications, which would then be reviewed by the panel of subject matter and educational experts. Their feedback would be returned to us as the basis for revisions to the designs. The final design specifications would then go to the steering committee to be signed off on prior to any development. Everything will go through Gordon, our project manager, whose job is to keep things on track overall.

"After the design specs are approved by the steering committee, they go to the development team from *ScarletMedia*, which is a company we haven't worked with before, although Jeff knows the director. After that point the design team would no longer be involved. By the way, the total timeline for the design work is three months. We need to decide how we can do the required work within this timeframe. So, what does everyone think?" asked Scott.

"Well, it depends," replied Tracey. "Do we know how many iterations of the review we will have to go through? That part of the process could take ages, especially if the other participants take their time getting feedback to us. I think we need to talk to everyone about setting some time limits."

"I agree," said Jeff. "We need to develop a timeline and see if we can get everyone to commit to it. Another thing I'm a little concerned about is how detailed the specifications for the design will need to be. They will need to be detailed enough so that the developers know what we are looking for, and also we need to be sure that we don't recommend something that exceeds the technical limitations involved in developing learning objects. We'll be out of the process by then so we won't have any input into the changes. How does everyone feel about that?"

Scott replied, "I think it's something we need to be aware of and be careful about. I was thinking that we might want to hold some workshop sessions in which we bring in the writers and the developers so that we clarify expectations for each team. I mentioned that to Gordon and he seemed to think it was a good idea."

Penny added, "It would be a good way to bring the developers into the process so that they understand the basis for the design. That way, if they need to make changes due to technical constraints, they are more likely to choose options that align with our original design."

"I'm wondering about the proposed working relationships among the different teams," Jeff said. "Do you know why they've done it like this, Scott?"

"Well, I think they used the whole-team approach in an earlier round of projects. But I got the impression that they weren't convinced that the whole-team approach provided the best combination of people to do the job well. I think they've decided to go this way so they have more say over who is involved," replied Scott.

Tracey added, "Well, whatever the reasons, we're not going to get much of a chance to work directly with the other teams. So if we have the workshops we can try to make sure we are all on the same wavelength."

"Alright, I'll work on a timeline and possible dates for meetings, and then get that out to everyone on e-mail," suggested Scott. "I can then negotiate with Gordon and the others.

As a next step for us, I think it would be worth working through one of the briefs. As I mentioned earlier, there are 32 design briefs, each about 2–3 pages long, that provide a short description of a design idea and possible means of implementing it as a learning object. I had the chance to read all of them on my way back from the project meeting last week and took the liberty of choosing one to start with. I think this might help us figure out how to approach our task of choosing the best ideas from among the 32 briefs and then shaping the good ones into workable learning objects."

Everyone nodded in agreement and Jeff said, "Good idea. I think we need to start with something concrete to get a better handle on the project."

"OK," replied Scott. "Let's start with *Mission to Mars*. It seems pretty straightforward. We could each consider it independently first and then put our heads together later." The others agreed. Scott suggested that they make a time to meet later in the week. Everyone checked their diaries and agreed on a meeting time two days later.

## Discussing the Brief

The team reconvened as planned to discuss the *Mission to Mars* brief (see Appendix 1–B). Scott began, "Has everyone had a chance to read through the brief?" Everyone indicated that they had. "Great. Let's start with the basis of the brief then. First of all, it's targeted at kindergarten to Year 2 students, and it's trying to get kids to see the difference between the things that they need and the things that they want."

"And it says it's also about how people contribute to the well-being of a community. That comes from a balance of needs and wants, I guess," added Penny.

"Right, so the students are starting a new community on Mars and they need to choose what they are going to take with them in the spaceship to do that. My first question is, do we think this concept is going to work?" asked Scott.

Jeff began by commenting that he saw the brief as focused and simple, but still with opportunity for learners to make decisions. For this reason, Jeff suggested that it would make a good learning object. Tracey added that engaging learners with a challenge could be very motivating, as would the fantasy element.

Penny looked a bit skeptical about this. "Yes, but it isn't that realistic, though, is it? I'm not sure the kids are really going to relate to this. And one of the principles mentioned in the project brief is setting the activities in authentic contexts."

"Traveling to Mars might not be that far off, you know," said Jeff.

"Yeah, right Jeff, but it's not as though it's something they can do now," replied Penny.

"OK, maybe it's not the right context. Can we think of some alternatives?" asked Scott. The team was quiet for a minute while they each read through the brief again and considered the issue.

"I think the essence is that they are in some kind of remote environment. Otherwise all the things a community needs would already be there," suggested Tracey.

Penny added, "And the difficulty with setting it in space is that they're going to need oxygen and water before they get anything else. That's just a bit advanced and might be too distracting. It's just not going to be something they can relate to. And the learning objects have to be pretty small, so we can't make it too involved."

"OK, I see your point. So what if it's something else? I don't know. What about a desert island?" suggested Jeff. "They could have to take things in a boat. We can include some things on the island, like it could have a freshwater lake, vegetation for building materials, and so on."

"And would they be able to come back to the mainland and swap things if they realized they don't have everything they need?" asked Tracey.

"I don't see why not. That would be important for the learning process. They would need to get some feedback on their decisions and have the opportunity to change their minds," replied Jeff.

"So, they would start a settlement or town on this island?" asked Scott.

"Yeah, they'd still need some of the people in the original brief, like a doctor or a police officer. So they could still explore the issues about people's roles and what they add to the community. And we can still show the consequences of their choices," said Jeff.

"Wait a second, this is starting to sound complicated. We're not making *SimCity*™. I don't see how we can fit all of this into a learning object. There's going to be too much content. I think we have to consider what a teacher can get through in a lesson. And we're talking about young children, with a fairly limited attention span," argued Tracey.

"That's true," said Scott. "From reading the project brief and from the discussion at the meeting, the learning objects should be pretty flexible. So we need to make sure that an individual student or a small group can use it without direct instruction from the teacher. But also a teacher could integrate the learning object into a lesson, as Tracey said. So we'll have to limit the options anyway to make it contained. One way is to have only so much room on the boat, so they can only take a limited number of items."

"We have to be careful how we limit it though or it won't be as realistic. I think we need to re-think the challenge," said Tracey.

"Maybe we need to think of a more confined setting then," suggested Scott.

"I agree. I still have a problem with the setting. And the desert island doesn't solve it," said Penny.

"Why not?" asked Jeff.

Penny explained, "Well, it's a bit of a cliché isn't it? It's more like something from a storybook than real life. Children of this age relate best to things in their immediate environments, which are basically their households. So if we consider the 'community' to be their families, that might help us."

"Good point, Penny. Perhaps we should ask ourselves how teachers would approach something like this in their classrooms. What kind of context might they use to set the scene for children of this age?" suggested Scott.

"What about a camping trip? Most kids would have some experience with that," offered Tracey.

Jeff agreed, "Yeah, that could work. They'd have to decide what to take with them. They'd only have so much space in their bags or the back of the cars or whatever. We could call it '*Let's Go Camping*.'"

"That would make it quite personal too, which is important for young children. We would have to lose the police officer and the doctor, but I'm not convinced they add much to the story anyway," said Penny.

"So what feedback will learners get about their choices? As I look at the writers' brief, it seems very behaviorist. For example, learners' choices are very limited and the feedback is not very authentic; if they haven't chosen the things they need, the planet starts to fade, which I think is nicer than people dying, but it's not very realistic. Whatever setting we choose, the learners will still need to get some feedback on the impact of their choices," suggested Tracey. "Maybe we should think of a character, like a guide or narrator, who could do this. Maybe feedback could come from another member of the family. So the scenario could be that they pack things for a camping trip, and then when they get to their destination they get the feedback."

Penny begins to draw the flowchart of the learning process on her laptop. She added, "And they only have so much space in their bags, so they have to make choices."

Jeff nodded his head and added, "They could be setting up camp and something happens because they haven't got the right equipment. Maybe they forget a warm hat so they get cold during the night."

"And they could get a stomachache if they only have chocolates and chips for dinner," Penny suggested as well. "And then they could change the items and run the whole thing again and see if they have made better choices. Just give me a second to map this out a bit."

The team waited while Penny finished the flowchart and then took a look at it (see Figure 1–2).

"Yeah, that would work. They could interact with the final scene somehow, maybe by clicking on parts of the scene to find out more. The guide could ask them what would have been a better choice," explained Jeff. "Does it still seem a bit behaviorist, though? Focusing on right and wrong answers and limiting the learners' choices isn't consistent with the constructivist approach for which we're aiming."

"It does raise questions about the nature of the feedback," said Penny thoughtfully. "I mean, how do we distinguish between a need and a want anyway? I might consider something absolutely essential that someone else thinks is completely frivolous. And for balance they'll have to be able to have some things they want but don't need. You could argue that's essential for happiness."

"I agree, but we still have to get across the idea that there is a difference between the things we need for survival and the things that we want," Jeff replied. "So there should be some choices that are better than others."

"What about including some way for learners to express their thinking about how the items they have chosen represent their needs or wants? So, the feedback would query them about their choices, rather than just telling them their choices are right or wrong. For example, there's nothing wrong with choosing to take some chocolate as a treat provided that's not the only food they have," offered Penny.

"It makes the package more complicated because there will be quite a few combinations," commented Scott. "One of the reasons for limiting the choices in the first place is that we need to keep the learning objects small."

**FIGURE 1–2**   Initial Flowchart for *Let's Go Camping.*

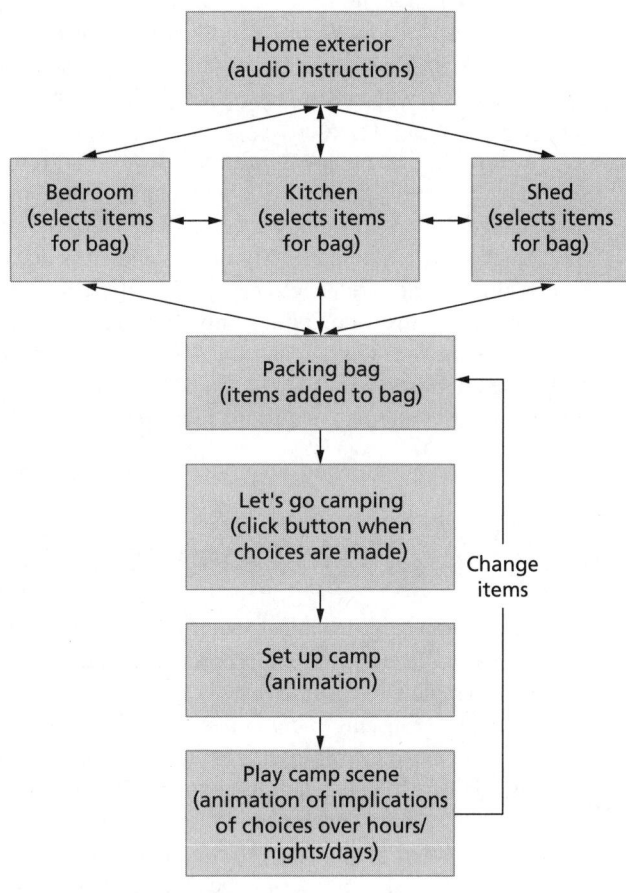

"I like the idea, though," said Jeff. "We could perhaps do it by giving feedback on their choices for categories of items, like Penny's food example. We could ask learners to decide what they would like to take to eat for three meals, for example. Then ask them some questions to get them thinking about their choices. The teacher could extend the ideas quite easily into some class discussion."

Scott added another thing for the team to think about. "*SchoolsOnline* is also quite keen for us to think about how a learning object can be adapted for different age groups. There were some ideas listed at the end of the design brief. It seems to me that this one could work with other age groups, too, if we wanted to extend it."

"I don't see why not. The objectives are still relevant to older learners, and we could use the same structure and adapt the content or increase the complexity," suggested Tracey.

Jeff added, "At least for Years 3 to 4 and Years 5 to 6. For secondary students we would need to bring in some more sophisticated concepts."

"You don't look so sure about this, Tracey," said Penny, having noticed that Tracey was still deep in thought.

Tracey responded, "Well, I still like the fantasy element. I think it would be motivating and different. I'm not sure how much the realism really matters. I can see your arguments and also how the camping trip would work, but it doesn't grab me. I'm just not sure which design would be better."

"Well, we're just about out of time, so we won't resolve it today. But it seems that the underlying concept is promising, even though we have moved well away from the original brief," added Jeff. "Can we do that, Scott? Can we recommend such substantial changes?"

"Absolutely," said Scott. "My understanding is that this is definitely part of our role. All parts of the brief are negotiable. In fact, the briefs represent ideas that we, the design team, should use as starting points only. We can accept, change, or discard them, provided that we can convince Gordon and the *SchoolsOnline* steering committee of our reasoning. If we have any reservations about the design briefs at all, now is the time for us to voice them and to offer alternative designs to achieve the objectives."

# Preliminary Analysis Questions

1. What criteria (e.g., technical specifications, design requirements) should the design team use to determine the appropriateness and merit of each design brief it has been asked to review?
2. Given the constraints under which the design team is working, suggest specific ways that it can move a draft brief from the form in which it is received (see Appendix 1–B) to that which is required by the project brief (see Appendix 1–A).
3. Apply the criteria, developed in response to question 1, to critique the two design ideas presented in this case: *Mission to Mars* and *Let's Go Camping*.
4. Outline the work flow among the three project teams by adding arrows to Figure 1–1. Discuss the potential challenges that arise because of this configuration.

# Implications for ID Practice

1. Discuss the skills needed by project managers in order to facilitate effective interaction among different teams (e.g., design, graphics, programming) working on an instructional design project.
2. Describe the core characteristics that define learning objects. What impact does each of these characteristics have on the reusability of a learning object?
3. Discuss the challenges involved in applying constructivist pedagogical strategies (e.g., authentic tasks, social interaction, and negotiation) within computer based learning object environments.

# APPENDIX 1–A

## Project Brief
### Our Nation and Society

*SchoolsOnline* is a national initiative to develop online digital learning resources (i.e., learning objects) in specified curricular areas. This project focuses on *Our Nation and Society* for years K–12.

This Project Brief provides an overview of the scope and major objectives of developing online curricular content for this area.

## Online Content

Within this initiative, the features of online content are expected to:

- engage students in meaningful, interactive learning experiences
- relate to intended outcomes and link to national, state, and territory syllabi
- support students' learning in new and effective ways
- exploit the potential of new media and technologies for promoting learning experiences not otherwise available
- cater to individuals or small groups
- adapt easily to a range of learning contexts
- support concept development, transfer of skills and understandings to and from real-world domains, and connections within and across learning areas
- support the development of lifelong learning skills
- encourage students to question and investigate
- provide real-life contexts and scenarios
- support literacy and numeracy development

# Project Content Focus

The online digital resources for this project should support the study of history, geography, indigenous studies, environmental studies, values and cultural studies, and study of civic life of particular regional and rural people.

# Project Objectives and Scope

This project will provide resources that support students to:

- develop understandings about contemporary society as a springboard for understanding self and others and for examining the contributions needed to bring about preferred futures
- investigate interconnecting social, cultural, ecological and economic systems, political and ethical issues, and alternative worldviews
- develop values, understandings, skills, dispositions, and behavior associated with civic decision making and with principles of the democratic process, sustainable futures, and social justice

The scope of the project is to design and develop high-quality online digital content organized around one or more of the following themes:

- geographical, economic, environmental, ethical, ideological, and political systems, and/or issues
- the way we are now
- what we want for the future

It should be noted that all of the above must be covered in the total body of content developed in the project but that not all elements need to be present in each individual learning object.

# Preferred Pedagogies

Constructivist pedagogies should underpin the design of all learning objects. Constructivism recognizes learners as the constructors of their own knowledge, values, and ethical outlook. Constructivist learning is based on tasks that:

- provide multiple representations of reality and the complexity of the real world
- present authentic tasks that encourage conceptualization

- provide real-world, case-based contexts
- support deep thinking
- often involve student collaboration featuring social negotiation and cooperative learning structures
- support students to choose from among variety of possible solutions or approaches to a problem
- enable learners to make connections across disciplines and perspectives

# APPENDIX 1–B

# Learning Object Design Brief

**Title:** Mission to Mars

**Target Audience:** Kindergarten–Grade 2

## Overall Concepts

The learning object will develop students' understanding of:

- values
- sustainability
- dimensions of well-being

## Subconcepts

The learning object will develop students' understanding of:

- how people contribute to the needs and well-being of the community
- how we all contribute to the community in productive and fair ways

## Learning Outcomes

Students will:

- identify the needs and wants of a community
- distinguish between needs and wants
- recognize healthy and unhealthy choices

# Interface Design Considerations

- clean interface
- large drag-and-drop areas
- large-font text
- audio instructions
- colorful, fun graphics

# Purpose of Learning Activity

The purpose of the learning activity for K–2 learners is to identify and understand the difference between their own needs and wants and to think about the needs and wants of others.

# Description of Learning Activities

**Step 1:** Students decide what is important to them—what they need to live in terms of people and resources. Students must discriminate between needs and wants.

A brightly colored spaceship appears in the foreground of the screen. Black space, stars, and planets appear in the background. Students are told that they are going to go on a mission to Mars and are asked what they need to take with them to live.

Students consider what they need to live and through appropriate selections, eventually populate the planet with the resources (i.e., people and things) they need.

Students are given a limited set of choices on a menu bar, and they are restricted in the number of resources they can choose. The choices may include family members, friends, a farmer, a builder, a police officer, water, healthy food, plants and animals, chocolate, TV, etc. The choices will cover a range of resources appropriate for different cultural groups, specifically including indigenous groups. The choices contain both needs and wants. The choices they make appear as graphical icons on the planet.

If students do not choose appropriate resources to satisfy basic needs such as water or other people, the planet starts to fade. An audio prompt asks them to consider what they really need.

With each appropriate choice, the students receive some form of affirmation (e.g., an audio applause, a smiling Martian). Students can remove resources from the planet and replace them with others until they are satisfied with the results.

Students explain the reasons for their choices either in written form on screen or orally.

**Step 2:** Students have to consider what the people and things they have previously chosen will need. There is another selection process whereby students must think about the needs of others in terms of resources and make appropriate selections from a set of choices. Students visually witness what happens when certain elements are missing or inserted in the scene. They can manipulate the scene until satisfied. The planet grows until a whole, sustainable community is reproduced.

**Step 3:** When the community is completed, students can select some "wants" from options provided. These "wants" include friends, pets, extra food such as chocolate, etc.

## Additional Information

The learning object can be replicated with other information and in other contexts.

It could also be extended in complexity for older learners. This could be done by increasing the size of the "ecological footprint" that the students' decisions leave. Reference could be made to the amount of water consumed, atmospheric pollution generated, and space occupied for farming, industry, and waste disposal.

# Michael Bishop

## Implementing Gaming Technologies in Traditional K–12 Contexts

*by Susan Pedersen*

Michael Bishop was at Oakdale Middle School last April when the results of the recent statewide proficiency tests were released. He'd been meeting with middle school teachers involved in pilot testing the educational games his team had developed for middle school science classes. As he left the training session he found Nancy Levin, the district-level science curriculum specialist, in the hallway, talking with Paul Russell, the Oakdale principal. Michael, a researcher at the university and the director of the project developing the science games, had been working with Nancy for two years now, and they had an easy relationship. So he approached her smiling, not yet realizing how serious the conversation was.

The news was grim. The previous year, the district average on the eighth-grade proficiency tests trailed the state average by 8%. This had prompted the district to implement new approaches in their middle schools designed to boost test scores in reading, math, and science. The new approaches included heavy use of software that offered individualized tutorials, as well as after-school programs for students who fell just short of proficiency in any of these subjects. Committees of teachers had convened over the summer to assess alignment of the curriculum to state standards and to select (and sometimes write) test items to be used for practice throughout the school year. Confidence in these approaches ran high in the district office, and school officials had waited eagerly for the confirmation of their effectiveness that the proficiency test results would provide. But the results showed exactly the opposite. The district average for eighth grade had fallen by 8% while the state average had risen by 2%. This left the district trailing the state average by a whopping 18%. The results of tests at the fifth-grade level were slightly better, but they still trailed state averages by 11%. Michael knew that in this state, such a drop typically had consequences for district personnel, and he wondered if some of this would fall on Nancy's shoulders.

So Michael was not entirely surprised six weeks later, after school was out for the summer, to get an e-mail from Nancy announcing that she was returning to the classroom to teach biology, and that her replacement would be Tara Jones. She did not mention Michael's project. Michael was surprised at the formality of the e-mail, so he tried calling

Nancy, both then and two days later. She returned neither call. Michael then contacted Tara to set up a time to meet to discuss the science game project.

Tara called Michael two days later. "I've had a chance to sit down with our superintendent to discuss your project, and I'm afraid that we've decided to withdraw," Tara told Michael. "We've decided that we just need to double down on essential skills and knowledge and that we can't afford to have our kids spend time playing games, even ones that are supposed to be educational. Each of your games takes over a week to play, and that's just too much time. The cohort you're working with will be eighth grade students next year, and since that's the grade in which kids take the science proficiency test, we've really got to work on preparing them. Now, I understand the problem we're causing for your project and that it will probably be an issue with your funding agency, but I'm sorry, the decision has been made."

# Finding a New Pilot Site

Michael was frustrated. Now in the middle of the project, he needed to recruit another school district to pilot test the games. So after taking a few days to consider his pitch, Michael called three different district offices and followed up with e-mails; one never responded and the other two formally declined to participate without even meeting with Michael. Michael decided to take a different approach and asked a colleague who had some contacts with district-level science coordinators to make some introductions. This led to conversations with administrators from four districts.

Michael felt as if he had to pitch the games to a skeptical audience, something he didn't like doing. He also knew that these administrators had full schedules, so he needed to give them enough detail to grab their interest but not overwhelm them, address issues head on, and make sure they could see the potential these games had for both learning and motivation. He sent a handout to each of the administrators before their conversation (see Figure 2–1). He began these conversations by explaining, "Each game addresses specific grade-level science concept standards, and does it in a way that makes it more likely that kids will understand and remember them. But more importantly, these games address inquiry standards. Kids ponder complex problems, ask questions, look for existing information, design investigations to gather data to answer their questions, support their decisions with evidence, and communicate their reasoning to classmates." Michael then walked the coordinator through the game model using the handout, answering questions as they arose. He made sure to emphasize how motivated students were during the game: "Even kids who normally seem unmotivated in science class stay on task and are enthusiastic. We really don't see much off-task behavior." Then he discussed the potential impact on standardized test results, citing results from the National Assessment of Educational Progress (NAEP) that suggested how games and other technology-based approaches that engage students in higher order thinking were correlated with higher outcomes on standardized tests than traditional approaches and tutorial software.

Bailey Richards, the science curriculum specialist in the Weyman independent school district (ISD), seemed genuinely interested in games as a means to engage students in

**FIGURE 2–1**    Game Description Sent to District Personnel Describing the Game Model, with Examples from One of the Games, *Rigglefish*.

| Rigglefish | |
|---|---|
| Game Description: *Rigglefish* is a game designed to address middle school standards related to genetics and scientific inquiry. In *Rigglefish,* learners take on the role of Dr. Waters, a geneticist tasked by the government with developing a source for Omega X, a fatty acid that can be used as a protectant against a deadly bioweapon. That source is the rigglefish, a recently discovered species of fish rich in Omega X. Rigglefish can be red, orange, or yellow, but only the yellow ones produce high concentrations of Omega X. Rigglefish also possess some traits that make them difficult to breed in captivity, including a sensitivity to low pressure environments, sharp spikes, and their distinctive wiggle. Players must breed a mating pair of rigglefish that can be farmed to provide a source for the needed protectant. | |

| Game Component | Example: *Rigglefish* |
|---|---|
| A Complex Task: Each game presents a complex, ill-structured task which requires students to engage in student-directed inquiry | Students must breed a mating pair of fish that are purebred for four key traits. To accomplish this task, students determine, through observation and testing, the phenotypes and genotypes of fish they collect, then breed these fish to obtain the target fish. |
| Opening Scenario: Video introduction to problem; provides a compelling backstory, but does not tell learners what to do | Student is cast in the role of Dr. Waters, a geneticist who receives an urgent request from the government to develop a source for Omega X, a protectant against a deadly new bioweapon. Task must be completed before enemy agents discover the lab where players are working. |
| A Virtual Environment: A confined space that contains all the tools and resources learners need; players spend very little time on navigation | Students work in a top-secret underwater lab with four rooms: bathysphere, sample room, pressure room, and breeding room. |
| Virtual Scientific Instruments: Virtual models of real-world scientific instruments, simplified to emphasize key characteristics relevant to student learning; students must interpret the data the instruments return | Sample Instruments: Bathysphere: Used to collect rigglefish for testing and breeding. Sample tanks: Used to observe rigglefish and determine phenotypes and genotypes of each. Gel electrophoresis and PCR: Determine a fish's genotype for wiggle trait. Breeding tanks: Breed rigglefish and select offspring for further testing and breeding. |
| Information Resources: All information needed to handle task is provided within game so that learners do not need to search online; information is divided among resources, which discourages reading without a purpose | Sample Resources: Genetics Guide: Information on topics such as dominant, recessive, co-dominant, and incompletely dominant alleles. Punnett square: Interactive square that players can use to determine possible offspring; connects genotypes with phenotypes. |

**FIGURE 2–1**   *Continued*

| Game Component | Example: *Rigglefish* |
|---|---|
| Expert Modeling Videos: An expert thinks aloud about how he or she would handle different tasks within game, making scientific thinking overt; videos available on demand | Menu allows students to ask questions such as: <br> What should I do first? <br> How can I tell the genotypes and phenotypes of different fish? <br> How do I breed a fish without a wiggle? |
| Tool Demonstration Videos: Shows how each tool within program functions | Videos on how to use: <br> Bathysphere <br> Sample tanks <br> Pressure tank <br> Gel electrophoresis <br> PCR <br> Punnett square <br> Breeding tanks |

scientific inquiry and agreed to meet with Michael and let him present the games to her. But, like Tara Jones, she balked at the amount of time required. "We hit a lot of topics in those middle grades and yes, we want depth, but we have to go deep quickly. So we want inquiry, but we really have to guide them through it so they don't spend a lot of time just trying to figure out what to do. Your games look great, but these kids aren't used to having to figure so much out for themselves. I think you would find a lot of kids wasting time not knowing what to do. Maybe advanced learners would be able to handle something like this, but I don't think this would be an efficient use of time for the average learner."

Laura Kenner and Daniel Brown, the science coordinators in two neighboring districts that had received ratings in the satisfactory range on the proficiency tests in the previous two years, raised other issues as well. Both districts were moving to a common curriculum in which lessons were developed by a group of teachers and then implemented in every classroom on the same day. The approach was new and many teachers were protesting. Laura explained, "At this point I just don't see how we could allow a few teachers to do something different. If we did, everyone would be asking to be allowed to bring in their pet projects." Daniel explained further, "We're trying to limit how much time our science classes use computers so that we can save computer lab time for math and language arts. If we had one or two science teachers getting to use computers for two weeks in a row, the other teachers and students would complain. I just don't think we could make that work."

Jim Harrington, the assistant superintendent for curriculum in Mason ISD, a large district where the middle school ratings fell into the excellent to exemplary categories, met with Michael for over an hour and seemed to really enjoy playing one of the games Michael's team had developed, even though he hit a couple of bugs. He was less concerned than the others about the length of the games themselves, but raised another issue about the time required. "I know some of these approaches have great potential, and I think that's certainly true for games. And I also know you have to pilot test them somewhere, but I feel like we really need to protect our kids from spending too much time on that sort of thing. We've had university folks come into our schools before, and they want to have kids complete a lot of surveys and tests and try out new materials and approaches. But not all of them are ready for prime time. Even in your game, there were some bugs; those could bring a class to a screeching halt and end up wasting time. And you want them to complete pretests and surveys and interviews. We just can't spend that sort of time on research."

Interestingly, none of the school personnel Michael spoke with argued that games were inappropriate in science education. In fact, many of them seemed enthusiastic about the use of games in education. In the end, Jim offered to let Michael implement the games in pre-AP classes in two middle schools and a magnet laptop program in another. Laura asked if he would like to work with the after-school science clubs at two of the schools in her district, and Daniel suggested he consider summer programs. They liked the games; they just didn't want them in their regular science classes.

A major purpose of the games Michael's team was developing, and the purpose for which they had received funding, was to hone an innovative model to use technology to increase the engagement of all students in scientific inquiry in their science classes. Restricting use of the games to gifted students, after-school programs, and science summer camps seemed like an admission that they weren't appropriate for regular kids in regular classes. Michael wondered if there were ways to make them more appealing to school districts. Though Nancy had given him some good advice, such as trying to keep the games to a maximum of eight days and including tool demonstration videos, and he had adjusted the original model for the games accordingly, it had been insufficient to make the games appealing to anyone who wasn't already an advocate of this type of approach. In considering what the options might be, Michael sought advice from people in diverse fields.

## Getting Advice

Michael recruited a small group of people with expertise in different areas to participate in an advisory session with him. Craig Dawson was the director of science education for the state education agency. He had 20 years of teaching experience in middle and high school science classes and was a strong advocate for inquiry-based learning. Michael had attended a couple of talks he had given, but did not know him well. Bob Blanchard was a game designer who had spent nine years in California working on some triple-A game titles, then moved two years ago to lead game design in a midsize company located in the same town as the university. Michael had met him the previous year when he was conducting interviews with gaming professionals as part of a research project led by a colleague at another university. Antonia Fisher was a professor of science education at Michael's university. She had projects of her own and had pleaded lack of time when Michael had invited her to be a co–principal investigator on his project. However, Michael had known her for years and valued her opinion, so he was glad she'd agreed to participate in the advisory session. Despite their busy schedules, they were able to meet for a four-hour block in early August.

**FIGURE 2–2** Players Use the Bathysphere in *Rigglefish* to Collect Fish They Can Study and Breed.

Michael began the meeting with introductions followed by a presentation of the game model, similar to the one he had given district administrators. He then showed them the opening scenario of *Rigglefish* and let them play for about 40 minutes (See Figure 2–2). This was enough time for everyone to capture fish and try out the different tools, including the breeding tank (see Figure 2–3). They all chatted as they played, commenting mostly on features they liked and asking questions about how to accomplish specific tasks. It was obvious they enjoyed the game and wanted to figure out how to breed the target fish.

Michael began transitioning the group from playing *Rigglefish* to discussing the project. "What I'd like from you is your advice on moving forward with the design of these games." He then explained about the withdrawal of one district from the pilot test and the responses from other districts. "We'd like to see these games implemented in middle school science classes, not only with pre-AP or gifted students, but with regular education classes as well. Is that reasonable? Do we need to design these games differently in order to make them attractive to teachers and districts? Or should we give up on that and design for a different audience?"

Craig Dawson shifted in his seat and at the same time seemed to shift roles from enthusiastic player to concerned educator. "That's a tough one, Michael. Teachers and administrators are concerned about those tests, but really what we're all concerned about is making the best use of instructional time. Games are highly engaging, but do students

**FIGURE 2–3**    The Breeding Tank in *Rigglefish* Allows Players to Cross Fish to Breed Offspring with Desired Traits.

learn as fast or as deeply as they do through other approaches? Unless you can build a case that these games engage students in real science and that this causes them to learn better and faster, you're going to continue to have the sort of pushback you've gotten so far. Now I know that standardized tests have a bad reputation among academics, and perhaps they're imperfect, but they're the best tool we have for identifying schools that are failing and students who need help. So you've got to be able to show that your games lead to learning that shows up on those tests."

Antonia Fisher responded, "I think that's a somewhat unrealistic expectation, Craig. Performance on those tests depends on a lot of factors. I would say that if you can show that you are successful in getting kids to engage in scientific practice within the games, that's enough to justify their use. The science education community has been trying for decades to incorporate better opportunities for kids to engage in authentic scientific practices and from what I noticed playing your game, I think it's pretty clear that players 'do science' in it. In particular what resonated with me was that I could see kids collaborating and debating the best ways to tackle various parts of this problem, just like the three of us did as we played. That type of critical thinking just doesn't happen often enough in our science classes."

"I agree that the game encourages higher level thinking," Craig replied. "I think that's great. All I'm saying is that if you want buy-in from schools, you're going to have to show an impact on performance. I'd recommend creating a bank of test items that teachers can use either as warm-up activities or homework, or perhaps even embed them in your games. Kids reach certain checkpoints and they answer a few questions to test their understanding. That would allow both the teachers and the students to see how much they understand."

Bob Blanchard objected, "Games are great at gathering data about players. There's no need to incorporate multiple-choice questions because you can tell through gameplay what a player does and doesn't understand. Now it's difficult to pull that data out of games and make it really usable for teachers, but it can give a much better picture of what players understand. Besides, incorporating multiple-choice or short-answer questions in a game will break up gameplay, distract the player, and kill motivation. You might be able to do some of that in a homework exercise, but I suspect that as soon as those worksheets come out, the type of critical thinking you're trying to get at here will disappear."

Antonia replied, "I think that's a real danger. You know, Michael, schools need alternatives. If the only types of learning materials out there are ones that prep students for tests, where are the models of alternative approaches? Where are the materials those innovative teachers can use? You have a vision here, and it's a pretty good one, so I say stick with it. These games won't be for everyone, but if you can find a few partners who believe in this work and show impact on the types of things that really matter, then you've done something important."

"What do you mean by 'really matter'?" Michael asked.

Antonia was growing passionate. "By the time a student finishes high school, he or she should have adopted the habits of mind that good scientists have. For example, they should bring the type of healthy skepticism that scientists have to making decisions in all areas of their lives. By that I mean that they should expect, no, *demand*, evidence for claims that others make. And they should think critically about whether that evidence is unbiased and valid. I think games like this can support that type of thinking. I think kids are likely to challenge each other about what claims they make and that they are going to want to defend what they are doing. In other words, they're going to ask each other for evidence and offer it themselves when challenged. That's incredible. That's what we should want out of our educational system. Achieving a goal like that—that should be the measure of success."

Craig smiled. "That's all fine and good, but you have to consider the realities of the classrooms where you want your games played. In addition, you have to think the teachers and students who play them."

Antonia nodded and said, "What I question about these games is whether you really support teachers in using them well. It takes time to learn to use an approach as different as this effectively."

Bob agreed. "I worked on an educational game and we did some testing in schools. As soon as the teacher was the one managing the implementation, we had problems. That's not a slam at the teachers; they were quite professional and enthusiastic, but they started telling the kids to do things that we'd never anticipated. In particular, they would show them specific strategies and tell them to play that way, even though there were multiple effective strategies. It undermined the whole gameplay experience in that the kids were not really figuring things out for themselves. You really have to provide good teacher training if you want them to support, rather than direct, the inquiry experience."

"But teachers are going to need to hold students accountable for learning while they are playing," Craig said. "Otherwise, what are you going to do about kids who get off-task?"

Michael responded, "Actually, we don't see a lot of off-task behavior."

"Perhaps you haven't seen it because you're there leading the class and the approach is novel," said Craig. "But when you've got a class with kids with diverse needs and a teacher who isn't entirely comfortable with the approach, you're going to have some kids get confused and off track. The teacher has got to have some control to bring them back on task. There have got to be checkpoints and at least a few definite assignments with due dates. Otherwise there's a danger of a lot of time being wasted."

"Michael," said Antonia, "if you are really looking for a pure implementation of your games, then you might seriously consider summer camps and homeschool markets. That would allow you to implement your vision of the games while at the same time learning about effective implementation strategies. Once you know how to optimize the player experience, you might be able to try that out in a school setting. There have been a variety of innovations that caught on outside of classrooms, and once they were really polished, started being adopted by schools."

Michael tried to get the group to identify areas of consensus about how he should move forward with the project, but didn't get very far. Beyond agreeing that the games had merit, their opinions diverged too much to coalesce into an action plan he could walk away with. The lofty principles Antonia espoused resonated with Michael's own beliefs about the goals of science education, but he also recognized that sticking with his vision might mean that the games were doomed to irrelevance. Even if he could find isolated teachers or schools willing to pilot test them, they would probably never achieve broad dissemination in middle schools under their current design. Michael left the meeting realizing he had a lot of thinking to do.

# Preliminary Analysis Questions

1. Identify the different barriers Michael encountered when he tried to convince school district personnel to implement the games in middle school classes. What questions do you think educational game designers must consider when designing a game for K–12 contexts?
2. What arguments could Michael make to convince school administrators and teachers about the potential benefits of educational games?
3. Why does Michael feel so strongly about *not* putting the game in an after-school program? Discuss the pros and cons of Michael's decision.

# Implications for ID Practice

1. What characteristics of middle school learners must designers consider when planning educational games? Provide specific examples.
2. Identify the different contexts in which an educational game might be played and how those contexts affect design decisions.
3. How can teachers assess student learning through educational games?
4. How are the factors affecting the adoption of a game in this case similar to or different from efforts to introduce other innovations in schools (e.g., problem-based learning, mobile devices)?

To learn more about or play *Rigglefish*, please visit www.velscience.com.

# CASE STUDY 3

# Denny Clifford

## Designing Learning Experiences for Middle School Science Teachers

*by Peggy A. Ertmer and Katherine S. Cennamo*

Denny Clifford, an independent instructional design (ID) consultant, had never felt so bewildered—Dr. Cynthia Oakes was one of the most complex clients he had ever worked for! Denny wasn't sure if this stemmed from the difference in their ages, genders, or educational experiences, or simply the nature of the project, but he found himself completely incapable of carrying on a meaningful conversation with Cynthia. They just didn't seem to speak the same language.

Denny was an experienced design consultant—he had worked for a media production firm for the past five years and was an Air Force technical designer/trainer before that. He had created a wide variety of instructional materials, including computer-based lessons, multimedia simulations, and distance education courses. Although Cynthia had personally requested his help with the development of a set of innovative materials for middle school science teachers, this was the most difficult job he had ever accepted. Originally, he had thought that his basic understanding of science and technology would be a distinct advantage, compared with other projects he had worked on; now he wasn't so sure. Maybe if he understood a little bit more about Cynthia's teaching philosophy, he wouldn't be so confused.

Cynthia, a professor of science education at the local university, believed wholeheartedly in a constructivist approach to teaching and learning. Denny learned, early on, that this translated into an aversion to such words as *objectives, criterion-referenced test items, directed instruction,* and *right answers.* Still, Cynthia had requested Denny's assistance in creating some instructional materials to help local middle school teachers teach in a manner consistent with science reform initiatives.

As in most middle schools, students at the local schools change classes for instruction in various content areas; thus, certain teachers are responsible for teaching science to multiple groups of students each day. Although some of these teachers have an interest in science, most are simply assigned to teach science without much training or interest in the subject. Several years ago, Cynthia received a large grant to develop science materials for this group of teachers.

As a national leader in the area of science education, Cynthia developed an innovative curriculum based on a social constructivist view of learning. Quite simply, the curriculum consisted of a set of "problems" for students to solve. Cynthia introduced the curriculum in local workshops where she explained her constructivist philosophy and provided an overview of the materials. The curriculum was wildly popular, leading to multiple requests from other school districts for Cynthia to present workshops and in-services at their localities.

Now, Cynthia has received a large grant to develop professional development materials for this audience. Money does not seem to be a concern; however, she has introduced a number of constraints to the project.

# The Middle School Science Project

First, Cynthia indicated that the purpose of this project was to help middle school science teachers (1) generate multiple ideas from their students about how to solve a scientific problem, (2) listen to and make sense of the students' ideas about science, and (3) know what to do with these ideas (i.e., respond in ways that value the students' ideas and provide opportunities for them to explicate their problem-solving strategies). Cynthia didn't really care what specific content from the science curriculum Denny focused on; instead, she wanted the teachers to learn an alternative way of teaching science to middle school students—that was the content she was most interested in teaching. In fact, she wasn't interested in *teaching* her content at all. She simply wanted to provide opportunities for teachers to "explore issues related to reform-based science teaching" in a "socially supportive" environment.

Second, Cynthia believed deeply in the effectiveness of her approach for developing scientific reasoning. From earlier discussions, Denny learned that science lessons typically began with pairs of students working on a problem from the curriculum and ended with them sharing their problem-solving strategies and solutions with the whole class in a large group discussion. Though her perspective sometimes conflicted with state mandates and policy, it didn't matter to Cynthia if the middle school students gave the right answers to the problems; her interest was in developing the problem-solving *process,* not achieving particular learning outcomes in terms of content. In fact, she mentioned that there *were* no absolute right answers, because "all knowledge is socially constructed." Thus, she wanted teachers to develop their pedagogical knowledge of science teaching in a similar manner.

Third, Cynthia was particularly sensitive to her participants' needs. She was well aware that classroom teachers were extremely busy people. She was hoping to provide instruction in a format that allowed teachers to work on their own time, possibly at school or home. Of course, she expected that teachers would start using innovative approaches to science instruction in their own classrooms.

Fourth, Cynthia didn't have the time, or the desire, to conduct a series of in-services or workshops for the local teachers. She had done this a number of times over the past few years and was no longer interested in continuing in this vein. Her main interest was research. She was deeply interested in the effects of the curriculum on students' scientific thinking. Typically, she provided extensive follow-up for each teacher who participated in her workshops. She observed their classes weekly and followed these with individual meetings in which she discussed her observations. In fact, she had published numerous articles in which she discussed children's learning in her problem-centered science curriculum.

It seemed to Denny that Cynthia was willing to find a way to meet the need for the workshops but wasn't interested in delivering them. In fact, it seemed that she had not really thought much about how to package the instruction. Denny wondered if much of her previous "instruction" on the curriculum had occurred during one-on-one meetings with the teachers. Although she did not want to spend her time conducting workshops, Cynthia indicated that she was willing to meet with teachers for an occasional half-day to "share experiences and stories." But, of course, that would be impossible if the program were eventually distributed nationally, as she envisioned. With the large number of requests for workshops, Cynthia just didn't have time to do it all. That's why she contacted Denny—to envision and design another way to distribute the information.

# What To Do?

At Denny's prior meeting with Cynthia, she had made it quite clear that she expected him to provide a list of suggestions regarding his proposed materials and delivery methods at their next meeting, scheduled within a week's time. Yet, to date, Denny hadn't completed *any* of his normal ID tasks. For example, he hadn't been able to develop a list of objectives or assessment instruments. He had no specific content to work with; Cynthia seemed to be the only subject matter expert available; in fact, he didn't even have a list of learner characteristics. Despite having had four meetings with Cynthia, Denny hadn't been able to obtain the information that he normally got from clients at the start of a project.

On reflection, however, Denny realized that the following resources, mentioned in conversations with Cynthia, might provide him with some direction, or at least a starting point:

- A list of 24 teachers who had completed the workshops in previous years; many of these people were teaching in local schools and, for the most part, were still practicing the techniques they had learned
- A box of DVDs, labeled by observation date, of these teachers in their classrooms as they were gaining experience with this approach
- A copy of the grant proposal that funded the development of the teacher materials
- A list of local teachers who expressed interest in learning to teach science in a new way
- A couple of articles that had been written by both Cynthia and a former participant who was entering her fifth year of teaching science in the manner Cynthia advocated

Denny had his notes (see Figure 3–1) from these meetings and the resources provided by Cynthia, but the information still seemed only remotely related to his assignment. How was he going to deliver effective instruction when he couldn't seem to begin designing it?

**FIGURE 3–1**   Denny's Notes from Meetings with Cynthia.

- Group discussions are important to allow opportunities for kids to create shared meaning of scientific ideas.
- Productive discussions allow kids to develop their scientific reasoning, to articulate their ideas, and to reflect on their reasoning and the reasoning of others.
- Teachers need assistance in becoming good discussion facilitators.
- Teachers need continual support while in the process of changing their practice.
- The teacher's role is critical in fostering students' ability to develop skills in scientific reasoning.
- Teaching in a manner consistent with reform initiatives requires a shift away from traditional teaching and change in teacher practice.
- Change in practice is especially important in terms of conducting successful class discussions during science, which are critical to the success of this approach.
- Teachers lack the time and social support necessary to reflect on their practice.
- Materials are targeted for both new and experienced teachers, reinforcing teaching in a manner consistent with reform initiatives in science education.
- Participants enroll voluntarily, so they usually have a positive attitude toward developing their practice. May have some anxiety about trying something new. Important to create trust and a nonjudgmental environment.
- Participating teachers are expected to reflect on classroom practices of their own and others, and to develop action plans for continual development of practice.

# Preliminary Analysis Questions

1. Describe the communication barriers operating in this case. Suggest strategies for circumventing or eliminating those barriers.
2. Describe how the identified resources can be repurposed to address specific ID needs.
3. What type of media, delivery mode, and instructional techniques might be appropriate for this content, audience, and client? Justify your recommendations.

# Implications for ID Practice

1. Suggest strategies to facilitate a mutually beneficial relationship between people with different philosophical backgrounds.
2. Draft an instructional strategy for a sample lesson that introduces teachers to a constructivist approach to science teaching.
3. Describe the importance of matching delivery mode, media, and instructional techniques to client and learner needs.
4. Consider settings in which the application of the ADDIE model may not work well. What alternative models can designers consider?

# Paul Lindley

## Designing a Video Game for History Education

*by William R. Watson*

"Quests and puzzles. Think an adventure game, like one of the Harry Potter games," Kevin said. "You're basically just running around in the castle the whole time."

"Did you see the awful reviews that game got?" Linda asked.

"Well, yeah, "Kevin responded." But it really wasn't a horrible game. It was the story, and the environment that hooked you."

"Yes, the environment," Paul agreed. "You get to be in the role of Harry in Hogwarts, and you can talk to anyone, and you can go anywhere on the grounds. It's a sandbox environment, like Grand Theft Auto."

"What's a sandbox?" Bo interrupted.

"Yeah, I haven't seen or played either of those games," Jamie added.

"It's where they make it seem like you're in the real world, because you can wander around and explore and try different things out and the game always responds, instead of just having one path through the game that you can't deviate from," Kevin replied.

Paul looked at his team of students. He'd been seeing this dynamic play out recently in the team's meetings. It was as if he had two teams of designers speaking two different languages. Kevin and Linda brought up specific games, and even particular moments or characters in games, when presenting design ideas, but without similar backgrounds in video games to pull from, Jamie and Bo were at a loss.

Paul looked around the table at the scattered books and DVDs his students had brought back with them. They'd previously borrowed a variety of materials to get a background on the human experiences and controversy surrounding the United States' decision to imprison its citizens of Japanese descent during World War II.

The graduate students were from Walker University and were members of the team responsible for designing an educational video game; Paul Lindley, their professor, specialized in educational technology and hoped to secure funding for game development. He had been approached by the principal of a local alternative high school about potentially developing an educational video game for the school. The school had a track record of taking students who had failed in the district's high school and, despite a small staff and limited resources, enabled them to succeed. Students were given more control over their own learning, through a project-based learning approach.

Paul had worked with the school previously and conducted research on learning from educational video games. Recently, he and the principal, Bob Reckowsky, sat down to brainstorm how they could make the game a reality. Bob, who apart from being the principal, was also one of two full-time teachers at the school, and had played professional baseball. He used that interest to develop an instructional module that examined the internment of Japanese Americans during World War II and the role baseball played in fostering morale in the camps. The original instruction went well, but Bob was left feeling there was still more that could be done with the content.

The school had no special resources, but Bob observed that a number of his students were really into video games. Knowing Paul's interest, Bob thought educational gaming was something worth exploring. In talking, the two identified a number of resources Bob already had; Paul then ordered some additional books and documentaries to learn more about the content. Paul also took a copy of Bob's workbook and the standards with which the module was aligned.

Paul then set about putting a team together, which currently consisted of four graduate students (Kevin Elkin, Jamie Tolliver, Linda Grimes, and Bo Chen) who would be working with him to design the game. None of the students had worked on educational game design before, and two of them had little experience with a wide range of game types. In fact, Jamie and Bo's past video game experiences had largely been limited to online card games. Nevertheless, they set out to develop an initial paper-based design of the game so that they could test out the game logic and mechanics before securing a grant to develop a digital version of the game.

Paul had only a cursory knowledge of the history that they were trying to teach; it had never been mentioned during his own K–12 history classes. However, after studying the books and documentaries he had ordered, as well as Bob's workbook, Paul felt he had gained a good knowledge base from which to proceed.

Paul learned that following the attack on Pearl Harbor, President Roosevelt signed Executive Order 9066, which banned all people of Japanese descent from the Pacific coast for the purposes of national security, unless they were held in internment camps. Following this order, Japanese and Japanese American citizens were forced to sell their property and all their belongings, often within a few days. The Supreme Court upheld the constitutional legality of this action in 1944; however, in 1988, President Reagan signed legislation apologizing for the internment on behalf of the government, declaring the act, among other things, to have been based on race prejudice.

During relocation, families were initially taken to centers, bringing with them only what they could carry. They were then sent to internment camps, often located on Native American reservations, where the families were housed with other families in buildings that lacked plumbing or cooking facilities. Baseball became one of the primary forms of entertainment in the camps. Camp leagues were created and internees built diamonds out of scrap materials and whatever they could piece together.

With this knowledge in place, Paul set about guiding his design team to consider content, design, and development issues.

## Back at the Meeting

Kevin finished telling the design team about the open worlds of Harry Potter and Grand Theft Auto, including ways in which the player was free to explore them.

Afterward, Paul remarked, "Well there's some more homework for you, Kevin." Paul considered Kevin to be a "hardcore gamer." He was familiar with almost every game on the market, and would describe specific gameplay from games over a decade old. "We'll find some copies of those games you can try out in the lab, and in the meantime, why don't the rest of you check out some gameplay videos of them on YouTube?"

"The thing is, both of those games still have violence," Linda said. "There's a lot of exploration, and there's the story, but you still cast spells at other characters in Harry Potter, and you get in gun and fist fights in Grand Theft Auto. Are those games still going to be fun if you're only exploring?" Linda was a graduate student in library science and was working with a group of other students and faculty on how to implement games within the context of the changing nature of modern libraries.

"Well, we know first that the story has to be engaging," Bo said. Bo, a student from China, had dutifully been borrowing a game to try out every couple of days in an effort to better understand the medium. A former public school teacher, he had a strong interest in motivating students but no real background in games. "And Jamie found an internment camp newsletter in the National Archives at archives.gov, so we can have real events in there. But we're talking about a camp of featureless buildings out in the desert, so I'm not sure how much fun the exploration will be. I was looking at a game online and I don't know if it's what you would call a sandbox, but there is a town that you walk around in, and you get to talk with different characters and go in different buildings. If everything looks the same it might be confusing."

"Remember, it's about the choices and about the goals," Paul added. "We need to give them interesting choices within the story. We have to let the players feel like they are in control."

"But that's where it gets tricky," Jamie said. "There's only so much we can do in terms of different outcomes in the story before all of the different choices make things unwieldy." Jamie, like Bo, had almost no experience with games. An older student, the only video games she had seen had been the games her children liked to play, but she had only watched them play. So this world of video games was entirely new to her.

"They can be choices that impact things in the immediate story but less so in the larger narrative," Kevin said. "Sorry, but think about Grand Theft Auto again. It seems like your choices must be having a huge outcome on the story, but if you play through it a couple of times, it's really an illusion, and the impact you have on the game is largely limited to the endings, except for a few things."

"And remember, we've got some of these big choices that the people in the camps had to make," Bo said. "Big decisions, like if they'd sign the oath swearing loyalty to the United States, the country that imprisoned them and forced them to sell everything they owned in a couple of days."

"Exactly," Paul approved. "It's important that the gameplay reflect the learning goals. We want an interesting story, and we want interesting choices, but we want them connected to the learning as well."

Paul flipped through his notes while the rest of the team continued their discussion. They had spent a considerable amount of time poring over historical documents, documentaries, and even a feature-length film about the role of baseball in the camps. They had found a couple of gold mines for ideas about events in the narrative and possible game activities, including camp newspapers and a book documenting the history of Japanese American baseball. Despite this, apart from stressing the importance of the game's story, they weren't any closer to actually designing gameplay or having a sense of the game's structure and focus.

"OK, OK!" Paul interrupted. "We've got a lot of ideas, but we need to start exploring some of these and get a better sense of what our constraints are. Bo, we know that there are states that specifically require that the history of the camps be taught. We need to be sure that we're able to match up with their standards, so I want you to start gathering that information so we can start to specify some of our learning goals." Bo hurriedly wrote in the notebook he always carried with him and nodded.

"We also need to have a better sense of our players and how the game might be used. I've got a list of some social studies teachers who have agreed to be interviewed, and we have a number of students at the alternative high school who have already completed a module about the history of baseball in the camps. Who wants to interview the students and the teachers? You'll need to drive to the school to interview the students; we can interview the teachers who aren't nearby by phone." Paul looked around and nodded as Jamie raised her hand. "Anyone else?" he asked.

"I can help," Linda said.

"Great. Most of these teachers have used games but not all of them. I want to know why they do or don't use games, how they use them, and what their primary goals for using a game like this might be. Also see if they're teaching about the camps, and why or why not.

"See what the students learned from taking the module. See what kind of games and gameplay they like and why. Linda, I want you and Kevin to keep brainstorming and also do some searching to get us some more examples of gameplay we might want to use. Keep thinking about commercial games that have considerable nonviolent gameplay, and also see what other educational games are doing, particularly if there are any historical games," Paul said. "And everyone keep adding to your notes about the people and events you run across that might have a place in the game. Everyone got that?"

# Linda and Jamie: Investigating Student and Teacher Needs

Linda moved her tray back to give Jamie room to sit at the café table. "What did you get?" Linda asked. "Veggie curry," Jamie replied. "They have a Meat-Free Monday deal for it." The two had just returned from visiting the alternative high school and were debriefing their experiences over lunch.

"So, what jumped out at you?" Jamie asked.

"That the kids have no idea what the camps have to do with them," Linda answered with a laugh.

"Yeah, absolutely," Jamie smiled. "For a second there I thought you were going to draw them a map, the way you were nudging them toward Guantanamo!" She shook her head and took a drink of water. "I heard the same thing from these teachers and the teachers I spoke with on the phone, too. They said the biggest thing with their students and history is that they can't make the connection between history and their own lives. The teachers seemed to think history can be an unpopular class for a lot of students because of that."

"Well, we certainly saw that here," Linda agreed, setting down her sandwich. "It seemed pretty clear that those two boys took the camps module because of their interest in baseball, not in history. They did seem interested in video games, though."

Jamie nodded. "They seemed to like most of the current popular games, and both mentioned they like to be able to develop and level up their characters, whether within a role-playing game or just getting new weapons and armor in a shooter, so we might think about if we can work in some sort of leveling or character customization. And the teachers at the school really seemed excited about the game. They thought the students would really like to play it."

"I'm sure," Linda answered. "It looked like they could use whatever resources they could get their hands on. They seemed to be spread pretty thin. They did mention it would be nice to be able to have the game e-mail them when a student completed it, so that it would be easier for them to track their progress, too. Did you get anything else from the teachers you spoke to on the phone?"

"The main thing over and over again was just how little time they have to teach anything anymore. I spoke to one guy who is teaching world history in one semester," Jamie exclaimed. "All of world history in one semester! Multiple teachers told me that they were very limited on time because of the standards they have to adhere to. So it's a chapter a week from the textbook and then move on. They were pretty clear that the game would need to be something that they could squeeze in. And the other thing was they had different class period times, too. So some, once they got the class down to the computer lab, might only have half an hour to actually play the game, and maybe only a couple of days of lab availability overall. I think we'd see teachers using it as homework as well as in class because of the limited access to computers," she finished, as Linda typed notes into her laptop. "Can you think of anything else?"

"Hmm, I wonder if homework is a problem because we don't know if all the kids have access to computers out of school. And if they do, what about the connection speed? And because the teachers all seem to have a lot on their plates, it's like Dr. Lindley said—we need to be sure to have guides for the teachers to make the game as easy to implement as possible, or it's not going to get used."

## Back Together Again: The Group Debriefs

"Let me get back to this idea of quests," Kevin said. It had been several weeks since the entire team had met together. In that time, Kevin had been reviewing all sorts of games, both commercial and educational, while Jamie and Linda had conducted interviews with teachers and students. Bo had been reviewing how and where the camps were taught in schools.

Kevin continued, "In a lot of RPGs—er, role-playing games—you have the main storyline and then you have smaller quests that get you an item or fill in some backstory but might not be required to advance the primary plot. Think of the kinds of mini-games that are in a lot of these sandbox games."

"Right," Bo agreed.

"We could have mini-games tied to some of what they did, like we already have the baseball component, but we know a lot of gambling occurred, and I read a story about people sneaking out of camp to fish at a nearby pond."

"Do we really want middle-schoolers playing gambling games?" Jamie laughed.

"Well, it's historically accurate," Linda mused, "but that's a good question."

"Yeah," Kevin said, "that's a question I had. We're wanting to highlight the race issue, but do we want to include the racial slurs that were used?"

"They were used in the newspapers," Bo said. "It would be changing the reality of that time if we removed them."

"But are parents going to be OK with their kids playing a game with that kind of language?" Kevin asked. "Will schools be OK with it? What does it matter how accurate it is if no one is allowed to play it?"

"Some of the teachers I talked with who hadn't really used games much did have some concerns about parents being against using them," Linda mentioned.

"Yeah, but we also had that teacher who has been using a history game for the past five years, and he said he'd never had a single parent complain or question what the kids were learning," Jamie countered.

"And the main thing we kept hearing again and again is how we have to make things relevant for the students. And if nothing else, racial issues are still relevant," Linda said.

"OK, let's slow down," Paul interrupted. "Let's put aside those decisions for now and focus on the gameplay again. So we've got mini-games and quests, Kevin."

"Right," Kevin said. "We know since we're trying to stay away from violent gameplay that we're going to focus on the story. A lot of these games have you going here and there and talking to different people so that you get an understanding of the story, and that action is a part of, or also includes, additional quests, mini-games, puzzles. That sort of thing."

"OK, but the thing is, a lot of those sandbox games and role-playing games are like 20 or 30 hours long!" Linda mused. "The teachers were very clear that their biggest challenge is time. Limited time in the computer lab. Limited time for the subject matter. And we don't want the students spending their time in class playing mini-games that don't contribute to the main plot."

"So let's talk about the story for a second and why we're wanting to focus on it," Paul said. "Why is narrative important for us?"

"Engagement," Bo said.

"Good, and . . . ?" Paul asked.

"If the learners identify with the main character, they will be able to see things from their point of view," Jamie said.

"Right—we're also wanting them to understand what life was like in these camps," Kevin said.

"So now we're starting to talk about topics that can lead to our learning objectives. Remember, that always needs to be what we're coming back to," Paul said. "What did you find about the standards, Bo?"

"Here are some of the standards I found," Bo said, pulling a paper out of his folder and placing it on the table. "It looks like it's the sophomore year when this is taught in California. It's also required in Arizona, and this is their set of standards."

The team passed the standards document around. "So what about national standards, Bo?" Linda asked.

"Well, it seems that there are no national standards for social studies," Bo answered. "Or, there are some, but adoption is up to the states. Each state has its own and there are some standards set by some social studies organizations, if that makes sense, as kind of guidelines. Furthermore, the standards for each state vary widely in length and specificity."

"So that's going to make identifying which standards to align with more challenging," Paul mused.

"We definitely heard from the teachers that anything we can do to make their jobs easier makes it more likely they would use the game," Linda stated. "So the teacher's guide is going to be really important. We'll want lesson plans, and they want things flexible, and they want the students to make the connection to what it has to do with them, and that's going to be the big challenge."

"Well, I know that there are lessons out there on teaching about the Supreme Court case, the Korematsu versus the United States case," Bo added. "So we could maybe connect that to some of the court cases about Guantanamo Bay, like Jamie suggested."

"But how are we going to work a Supreme Court case into the game?" Kevin asked.

"Why does it have to be in the game?" Paul responded. "Remember, we want the game to be the hook to get them interested in the topic. The game does not replace the teacher. Our job is to get them interested and make that connection to their own lives. Get them hooked, get them interested, and exploration can happen inside and outside of the game. So the question is how to make them see the relevance and get them interested in exploring the topic. So why is it relevant to modern issues?"

"We're talking about individual rights versus the rights of the nation," Jamie added.

"Exactly," Paul said. "We're talking about classic issues of a democracy. We don't need to limit ourselves to just a history game or history in a void. We're looking at history as a part of social studies, which has a larger goal of citizenship education. So we need to look at controversies of today and tie them to the past. Guantanamo Bay. Habeas corpus. The Patriot Act. Drones targeting individuals with bombs."

"Sounds like a lot of issues related to 9/11," Jamie mused. "And 9/11 casts a long shadow. Even if the kids didn't experience that day, they will still be really aware of it. And we could be teaching them the relevance of that history as well as the history of the camps. Showing them the connection between history and today."

"We might make some out-of-game connections to current events in the instructor guide and lesson plans, then," Bo said. "But don't we want something in-game as well? How can we make some sort of connection there?"

"So let's review where we are," Paul said. "You know what I always say—ID is a process of considering goals within constraints and resources. So let's start there."

# Preliminary Analysis Questions

1. This case ends with Paul directing the team to list the constraints and resources in the case. What do you think the team came up with?
2. Initially, not all of the team members were knowledgeable about the subject matter or the genre of gaming. Critique the process the team used to develop their understanding in the subject matter and gaming genre. From an instructional analysis perspective, should they have done anything differently?
3. How should the team balance historical accuracy with age-appropriate and racially sensitive content? What instructional design approaches can help the team make informed choices on these decisions?

# Implications for ID Practice

1. What learning theories or instructional design approaches might inform the design and use of games for learning?
2. What are the roles of the instructor when implementing video games for learning? Can a game effectively educate on its own?
3. Should educational game designers try to compete with commercially produced games when educational designers lack the resources to produce the same levels of quality and engagement? Provide a rationale for your response.

# Sandra Sanchez and Vincent Peters
## Helping a School Prepare for a New Mandate

*by Theresa A. Cullen and Sheila Rulison*

## Another Initiative

Sandra Sanchez has been vice principal of the Los Santos High School, a small urban high school with a diverse set of students, for two years now. Although official statistics are not available, a high percentage of students do not speak English at home. When moving between classrooms, students often speak Spanish with each other; however, school policy does not allow Spanish to be used as part of the classroom interactions, even if the teacher is bilingual.

Sandra's background is representative of many of the students of the school district. She was the first in her family to graduate from high school and college. She was born in the United States, but her parents do not speak English fluently. Sandra is bilingual and, as such, is able to communicate effectively with parents and community members in both English and Spanish.

The project started this past fall when the principal and the superintendent told Sandra that her school would be the pilot school to prepare teachers to teach in alignment with the new Common Core, a national initiative to establish a set of academic standards for math and language arts. They specifically selected her school because Sandra was working on her PhD in assessment, and they knew that she would be amenable to the project. Although Sandra always liked a challenge, she knew that her teachers and staff would resist being the "test" school yet again. The plan in year 1 was for Los Santos to implement training and new teacher evaluations based on the Common Core. During year 2, the process would be repeated at all the other schools in the district. The school district administrators felt that Sandra would work effectively with an outside consultant, an instructional designer named Vincent Peters. Their job was to create both the training materials and teacher assessments to be piloted at Los Santos and then modified for full district deployment. Sandra knew that recent budget cuts and pay rate freezes experienced by the teachers might make things a little difficult for Vincent. The teachers likely would not be happy that the district was paying an outside consultant to oversee this new initiative when they were being asked to personally pay for some of their own daily teaching materials, such as their own copy paper, for class.

After receiving the charge from the superintendent, Sandra arranged her first meeting with Vincent. They met at her office one day after school. Sandra started the meeting by introducing herself and her background, and then invited Vincent to speak about his background.

Vincent spoke eagerly about his background. "I grew up in the suburbs of this city, but I live near here now. My bachelor's degree is in psychology and after working for several years as an assessment specialist in a hospital, I was frustrated by how some of the assessments I administered did not seem to measure the things they were supposed to. So, I went back and got my masters in instructional design. I really enjoyed learning about assessment techniques, and now I'm excited to design assessments myself."

Sandra asked him, "What projects have you worked on in the past?"

Vincent recounted, "I have mainly been involved in business projects where I introduced new processes to increase efficiency for employees and customers. For example, I designed training for a new checkout procedure at an auto dealership that streamlined the purchase, trade-in, and financial aspects for customers buying both new and used cars. I also designed an evaluation system for probationary employees in their first 90 days on the job at a local retail chain. The system ensured that new employees were systematically assessed on their basic skills, such as running the register, maintaining the inventory, and performing the sales and customer satisfaction skills. Most recently, I designed a system for certification evaluation of instructors at the local YMCA."

Sandra was disappointed not to hear K–12 in any of his answers, so she continued, "Have you ever designed a program for a school district along the lines of what we have in mind for this project?"

Vincent paused a moment, and tried to put a positive spin on his past experiences. "Your project sounds like it will require the incorporation of both the evaluation and training experiences that are similar to what I have previously designed."

Sandra realized that he did not have a lot of experience in the K–12 context beyond his own school experiences. She needed to be sure he understood the Los Santos context.

Sandra decided to dive into the project, explaining, "I am not sure what you have discussed yet with the superintendent, but let me give you a little background on the Common Core Standards. Forty-eight states, the District of Columbia, and two territories convened about two years ago and developed the document known as the Common Core State Standards. These standards have now been adopted by 46 states. The full implementation with accompanying assessments will not be in place for another two years, but in the meantime, school districts across the nation will be transitioning toward replacing their individual state standards with a national set of standards. English language arts and mathematics will be the primary focus, but all subject areas will be emphasizing higher literacy requirements. The goal is that students will graduate with the kind of knowledge and skills that will allow them to be successful in college and their future careers. If you want to read more about it yourself, you can visit their website at corestandards.org. Your charge is to design a program that will help Los Santos High School accomplish this."

Vincent promised to visit the website as he prepared for their next meeting so he could brainstorm some more ideas.

Sandra cautioned him, "This project may seem very straightforward, but there are also some complex federal mandates to be aware of. In our school we will also need to focus on some special populations that Los Santos serves, namely students with disabilities and students who are English language learners. Now that I know a little more about your background, I can gather some informational materials that tell you more about our school, and some of the materials we already use for federal mandates. I think I will arrange for a group of people who can help you if you need it, too. They can give you feedback and help you learn more about our school. How does that sound to you? Is there anyone that you would want me to be sure to invite?"

Vincent replied, "That would be great—the more I know about the people I will be working with, the better. Would it be possible to have both experienced and newer teachers and maybe even some parents? Oh, and can I also get an account on your school's intranet so that I can see what kinds of technologies your teachers are accustomed to using?"

"Absolutely," answered Sandra. "I will gather a group that will represent our faculty and our stakeholders, and I can get you a login ID for our district. One more thing—the teachers have requested some time to work together during the school day, but I can't see how we can take valuable instructional time away from the students. Do you have any suggestions?"

Vincent responded, "As a matter of fact, I have been doing some research on that very topic to prepare for this project, and I have an idea that would allow each department to collaborate weekly. I read a summary online that described an approach in other high-achieving countries that involves teachers spending a little over half their day with students. The remaining time is spent with colleagues planning the kind of instruction that challenges their students to engage in high levels of critical and analytical thinking. I'll send you the article—the research results were impressive. I'd like to think of it as time invested in good teaching that will benefit the students in the long run, rather than instructional time lost—quality over quantity, so to speak."

Sandra nodded. "Since we are a pilot school for your instructional design, it may be a good time to incorporate collaboration time as one of the changes. Let's see what the teachers think about it next time we meet."

As they parted ways, Sandra and Vincent both realized that the next meeting with the teacher committee would be crucial to a smooth implementation of the instructional design.

## Gathering Resources

Sandra went back to her office and began to think about the problem. Even though Vincent did not ask for it specifically, she knew that the school had a high population of students who were receiving special services, and Vincent would need to learn more about them as a group. She gathered materials about special education at the school, set up accounts for Vincent on the school's servers and management systems, and e-mailed him the information. (See Figures 5–1 and 5–2.)

**FIGURE 5–1**   E-mail Message from Sandra to Vincent.

From: Sandra Sanchez
Date: Wednesday, September 1 4:26 PM
To: Vincent Peters
Subject: Resources and Information

Vincent:

I arranged a few resources that I thought would be useful for you. Because of our large numbers of students with disabilities, first I wanted to provide you more information on this.

I will forward you the annual letter from our special ed department head explaining Individualized Education Plans (IEPs) and Universal Design for Learning (UDL). In addition, I am including a sample IEP accommodations page so you can see the kinds of alternatives that students may be allowed to complete a test.

If you would like further information about special education issues, then consider visiting the U.S. Department of Education website and reviewing the information about IEPs: http://nichcy.org/schools-administrators.

Of course, the Common Core State Standards (www.corestandards.org) will be an important tool for you as well.

I have also included general information on the school for you including a copy of the school year schedule, which lists our four professional development dates.

Finally, I set up an account for you on the school's content management system that is used to provide messages to parents and teachers, maintain class web pages, and sign up for workshops. You can access the portal through the school homepage under the "Faculty and Staff" tab.

Your account name is Vincent001.

Your password is the same, but it will ask you to change it upon first login.

I hope that these resources will help you get started.


Sandra Sanchez
Vice Principal
Los Santos School

Following up on their earlier conversation, she began to organize a committee to help him in the process. In addition to herself as the committee chair, she listed the following potential members:

Teacher:  Edward Contreras, English teacher who has taught freshman English at the school for 20 years. He is bilingual and prides himself on picking reading material that celebrates the culture of the students who attend the school even if that means deviating slightly from the state recommended reading list. Regularly describes his language abilities as helping him connect with the students and their parents.

**FIGURE 5–2** Annual Special Education E-mail Sent to All Teachers.

From: Sandra Sanchez
Sent: Wednesday, September 1 4:48 PM
To: Vincent Peters
Subject: FW: Special Education Reminders

---

From: Joyce Brown
Sent: Thursday, August 10th 9:17 AM
To: all teachers group
Subject: Special Education Reminders

Welcome back to another school year at Los Santos!

This is my annual e-mail message to all of you to remind you of our special education policies and where you can find more information.

Any student can be evaluated for special education services after a teacher makes a referral to any of the special education faculty. In order for a child to receive special education services, he or she must be tested and a gap in performance must be identified.

Students identified as needing services will have an IEP—Individualized Education Plan—written for them by a committee made up of their parents, the child, all of their teachers, a school administrator, and other support personnel. The IEP will include their accommodations, special instructions, or procedures that the committee decides will help them be successful in the Least Restrictive Environment (LRE). Furthermore, if a student's IEP allows them to use calculators in math class, that means that they will get to use them on state tests as well. A student's IEP is reviewed each year and is considered a contract between the school and the parents and the child about their educational plan.

Everyone's participation in referring students for testing, participating in their IEP plans, and allowing them to use their prescribed accommodations is vital to their education.

I want to encourage you to think about these students and all your students when you are designing activities for your class. Many times I have found that when teachers design activities with these students in mind, assignments for the entire class improve. This is a concept called Universal Design for Learning (UDL) and can really benefit all of your students.

The special education teachers are available to consult with you about students and help you identify how they can be more successful in your classrooms. Please use us as resources!

If you would like to read more information about special education laws, UDL, and the IEP process, please refer to: http://nichcy.org/schools-administrators. This site will answer many of your questions and give you some ideas for your classroom.

Thank you again, and I look forward to it being an exciting and effective year.

Joyce Brown
Special Education Department Head

Special Education Teacher: Joyce Brown, head of the department and knowledgeable about special education laws and compliance. She works mainly with children with autism, and particularly Asperger's syndrome. Each year she sends out a letter to all teachers reminding

| | |
|---|---|
| | them of the Individualized Education Plan (IEP) process and explaining the benefits of Universal Design for Learning (UDL) to all their students. |
| Curricular Coach: | Chris Collings, math curriculum coach for the high school. Her role is to support the other math teachers and plan the curriculum. Her job includes mentoring younger teachers, observing all teachers, and modifying common course assignments. She teaches AP Calculus and Algebra II/Trig in the morning, and her afternoons are dedicated to curricular duties. |
| Parent: | Carmen Vasquez, parent who speaks very little English and whose oldest child is a sophomore. She also has a son, Diego, who is in the middle school. She is interested in being involved in the school but is often reluctant to interact in groups because of her language challenges. She regularly comes by the school and speaks with either the vice principal or other teachers who are bilingual. |
| English Language Learner (ELL) Coordinator: | Josie Galvan, former foreign language teacher at a large urban district, has been coordinating the district's ELL program for about five years. The program pulls students out of their regular classes for two hours a week at the high school level to work on their English language skills. She also serves as a support for classroom teachers who have students who have not yet mastered English. |

Sandra sent the materials to Vincent and told him about the committee. She invited him to come back to the school in a week to meet with the committee, to ask questions, and to begin to form his plans for assessing teachers' readiness and training them for the new initiative. Sandra assured Vincent that the meeting would be under his direction, and she would help him in any way necessary.

## The Meeting

Vincent arrived at the school about 30 minutes early to give himself time to look around and familiarize himself with the environment. When the committee members began arriving at the conference room, he noticed that the group was quiet, and no one seemed too interested in being there. He cleared his throat and started the meeting.

Vincent introduced himself and his background. He explained some of his recent project designs just as he had done with Sandra. He then focused the rest of the meeting on the instructional design for implementation of the Common Core at Los Santos High.

Vincent continued by describing his assignment. "I see my task as designing training for teachers that enables them to adapt how they are teaching in order to meet the new requirements of the Common Core Standards and to develop a way to assess how well teachers are moving toward this goal. The standards are very performance-based for the students, so this will be exciting. Teachers will be able to employ inquiry-based learning in their instruction. There will be lots of new things for the teachers to learn."

Edward sat with his arms crossed and was the first to speak. "Sorry to interrupt you, Vincent, but we need to make sure that we don't get too excited. You know the saying . . . 'This too shall pass.' I have been here for over 20 years and the state will move onto something new in no time. We really should not put too much effort into this change because they never see these sorts of things all the way through."

Joyce spoke up, adding, "Edward, I agree with you about the state, but this might be a really good opportunity to make some changes that could help my kids succeed in mainstream classrooms. These new standards would allow them to show what they can do and not just recite facts. For example, these standards are supposed to be performance-based, as Vincent mentioned, and I know that some of our special ed students can do better on performance tasks than standardized tests."

Josie chimed in, "I like the idea of these performance-based assessments for kids, but honestly, my kids in the ELL program have a hard enough time with straightforward tasks. I worry that the teachers will have a hard time communicating what is expected to my kids and they might do even worse on tests because they have difficulty understanding the tasks presented to them."

Chris seemed a little miffed at that comment and reminded her, "Josie, helping teachers develop clear expectations and assessments is part of our job as curriculum coaches, and if you have a concern, you should raise it in specific cases."

Carmen did not say anything through this whole exchange, so Vincent addressed her directly and asked her what she thought. With translation assistance from Edward, she explained, "I just want my son to get a diploma when he's done, and be on the path to a successful life."

Vincent realized there were several agendas at work here. First, he realized that teachers were frustrated by what seemed to be a constant stream of new mandates. Also, he observed that each teacher thought that he/she had a role or a specific audience to serve; furthermore, the teachers were very protective of the students.

Vincent asked the group, "When can we do training? Could we use one Saturday a month or maybe a few evening sessions to sit down together and plan this out?"

There was an initial awkward silence, and it was Edward who addressed the elephant in the room as he blurted out, "Evenings or Saturdays? I already have bus duty before and after school, and I'm the sponsor for the Honor Society and the Multicultural Club. I just don't have any more free time to give."

Chris also added her perspective. "I am the past president of our Educator Association, and I want you to be aware of how our contract works. Our contract is for 180 days, including these four professional days. Extra days or extra duties are contracted and *compensated* beyond that. Teachers can't be required to come to extra sessions or trainings without appropriate compensation that would be offered to any other professional."

Sandra pointed him to the school schedule, which included four professional development (PD) days. She pointed out, "Each PD day has six hours available. We also have monthly faculty meetings after school that might have 10 to 20 minutes available in them for discussing the Common Core."

Knowing that meetings often run over, Vincent realized that 10 to 20 minutes at the end of a faculty meeting would not accomplish the task set before them. He was also well aware of the need for the additional collaboration time to be included within the contract workday. He and Sandra had briefly discussed the topic of dedicated collaboration time before the meeting, and he felt this was the perfect time to introduce a potential resolution to this dilemma. He had discovered through his own research that improving teacher efficacy and student achievement could be accomplished by creating a 40-minute enhancement period at the beginning of each school day and shaving five minutes off each class. This enhancement time could be used for teacher collaboration in teams and also provide extra time to tutor struggling students. Vincent passed out a handout that illustrated what this kind of schedule might look like (see Figure 5–3). "As you'll notice, responsibilities for facilitation during the enhancement period rotate across academic departments, so each one receives a common planning time each week."

After a cursory glance at the schedule, Edward exclaimed, "We are losing five minutes of instructional time for every class period? I have trouble finishing a daily lesson as it is."

Chris chimed in, "The math teachers will also be reluctant to give up any instructional and practice time, and I'm betting the science teachers will be even more vocal about losing time for labs. What will we say to them?"

**FIGURE 5–3**   Rotation Schedule of Enhancement/Collaboration Period.

| 7:45 | Teachers report |
| --- | --- |
| 8:00–8:40 | Enhancement period |
| 8:45–9:25 | 1st Period |
| 9:30–10:10 | 2nd Period |
| 10:15–10:55 | 3rd Period |
| 11:00–11:40 | 4th Period |
| 11:45–12:15 | Lunch |
| 12:20–1:00 | 5th Period |
| 1:05–1:45 | 6th Period |
| 1:50–2:30 | 7th Period |
| 2:35–3:15 | 8th Period |
| Monday | All teachers facilitate student enhancement |
| Tuesday | English Department collaboration |
| Wednesday | Science Department collaboration |
| Thursday | Math Department collaboration |
| Friday | History Department collaboration |

Vincent, expecting reluctance to change, defused the situation by explaining, "We have got to think of this enhancement period as an investment in the teachers as a collaborative group of professionals who can share ideas or concerns as a means of eliminating the isolation that can make being a teacher so difficult. With the new assessments for the Common Core Standards approaching, it will be important to boost the teachers' knowledge and capacities to meet the different expectations required under the new standards, and having a common planning time by content area is a step in the right direction. This could translate into improved instructional strategies and, in turn, increased student achievement that we can track through their test scores."

Sandra agreed. "Teachers actually want more time to plan together; we've just never had a workable solution that would be both fair and productive. If teachers have an agenda and set goals for each meeting, they will begin to see results. I think it's a win-win for the teachers and the students."

Joyce added, "In special education, we share a lot of ideas to find the best solutions for each of our kids, and that has been key to our success. Extra time to do this would be great."

Josie interjected, "I could sit in on different content area meetings to help teachers develop with proactive strategies for the ELL students rather than waiting until they fall behind."

Joyce agreed, "The special education department would love to be able to do that, too!"

Members of the committee were interested in the enhancement program, and the teachers were encouraged by the opportunity to work as a team toward their goal of implementing the Common Core. More discussion would certainly follow at subsequent meetings.

Vincent went to his next item. "Sandra gave me an account on your teacher and parent communication system, and I looked around. I saw that it could send out e-mails, host discussion forums, and even have websites that are available to groups that log in to the system. How many of you use it?"

All of the people at the table agreed that they logged in several times a week and were quite comfortable with it.

Edward reported, "We have to put our attendance and grades in there, so it's always open on my computer when I am at work."

Carmen was also a very frequent user, and voiced her thoughts while Edward translated. "I check it twice a day. It has upcoming meetings and messages from the teachers on it. I can see if my kids are missing any assignments."

Vincent had been warned by Sandra that all students, even those receiving special services for disabilities, would be taking the test based on the Common Core, so he asked, "How do you help your students prepare for the state tests right now?"

Chris explained, "Each teacher spends about 30% of their time currently on test preparation. They do it in a variety of ways. Some teachers used an Integrated Learning System, which is computer-based, and students are able to practice standardized test items. The curriculum coaches also prepare and distribute sample items for the teachers to use with their classes. They often go through the sample items in small groups and model test-taking strategies with them."

Vincent followed up, "So that is for your general population students. What kind of special preparation is done for ELLs and kids with IEPs?"

Suddenly Vincent heard snickering at the table, and both Joyce and Josie grimaced. "Not a whole lot," Joyce said. "Generally if students have a study hour in the resource room, if we have extra time, which we rarely do, we sometimes work on test skills."

Josie added, "We never have extra time in the ELL classroom, and during any given hour, I have students at different grade levels, with different language abilities, and speaking different languages in my classroom. We never get to testing skills."

Vincent acknowledged their response. "Okay, so I see where the need exists. Some of this can be addressed through incorporation of an enhancement/collaboration period, which should provide an avenue for re-teaching or test prep. Do content teachers receive any special training on how to prepare students who are ELLs or have IEPs for taking the tests?"

The whole table responded, "No."

Joyce added, "Unless you count the one required special education course that most teachers took as undergraduates."

Chris quickly added, "That is, if they are certified teachers."

Vincent redirected their discussion. "Chris, if the curriculum coaches take the lead on this test prep, how do they document and report that it's being done?"

Chris remarked, "We really don't. I know I talk with each of my teachers at our bi-weekly content meetings. I also observe them when I can. It is not part of our formal teaching evaluation, and even though we turn in lesson plans weekly, I have never checked to be sure the test preparation items are being included. I trust my colleagues. They are professionals and good teachers. They have the best interests of students at heart."

Sandra clarified, "When the test scores come out each year, we discuss them as a faculty and identify strategies we could be using to improve them."

Vincent back stepped a little. "I was not implying that teachers were not preparing their students for the tests. I just wanted to know what you were already doing. If you already have a way to check that this preparation is being done, I wanted to use it. Just because something new is about to happen, does not mean that everything you do has to change. Are there any special concerns that I should be aware of when considering kids who are ELLs or have IEPs?"

Josie sat up in her chair, and looked excited to be asked. She cautioned Vincent, "Students who are English language learners often have difficulties with idioms and other general conventions of the English language. Because of that, they may not know a common English saying or special words used in the test question. English language learners sometimes struggle to figure out what the questions mean, let alone what the correct answer is. They need more strategies to decode the questions, even if they don't know all the words."

Joyce added, "Kids with IEPs are given accommodations—ways in which the test can be modified. For example, some get extra time on tests, and others can take them in quiet places. Some kids are really embarrassed by this and if the teacher does not initiate it, they often fail to ask for it. However, having extra test time can really make a big difference in their success."

Sandra added, "I shared a sample accommodation page with Vincent. Maybe Vincent and Joyce can sit down later and discuss it in more detail. In fact, Vincent, maybe you can arrange to shadow several of the committee members or sit in on their classes to get a better idea of how things work at Los Santos." (See Figure 5–4.)

**FIGURE 5–4**    Sample Accommodations Page.

> **Student Summary for Individualized Education Plan (IEP)**
>
> **Student Strengths**
> The student is very social and gets along with others.
>
> The student is very verbal and can explain things verbally effectively.
>
> **Student Weaknesses**
> The student has difficulty processing written text, and therefore needs extra time to read and take tests.
>
> The student has difficulties doing arithmetic. The student needs to use a calculator in class and on tests to check her work.
>
> **Possible Classroom Difficulties**
> The social nature of this student can cause her to be distracted or to distract other students, especially when she is frustrated. The student may need to be excused to a quiet area or the resource room in order to concentrate on tasks and not distract other students.

Vincent looked over his notes and realized that most of his questions had been answered. He had a good idea of what the teachers were currently doing. One more question occurred to him.

He asked, "What role do parents currently play in preparing students for the state exams?"

Carmen responded, again with translation assistance. "I know we have gotten some letters from the school and e-mails. On the days of the tests they remind us to have our kids get a good night's rest and eat breakfast. When my son was struggling in math, they told him to go to math camp in the summer. But he didn't go because we were going to visit family then."

Vincent directed his question to the rest of the table.

Edward remarked, "Carmen is a very involved parent, but I can't say that for everyone. We really have not included parents in preparing students for assessments. A few parents come by each year and ask for suggestions to help their children do better, but for the most part we focus on remediation and providing camps and extra tutoring to kids who do not pass the test."

Vincent thanked everyone for coming and asked if he could contact the committee if he had any follow-up questions.

As Vincent left the meeting, he overheard two of the teachers talking in the hallway. Chris was reassuring Edward. She said, "I think we just need to see what happens here. As with anything else new, it takes a while to work the bugs out of the system."

Edward replied, "But if it's like No Child Left Behind, it does not matter what I do to get ready for this test, it all comes down to how the students do on the test. What I am doing differently is never acknowledged. With so many students coming in and out of the district during the year, it makes me nervous when they use those test scores to decide if I am doing a good job or not."

Chris responded, "We will just have to wait and see—maybe this time it will be different."

Vincent realized that he had a great deal of work ahead of him if he were going to get ready for the first professional development day that would occur in about a month. He went home and looked at all the materials he'd been given and at his meeting notes.

He began to create a list of things that his plan would need to include if he were going to create a successful design along with an accompanying plan for teacher evaluation. He was especially concerned about the amount of time that he had available to him for professional development in this project. He quickly realized that he would have to consider time differently and plan to evaluate in creative ways if he were going to collect enough evidence of teacher readiness.

# Preliminary Analysis Questions

1. How are Vincent's previous ID experiences, outside of K–12, relevant to this situation? How could he use those previous experiences to his benefit here?
2. Why is it important for Vincent to use existing processes within the school for his training approach?
3. How might Vincent be able to obtain buy-in for the training and preparation processes if the teachers are tired of new programs and projects being regularly introduced at the school?
4. How can Vincent be sure that he is involving all of the important stakeholders? How does that affect his training plans? His assessment plans?
5. The school district has hired Vincent to design the training program but not administer it. How does this affect his design choices? How can he be sure that the program he designed is completed in the way he intended?

# Implications for ID Practice

1. Discuss how diffusion research (such as Rogers, 2003) is relevant to this instructional design situation. How can you develop a plan that uses individuals at all different stages of adoption? How can all the stakeholders be involved and have their needs met?
2. Using Kirkpatrick's (2006) model of evaluation, discuss the levels of assessment that could be employed to involve all stakeholders and determine the success of a professional development program.
3. Weigh the pros and cons of using teacher data versus student data for evaluation.

# Resources

*Common Core State Standards*. (2010). National Governors Association Center for Best Practices, Council of Chief State School Officers, Washington, DC. Retrieved from http://www.corestandards.org.

Kirkpatrick, D. L., & Kirkpatrick, J. D. (2006). *Evaluating training programs: The four levels* (3rd ed.). San Francisco, CA: Berrett-Koehler.

Rogers, E. (2003). *Diffusion of innovations* (5th ed.). New York: Simon & Schuster.

# CASE STUDY 6

# Tina Sears

## Evaluating the Impact of a K–12 Laptop Program

*by Michael M. Grant, Deborah L. Lowther, and Steven M. Ross*

Andersen was a rural, southern community tucked in at the base of the Blue Ridge Mountains in upstate South Carolina. Like other small, close-knit towns in the state, more than half the students in the four-school district qualified for free or reduced lunch. Furthermore, a number of students were minorities, at least in part because a large number of Mexican American families had recently moved into the area.

Hillendale Textiles was an anchor of the community. Not only did many of the parents work one of the three shifts, but CEO and owner Bradley Cook had often stepped in to provide the school district with funds for special projects, such as the high school's football stadium and new band uniforms. It was easy to see why the rotund Mr. Cook had the ear of the school administrators and the school board.

## The Pilot Laptop Program

Another special project was now in the works: In late October, Mr. Cook received a call from Darren Chaude, a business associate at Toh, Inc., an aggressive computer systems firm headquartered in Southeast Asia but well established in the United States. (Hillendale Textiles used Toh, Inc. hardware for its fabric manufacturing lines.) Darren called because he knew that Mr. Cook was an active supporter of his local school district and might be interested in Toh, Inc.'s laptop program for K–12 schools. Toh, Inc. had just become highly visible in portable technologies and was vying for market share with extreme competitive pricing. Darren shared his opinion that the program had been shown to not only improve students' learning, but also to prepare them for the high-tech job market. He further explained that the program included 60 hours of teacher training from a national expert, free teacher laptops, full technical support, and discounted prices on volume purchases of laptops. Mr. Cook was very impressed with Darren's description of a recent visit he had made to a fifth-grade laptop classroom. Darren said he had never seen students with such a high level of computer skills or who appeared so motivated to learn.

The conversation piqued Mr. Cook's interest, so he decided to investigate the possibility of funding laptops in Andersen County School District. After some initial investigation, and following further discussion with Darren, he decided on a pilot program with the eight fifth-grade classrooms. He did not want to buy laptops for all grades, particularly if the program proved to be unsuccessful. His two primary reasons for funding the program were to improve student learning and to increase employee loyalty by supporting a program that benefited their children. Of course, it wouldn't hurt that he'd get a great tax write-off as well!

Capriciously, Mr. Cook skipped consulting the district before signing the contract with Toh, Inc. He wanted to present the news at the Winter Teacher Meeting, which was attended by all teachers and administrators—and the newspaper. With a certain amount of shock (which was to be expected) and an equal amount of gratitude (which was also to be expected), Andersen County School District set about to make Mr. Cook's vision a reality.

As District Technology Coordinator, Tina Sears was appointed project director. Plucky and adventurous, Tina, with a small committee of committed parents, fifth-grade teachers, and the school principals, ordered the equipment from Toh, Inc., scheduled the teacher professional development sessions, and prepared to document the changes in teaching and learning. The committee wrote some program goals and distributed them in a flyer to the parents and school board (see Figure 6–1).

**FIGURE 6–1**  Pilot Laptop Program Goals and Professional Development Plan.

Andersen County School District
Pilot Laptop Program

**PROGRAM GOALS**

The purpose of the pilot laptop program is to:

1. Equip each 5th-grade classroom with high-performance laptop computers
2. Ensure students and teachers are computer literate
3. Increase student achievement through the use of laptop computers

**PROFESSIONAL DEVELOPMENT PLAN**

In order to achieve the program goals, the 5th-grade teachers will participate in a comprehensive two-week professional development (PD) summer seminar and monthly three-hour sessions during the school year. The training activities will engage teachers in three types of activities: *experiencing* classroom simulations, *creating* materials and resources to support technology integration efforts, and practice *modeling* scenarios to build implementation and management skills. The specific PD objectives are below.

The teachers will be able to:

• Create lesson plans that engage students in effective use of laptop computers as a tool to improve achievement on the district's standardized assessments
• Integrate effective student use of laptop computers into everyday teaching and learning
• Manage classrooms that have students using laptop computers

# Teacher Professional Development

With the equipment on the way and the summer holiday steadily marching by, Tina spoke with Toh, Inc.'s teacher trainer, Mark Waters, a nationally recognized expert in the field of K–12 technology integration, about running the professional development workshops for her teachers. His full-time job was as a professor at a large mid-Atlantic university; he also consulted for Toh, Inc. with schools that were beginning new laptop programs. Mark's approach centered on encouraging teachers to engage students in using the computer as a tool during problem-based activities. In essence, the teachers wouldn't just learn how to use computers, they would learn how to teach while using computers to meet their objectives. Mark emphasized that computers wouldn't just be an add-on to the curriculum; they would be integral to achieving the objectives outlined in the curriculum. Computers would not be a reward for the "smart kids" or for finishing work early; every student would use computers to support and enhance classroom activities.

Essential to the two weeks of professional development in the summer was a series of simulation activities in which Mark modeled the role of a fifth-grade teacher while the teachers assumed the roles of fifth-grade students. For example, while learning about plate tectonics, the teachers/fifth graders would use concept-mapping software, or while learning about similes, the teachers/fifth graders would use presentation software. Mark began each lesson, "Today, we're going to learn about . . ." and filled in with "science, social studies, math, or language arts." Then he would say, "The point of this lesson is not to learn everything there is to know about . . ." and filled in with "Word," "PowerPoint," "Excel," or some other popular software package. Throughout the two weeks, Mark illustrated how the software applications had specific uses, and how teachers should match each application's use to their curricular objectives.

# Implementing the Laptop Program

As school began in mid-August, the heat didn't give in, and neither did Tina and her newly trained fifth-grade teachers. During the school year, three-hour follow-up workshops were conducted monthly to maintain the momentum generated during the summer workshops. The teachers planned lessons collaboratively, and Tina guided them through making the best uses of technology for learning.

Documenting progress continued to nag at Tina. She couldn't let the evaluation slip her mind. To move this task along, Tina called on a friend from a neighboring district who had received computers for her library from a local literacy council. Her friend reported that she had used student, teacher, and parent surveys, but had also wanted to tell the "true" story of how the computers were being used. To do this, she regularly video recorded the students as they were accomplishing different activities, and then created an edited version to show at the annual literacy council's fund-raising dinner. The video recording was an incredible hit and resulted in the library receiving 10 more computers.

Tina decided she would definitely include video, but she wanted to go even further. So she decided to hold focus groups with the teachers and students to obtain information that wouldn't show up on a survey. She also added technology to the district's annual teacher evaluation form, which was a huge improvement because the evaluation hadn't been changed in years. And, of course, she needed to include the Iowa Test of Basic Skills (ITBS) scores as part of the data collection as well. She dashed off these descriptions in a fax to Andersen County's school superintendent, Dr. Tammy Burns (see Figure 6–2).

It was unseasonably warm for January, and Dryer Elementary was alive with activity for fifth-grade parent night. Tina beamed throughout the whole evening. The shiny laptops were on display, and streaming videos of students using the laptops were projected in the classrooms. As the images on the screens changed, Tina recalled seeing students retrieve census data from the web and then place it in Excel to make predictions on future population trends. She also saw students team-writing a paper using a web-based word processor. The video revealed that students used technology tools seamlessly to support their learning, including the thesaurus, online dictionaries and encyclopedias, concept mapping software, and graphing calculators. The students also instantaneously searched the web when questions arose during discussions or problem-solving exercises.

It was obvious to Tina the changes were not just with the students; video clips affirmed that the teachers were changing, too. They were not glued to the front of their classrooms. They moved about, talking with individual students and small groups.

The next day it seemed cooler—closer to normal for January—as Tina met with the fifth-grade teachers and recorded their pride from parents' night. As expected, a photo of Mr. Cook surrounded by laptops and excited fifth-grade students made the newspaper front page.

Spring announced its arrival early in March, and now, everyone was sweating again. Tina was pleased that the time in her muggy, yellow office was abbreviated today. She had scheduled video recording two of the fifth-grade laptop classrooms. This was always a highlight in her day because of the amount of progress that had been made in many of the classrooms. In the most innovative classrooms, students were so engaged in their assignments that they hardly noticed the digital recorder (an enthusiasm she wished would transfer to all the classrooms). Teachers were busily moving from group to group answering and asking questions. Students and teachers frequently used the digital projector to share and discuss their work.

With a subtle smile on her face, Tina reminisced. All the classrooms' activities and excitement reminded her of when she was selected as the only teacher in the district to have computers placed in her classroom. Back then, students were limited to basic programming and using rudimentary software like Logo. Many students were motivated with turtles and geometry. Yet, even with her limited resources, she used the computers to create a learning environment where more students wanted to learn. Her class was even on the front page of the newspaper, which probably contributed to her appointment as district technology director. Her pluckiness surely helped, too.

Tina collected the last of the parent, teacher, and student surveys, which had straggled in. It was a 70% response rate; the phone calls to homes had eked out a remarkable number of returned surveys. She felt quite pleased that almost everyone marked "Yes" to her two key questions: (1) Do you think students are learning more? and (2) Have the laptops made students more interested in learning?

**FIGURE 6–2**    Tina Sears' Evaluation Plan.

---

# FAX Transmittal Form

| | |
|---|---|
| **To:** | **Dr. Tammy Burns** |
| | **Andersen County School District** |
| FAX: | 864-555-5234 |
| Phone: | 864-555-5235 |
| **From:** | **Tina Sears** |
| | **District Technology Director** |
| FAX: | 864-555-5123 |
| Phone: | 864-555-5124 |
| **Subject:** | **Pilot Laptop Program Evaluation** |
| **No. of Pages:** | 1 page |

Dr. Burns,
See the evaluation plan below for the pilot laptop program for the eight fifth-grade classrooms.
Thanks, Tina

## Pilot Laptop Program Evaluation

### Purpose
Mr. Bradley Cook, CEO of Hillendale Textiles, generously donated laptop computers to our eight fifth-grade classrooms. He has agreed to provide laptops for all elementary classrooms, if evidence can be provided to show that use of the laptops improved student learning. Therefore, the purpose of this evaluation is to demonstrate how providing laptops for each fifth-grade classroom improves student learning.

### Evaluation Plan
Our district has planned the following activities to demonstrate the positive impacts of having laptop computers:

1. Add "Technology Use" to the district annual teacher observation form.
2. Throughout the year: Collect videotapes of successful laptop use.
3. At the end of the year: Conduct teacher focus groups to see how the teachers feel about using laptops.
4. At the end of the year: Give teachers, students, and parents a survey to see how they feel about the use of laptops.
5. Compare last year's ITBS scores with this year's scores.

# Initial Evaluation Results

School had been out for a couple of weeks now, and so had Tina's air conditioning. She carefully transferred the data—the bulk of which were positive survey results and teacher focus group responses—to the final report that she had written. For example, one teacher said, "I've never seen so many of my students so excited to learn." Another commented, "I've been teaching for 15 years and have rarely seen so many student products that were written so clearly and demonstrated such deep levels of learning." Tina also created an edited version of the videos that showed multiple examples of classroom environments that were improved because of the use of laptops. She was confident that the report and video would please Mr. Cook and would be a great springboard to expand to the other grades. She printed out the report and dropped it in the mail, along with the videotape. The smile on her face showed her elation over the report; the sweat on her brow divulged her prayer for the HVAC repairman.

Torrents of rain pounded outside. The almost 100-degree weather was a constant for summer in South Carolina, and Tina's small air conditioner strained to keep up. Adding insult to injury, it was only hotter after it rained.

*BOING!*

The e-mail alert was a welcomed distraction. Tina quickly opened the message and followed the lines of text across the bright screen (see Figure 6–3).

The message was from Dr. Burns and included an original message from Mr. Cook, sponsor of the laptop program. It was obvious that Mr. Cook was unhappy with the evaluation results.

As she read Mr. Cook's message, Tina's usual effervescence quickly diminished. How wrong could she be? It had been a whirlwind year, but how could Mr. Cook think that the program was not a success? He had focused on the lack of change in the test scores and had discounted positive survey results. He had also dismissed her reports from the teacher focus groups and the video. The fifth-grade teachers had accomplished so much; she had witnessed it first-hand. Luckily Mr. Cook conceded funding for a formal evaluation the following school year, postponing his decision about discontinuing the laptop program.

Maybe the information in the report had not been definitive enough. Maybe the data she had collected were not convincing enough to warrant another significant expenditure from the textile manufacturing company's foundation. Cook's threat to kill the funding flooded her mind. "I've got to do something about this evaluation," she thought. "I can't let the other teachers and students down. I've seen so much progress with the laptops." She began to question herself, and now she needed to host a meeting with all the stakeholders.

Without a doubt, she needed help with the requested evaluation. Fortunately, Mr. Cook was willing to pay for it, so she should get some outside help. That would relieve some of her pressure and help mitigate her bias. She decided to contact the Toh, Inc. consultant, Mark Waters, who helped with the teachers' professional development. He had been a breath of fresh air with the teachers and the professional development. Somewhere in the back of her mind she recalled him mentioning something about program evaluation.

**FIGURE 6–3**    E-mail from Superintendent, Dr. Tammy Burns, to Tina Sears, District Technology Director.

| Subject: | FW:  Laptop Evaluation Report |
| --- | --- |
| To: | Tina Sears <tsears@andersen.k12.sc.us> |
| From: | Dr. Tammy Burns <tburns@andersen.k12.sc.us> |
| Date: | July 25 |

Tina,
Below is an e-mail from Mr. Cook regarding your laptop report.

Begin to schedule the stakeholders' meeting so that we can have an evaluation plan in place for Mr. Cook by October 1.

Thank you,
Dr. Burns

| Subject: | Laptop Evaluation Report |
| --- | --- |
| To: | Dr. Tammy Burns <tburns@andersen.k12.sc.us> |
| From: | Bradley Cook <bcook@hillendaletextiles.com> |
| Date: | July 25 |

Tammy,

I am disappointed in the lackluster results documented in the Pilot Laptop Evaluation Report submitted by Ms. Tina Sears, Andersen County School District Technology Coordinator. The report documents the positive attitudes by teachers, students, parents, and administrators, and the video clips were moving. But most important to me, this report documents no improvements in student scores on the ITBS. I am considering pulling the funding and dropping the expansion to the other grade levels.

However, if the district can produce a solid evaluation plan that better demonstrates the impact of laptop computers on student learning, I will fund a full evaluation to occur during the next school year. If this report yields positive results, I will extend the laptop program to the remaining elementary grades. For me to consider this new evaluation to be thorough, the school district will need to host a meeting to discuss points of view from teachers, principals, parents, and parent-teacher associations. In addition, the Hillendale Textiles foundation board and myself will need to be present as the sponsors of this program.

Let's talk soon,

Bradley

# Planning the Future Evaluation

School started back. Mark had been a gold mine. Tina couldn't believe her luck. Mark worked within a center on campus that helped local and nationwide schools with documenting changes from instructional interventions, just like her laptop pilot program. The unassuming director of the center, Dr. Lisa Colm, was a nationally recognized and well-respected leader in the field of school evaluation. She had backgrounds in educational psychology, statistics, and psychometrics, but her personality tempered audiences' reactions to these sometimes challenging topics. While discussing program results with legislators, school boards, and other bigwigs, she often asked, "Is this in the best interest of children?" She made the results and numbers real—because they represented real teachers and real children.

After some discussion, the center agreed to handle the laptop pilot's external evaluation. Together with a team from the center, Dr. Colm agreed to facilitate a meeting, a week later, among Andersen County School District's stakeholders: teachers, principals, parents, the PTA president, community members, Mr. Cook, and the Hillendale Textiles foundation board, as well as the school board members. "A tough crowd for sure," Tina sighed. She was just relieved she didn't have to lead the meeting.

In the small, cramped boardroom at the school district office, all of the chairs were filled. Tina sat quietly in the back and fanned herself. While Dr. Colm expertly maneuvered the discussion around the laptop pilot program's purpose and goals to the various attendees, three members of the evaluation team scrawled copious notes. The purpose of the project, how the teachers and students had used the laptops, anecdotes from teachers and parents, and emphases on student test scores were all covered.

As purses and yellow notepads were picked up, sweat-soaked tissues were tossed, and the various stakeholders filed out, Tina approached Dr. Colm and the evaluation team. She was apprehensive; she knew these folks were her best help, or the project was sunk. Dr. Colm smiled and reassured Tina: "I'm confident we can help."

## The Next Day

Back at the university, Dr. Colm and the evaluation team met in their cool, blue conference room to debrief the stakeholder meeting from the day before. The relaxed team compiled all their notes onto a large whiteboard wallpapering one side of the room (see Figure 6–4).

**FIGURE 6–4** Whiteboard Notes from Dr. Colm's Evaluation Team Meeting.

### Stakeholder Questions

Do teachers teach differently when lessons include student use of computers?

In what ways do parents support the laptop program?

How do students' scores change, if at all, on the ITBS?

In which subject areas do student ITBS scores increase the most?

How often do students use the laptops?

In which subjects do students use the laptops the most?

Do students behave differently when they use the laptops?

How confident do teachers feel to integrate students' use of laptop computers into their instruction?

Reviewing the whiteboard, Dr. Colm sighed. She was confident that her team could readily craft a proposal within the timeline. However, addressing all the stakeholders' questions, particularly those focused on the ITBS test scores, would be more difficult to achieve, and it would be even harder to make others understand why it was difficult. Yet, with a confidence that came from having addressed these issues many times before, she turned to her team and smiled, "Well, team. Let's get to work!"

# Preliminary Analysis Questions

1. You are a member of Dr. Colm's evaluation team. Consider questions raised by stakeholders in the meeting (see Figure 6–4). What other questions might have been raised at the meeting? Be sure all viewpoints are represented.
2. Why do you think Mr. Cook decided to fund one more year of the laptop program even though student achievement gains were not realized?
3. In what ways should the "formal" evaluation be different from the evaluation conducted by Tina Sears?
4. In addition to student achievement, what other factors could be examined to determine whether or not student use of laptops affects student learning?
5. Describe the evaluation method (instruments, data collection, and analysis) needed to measure the achievement of program goals and to address the stakeholders' questions.

# Implications for ID Practice

1. What influence should testimonials have on making technology purchasing decisions?
2. How can evaluators convince stakeholders that alternative evaluation measures, other than standardized tests, are needed to answer complex questions related to measuring student achievement?
3. What techniques can evaluators use to ensure that results are unbiased?
4. What are some of the challenges evaluators face when scaling up from a small program to a larger program with the same goals? How would data collection and analysis methods differ depending on the size of the program?

# CASE STUDY 7

# Maya Thomas

## Implementing New Instructional Approaches in a K–12 Setting

*by Chandra Orrill and Janette R. Hill*

---

**Subject:** Math ideas
**Date:** Wed., April 21 08:10 GMT
**From:** r.ponten@middlecity.k12.ga.us
**To:** m.thomas@middlecity.k12.ga.us

Maya,

Next year, I will be teaching struggling 7th-grade math students. For self-survival, I have got to find an innovative way to reach and teach these kids. I am open to trying *anything!* I envision making this like a laboratory class, where we "do math" by doing activities and lots of different things. They have got to learn by doing. I have regular access to a laptop cart with 10 computers and one teacher computer. All are connected to our wireless network, so the possibilities are not limitless but are promising.

What do you think?

Ruth Ann Ponten

---

Maya Thomas, the staff development and instructional consultant for the Middle City School District, looked up from her e-mail and remembered her most recent science class with similar kids. She knew that there had to be some way to help Ruth Ann succeed with her students. She picked up the phone to call Ruth Ann and set up a time to talk.

    The next afternoon, Maya drove out to the middle school. As she drove through the rural area, she reflected on the changes that had occurred in the past decade. This once-quiet community of farmers and working-class folks was in a major state of transition. College-educated professionals were moving in because they were attracted to the community's tight-knit feeling and immaculate old houses. This change was also bringing other modifications, such as different expectations about education and a willingness to try new ideas for teaching and learning. These changes made Maya's job exciting as well as challenging.

Maya arrived at the school at the beginning of Ruth Ann's planning period. Maya entered the room, dodging a couple of students who were rushing off to their next classes. She quickly got inside and sat down at a desk. Ruth Ann, who was writing something on the board, turned and greeted Maya, then resumed what she was doing. After she finished writing, she came over to talk. She explained to Maya that she was so frustrated the last time she taught this population that she just couldn't bear to do it the same way again. Maya listened patiently, knowing that often teachers need time to vent before being able to get to work. Maya found herself thinking about the last class that she taught before becoming a staff development specialist after seven years of teaching. They were a bright group but simply were not motivated to succeed in school. She remembered the helpless feeling of knowing there must be better ways to help her students learn and the frustration of not knowing what those ways were. She empathized with Ruth Ann's stress and feeling of helplessness—this was a tough situation.

They talked for about an hour, and, as they talked, Maya took notes identifying some of the assumptions and beliefs that Ruth Ann seemed to hold. Maya began asking Ruth Ann questions about her previous class and about the students she was likely to have next year. Ruth Ann explained that the previous class had been very difficult because the students were out of control. A few of the kids just did not care about what was going on in the class and distracted the rest of the students. Ruth Ann continued noting that, even when the students were on task, they were so deficient in their basic mathematical skills that she just was not sure where to begin with them. She also mentioned that many of the kids seemed really interested in the technology, which is why she had mentioned that in her e-mail. But Ruth Ann also pointed out that other students didn't seem to like the computers at all. She finished by noting her extreme frustration that the students simply would not do their homework.

Maya asked about the kinds of students that tended to be placed in the class. Ruth Ann commented that it was almost never the farmers' kids or the kids of the college-educated professionals who were tracked into these classes, but ones who tended to move between parents and between schools. In addition, they tended to be unsupervised after school and did not have parental support when they got home in the afternoon. Maya pondered how these factors might influence students' reactions to being immersed in a laboratory setting such as the one that Ruth Ann envisioned.

As Ruth Ann talked, Maya realized how often she mentioned getting the kids to work more math problems. Even though Ruth Ann had originally said that she would be open to doing anything to help her kids, Maya realized it might not be as easy as just *saying* it. It was apparent to Maya that Ruth Ann typically taught from the front of the room, giving assignments with many problems, so that students had a lot of opportunities for practice. Learning in this environment meant memorizing formulas and calculating accurately. Ruth Ann had mentioned a laboratory-style class in her e-mail; now she also added that she thought the math needed to bring in more "real-world" experiences. Ruth Ann also mentioned that she knew that having students work problems at the board was not enough—that there had to be a better way to teach math. But, she added, she did not know any other way to teach math.

Maya realized that helping Ruth Ann develop a more hands-on, real-world learning environment would be difficult, given the differences in Ruth Ann's desired outcomes and her

**TABLE 7–1**   *Summary of Field Notes from Student Interviews*

| Source | Notes |
| --- | --- |
| High 7th-grade math achievers at Middle City | – "6th- and 7th-grade math was okay, but I don't see how this will help me when I grow up."<br>– Many like some group work but don't like being graded in groups because students don't always do their part in a group.<br>– The overwhelming student definition for math is that it means working a lot of problems.<br>– Many students claim to like using the calculator because it makes things easier.<br>– Several commented that their favorite part of math is the puzzles (number and shape) that they get to work on when they have extra time in class.<br>– Most students don't really like the computers because they do only drill and practice. |
| Poor 7th-grade math achievers at Middle City | – "6th- and 7th-grade math was boring."<br>– "6th- and 7th-grade math didn't make any sense to me."<br>– "All the teacher did was work problems on the board and expect us to do them at our desks."<br>– "There was too much homework."<br>– "My mom works and can't help me with my homework."<br>– "I hate math."<br>– "Man, my dad says that this math is useless. I don't know why I have to do it."<br>– Students reported liking classes that involve hands-on activities, such as science.<br>– Most of the students said they like working in groups.<br>– Most said that they like solving problems.<br>– A few commented that they used to like math but that it is not fun anymore.<br>– They don't really like the computers because they do only drill and practice. |
| Poor 6th-grade achievers (next year's 7th-grade low-level class) | – "I can't get any help with my homework at home."<br>– "This math won't matter when I grow up—just as long as I can add and stuff. I can just use a calculator."<br>– None like math—it's boring and hard.<br>– None see connection to real life.<br>– Most like hands-on work in science.<br>– None want a teacher who makes them do a lot of homework.<br>– They all hope that the teacher will help them more than just talking at the board because that is boring and because they don't always understand what the teacher is doing.<br>– Most haven't really used the computers a lot.<br>– They all seemed to think that there are too many problems to work in the book. Their homework takes too long, and they don't know how to do it. |

**TABLE 7–2** *Summary of Field Notes from Interviews with Ruth Ann and Assistant Principal*

| Source | Notes |
|---|---|
| Ruth Ann | – Feels the regular curriculum doesn't work for this kind of learner |
| | – Hates to teach at the board and let students practice yet does this all the time in all of her classes |
| | – Believes that low-achieving kids can benefit from doing hands-on activities in authentic situations |
| | – Worries about class conduct—the struggling kids tend to be rowdy and off-task and often skip class. She knows there will be little parent support to rely on. |
| | – Wants to look at innovative ways to grade, but is bound to the *A, B, C, D, F* policy of the school |
| | – Doesn't like the current book used for these kids because it is too choppy—ideas are covered in strange orders and for the wrong amount of time |
| Assistant principal for curriculum | – Supports Ruth Ann in whatever efforts she takes; these kids aren't succeeding. So any success is a giant step. |
| | – Would like to see a more progressive approach to math but stressed that the state Common Core Standards *must* be met and students must pass the end-of-year test |
| | – Wants to have pretests and posttests for each unit as well as quarterly benchmark assessments |
| | – Knows that there is little money to support the purchase of materials for the students |
| | – Wants synergy with other in-school programs, if possible |

current practices. Maya knew from personal experience that changing teaching styles was a lot of hard work. She wondered how best to support Ruth Ann in helping the kids succeed.

Maya went home that evening, thinking about Ruth Ann's situation. On her run that night, she formulated a plan to help support Ruth Ann: she would talk to some students and teachers to explore the current seventh-grade curriculum, as well as the kinds of things that might improve it. She was determined to begin the next day.

First thing the next morning, Maya started her detective work. She began at the curriculum office to find out which students had been placed in the low-level course the previous year and to collect information about the current sixth-grade class. She deliberately selected a few students from each group, dividing them into three categories: those who had done very well, those who had struggled, and those who were likely to be in the low-level class the following year. One-by-one, she talked to about 10 kids over the next week and a half. To round out the analysis, Maya also interviewed each of the teachers about the curriculum and their perceptions regarding students' performances. She also talked with the assistant principal for curriculum about her thoughts on the course (see Tables 7–1 and 7–2 for a summary of student, teacher, and administrator information).

In addition to talking to various people during data gathering, Maya spent time combing through the state's Common Core Standards and the school's textbook (see Table 7–3 for a summary of curricular information).

**TABLE 7–3** *Summary of Curriculum Information from State Standards and Textbook*

| Source | Notes |
|---|---|
| State standards | – Include a lot of computational skills. |
| | – Include standards for practice, but they are separate from the content standards. How are they assessed? |
| | – Include some explicit practical links (e.g., calculate sales tax and raises). |
| | – Require considerable mastery of concepts involving variable use. |
| | – Include proportions and integers. Students should have mastered fractions already. |
| | – The geometry and statistics standards seem like they would be easy to do hands-on (drawing constructions, exploring probability, and learning about random samples). |
| Textbook | – Includes a lot of practice in computation. |
| | – Includes the topics listed in the state standards. |
| | – Does not focus on standards of practice (e.g., problem solving, mathematical argument, mathematical reasoning, modeling, using tools to solve problems, making use of structure and patterns). |
| | – Is visually appealing and interesting. |
| | – Includes a link to everyday life in each chapter, but problems do not come from that. |
| | – Includes regular multiple-choice test-practice activities to prepare students for annual assessments. |
| | – Review problems are offered regularly throughout each chapter to review previously learned skills. |
| | – Includes a technology integration idea in every unit. |
| | – Chapter problems include one or two higher-order thinking problems. |
| | – There is no explicit call for manipulatives or alternative materials; everything can be done with paper and pencil. |

Once she had completed the interviews and reviewed the curricular materials, Maya analyzed the data she had collected. She wanted to be well prepared for her meeting with Ruth Ann the next week. She was alarmed to see that the factors working against success in mathematics went beyond those she expected. Maya had anticipated that students whose parents were not college graduates would be lower performers and would demonstrate lower achievement than other students. However, she also found, among a segment of the population, what looked like a cultural tendency to be resistant to education in general. There was an attitude of "My mom and dad didn't get a high school education and they're doing fine," or "My friends aren't doing well in school," or "My community doesn't care if I succeed here because school isn't an important part of my life," or a combination of these. This saddened Maya. She wondered, "How do you help students with these kinds of attitudes see the value of school mathematics in their everyday lives?"

About three weeks later, Maya and Ruth Ann finally got to spend half a day working on ideas for the class. Maya presented a short synopsis of her findings. Ruth Ann was surprised, and, like Maya, she was saddened by the poor attitudes of the lower-achieving students. Ruth Ann was also surprised at the discrepancies between what the standards called for and what her book was actually providing. She told Maya that she knew the book had problems but did not realize that it neglected so many important concepts. Then, Ruth Ann and Maya looked over a variety of new curricular materials and discussed the issues involved in integrating them into the math curriculum.

| | |
|---|---|
| Ruth Ann: | My first reaction to these materials is that I have no idea where to start. I mean, I can see that these problems are really good—they are open-ended and would get the kids engaged. But how would I help them solve these problems when they don't even have the basics? I'm a person who believes that you need the foundations, first. Develop the skills—then you can move on to these problems. |
| Maya: | OK. I can understand your point. The students you're targeting do come in with really low skills. But don't you think that we need to explore some different ways to help them? I mean, after all, if the traditional drill and practice worked for these kids, you wouldn't have them in this class, would you? |
| Ruth Ann: | That's true, and I can see how these materials could really make the kids think. But how do I know I'm meeting the Common Core Standards? I don't see how this is going to help them do better on the test. |
| Maya: | I'm glad you see some potential here. Maybe you and I can work together to see how they meet the standards. |
| Ruth Ann: | Won't the kids panic when they see these? I mean, these kids don't like school—they don't do their homework and they certainly aren't going to like all the writing. |
| Maya: | You might be right about the writing. Do you think that the kids will see these materials as more relevant to their everyday lives? |
| Ruth Ann: | Well, yeah. Still, what if the students refuse to do the work? And what if *I* can't work the problems? |
| Maya: | Maybe we can come up with some incentives to help get the kids interested. As for you not being able to work the problems, we'll make sure that you have some practice ahead of time, so you'll be fine. It may actually be a great way to get the students interested: Have them help you! |
| Ruth Ann: | Well, I can see that the students would at least have answers to some of their questions about how they'll use it in the real world. I worry, though, about the grading. How will I grade this work? |
| Maya: | Yeah, grading will be different in this kind of class. This is something I think we can work on together. |
| Ruth Ann: | I mean, all this writing—how will I know what they're thinking? I'm afraid that I won't see where they are having problems in this. They just don't have to do enough problems to indicate where the gaps are in their skills. |

| | |
|---|---|
| Maya: | I think you'll be surprised. I talked to a teacher at a workshop a couple weeks ago who is using this kind of approach. She said she actually knows *more* about her students' thinking now than she did when they were just working problems. She says it's been wonderful. |
| Ruth Ann: | And what about the parents? I know that they'll be screaming at me—this isn't what they know as math! |
| Maya: | I can see your point here. |
| Ruth Ann: | Hmm, I just don't know, Maya. I mean, we just went through textbook adoption a couple years ago, and we were so sure that we chose the best stuff out there. How can I go and change what I do now? I know the kids need something more than the textbooks, but this is a big change. Well, let me keep these materials and look at them more closely. [Ruth Ann is flipping through the notebooks.] Hey, here's an activity for graphing. We'll be doing that in one of my classes later in the week—maybe I can try it there. |
| Maya: | Great. How about if we sit down again next week and talk about this some more? |
| Ruth Ann: | Sounds good! |

Maya left feeling hopeful, but there was still no firm commitment to a new approach. Ruth Ann had raised a number of issues that seemed to indicate that she might not be comfortable with adopting a new method—that, although Ruth Ann wanted to implement a new approach in her classroom, she was reluctant to jump in. Maya believed that Ruth Ann wanted to change and was working in a system that valued change. However, there was still a strong core in the community that held tight to tradition, and Maya thought that Ruth Ann might be a little uncomfortable actually implementing the approach that she had initially said she wanted.

How could she and Ruth Ann work together to create a better math experience, given all these constraints? What kinds of support could she offer Ruth Ann that might help her use innovative curricula to get the kids interested in math? How could they meet the assessment requirements set forth by the assistant principal and still keep the instruction focused on the learning and development of mathematical knowledge? These were the questions that were going through Maya's head as she reflected on the conversation with Ruth Ann. Although she knew that it would be a lot of work, she felt confident that she could help. This was what she enjoyed about her work.

# Preliminary Analysis Questions

1. Critique the steps Maya took to identify the needs in the case, including the collection and analysis of data. What are some things she did well? What would you suggest to improve her practice?
2. What are some of the options Maya can explore to support the learning environment Ruth Ann requested?

3. What are some of the critical factors Maya needs to attend to if this effort is to be successful?
4. Consider how the work with Ruth Ann could be used as a starting place for schoolwide mathematics reform. Does that change the way Maya should work with Ruth Ann and the other math teachers? Does it change the options they should consider?
5. How might the community and parents influence the success of this effort? How might Ruth Ann tap into various resources available in the community, and how might that affect success?

# Implications for ID Practice

1. Discuss how characteristics of an organization affect the outcomes of a needs assessment.
2. Discuss how factors such as culture and resource availability affect change management.
3. To what extent should a change manager determine the direction a change should go? Who owns the change process? How should the needs of secondary adopters, such as learners affected by the adoption decisions of teachers, be addressed?
4. What are some ways to move people from one stage of adoption to the next?

# PART II

# Case Studies

## Section 2: Post-secondary Audience/Context

# Jackie Adams

## Evaluating a Federally Funded Faculty Training Program

*by Melissa J. Dark*

## Creating an Evaluation Plan

After graduating with a master's degree in instructional design, Jackie Adams accepted an instructional design position with a federally funded project at a large university. As the instructional designer on the project, Jackie's main responsibilities were to work with technical subject matter experts in the development, delivery, and evaluation of in-service faculty education. The Advanced Manufacturing Technology Education (AMTE) project was a new venture, which meant that Jackie would be clarifying her job at the same time she was developing the in-service faculty education program. The first thing Jackie did was read the grant proposal and talk with her new boss, Ray DeMilo.

Jackie learned that the AMTE project was one of many projects funded by the Advanced Technology Education (ATE) program. The goal of the ATE program was to improve science and engineering technician education at the undergraduate and secondary school levels. The ATE projects focused on one or more of the following aspects: curriculum development, instructional materials development, teacher/faculty enhancement, or student recruitment. The AMTE project focused specifically on teacher enhancement as a means of advancing technology education. The rationale behind AMTE was to provide educators with state-of-the-art knowledge in their technical disciplines, so that their students, in turn, would benefit from the most current advances in technology. During each year of the three-year grant, the AMTE project was to provide faculty development to 100 science, math, and engineering technology educators.

Over the course of the next several months, Jackie worked with several subject matter experts to plan in-service workshops in high-tech areas, such as computer numerical control, programmable logic controllers, robotics, electromechanical controls, lasers, solid modeling, and rapid prototyping.

Jackie had been on the job about four months when Ray asked to discuss her progress to date. Ray told Jackie that he was pleased with the progress of the project and that her skills in instructional design had significantly contributed to this progress. Jackie felt great.

**FIGURE 8–1**    AMTE Evaluation Plan.

The focus for the AMTE evaluation plan will be the development of a quality system that will provide a well-defined and agreed-upon standard for evaluating and continuously improving AMTE's operations. The use of standards to establish quality systems in industrial and education settings is growing rapidly and provides an excellent framework for the development of AMTE's evaluation plan.

Quality systems based on such standards typically include the development of both a program for assuring an organization's quality and all the activities and operations required to implement it effectively. AMTE is proposing to establish a comprehensive quality system, which will cover elements such as documentation, implementation, review and correction for all activities having a bearing on the quality of the information, and services and activities supplied by AMTE.

A key factor in the management of AMTE's quality system will be the development of a quality audit, which will be used to provide the data for evaluating and improving the effectiveness of its quality system. The objectives of AMTE's quality system audits will be to a) maintain or improve efficiency of its operations and image, b) determine how disciplined and effective the organization's operations are, and c) meet an appropriate level of quality assurance as specified by an agreed-upon standard or contractual agreement. The standard for the AMTE quality system audits will define its policies, lines of responsibility and accountability, and procedures, in addition to work instructions, and recordkeeping requirements as appropriate. Audits will be conducted periodically by internal AMTE auditors in order to maintain and improve the quality system, as well as external reviewers who may provide a more objective assessment of the project.

He went on to explain that he had just received a memo announcing new legislation that was going to have an impact on all federally funded projects, including AMTE. The new legislation required greater and more stringent performance assessment of all federally funded projects. Jackie asked Ray what that meant for AMTE. According to Ray, they needed a more detailed evaluation plan to assess the performance of their project. Ray delegated the evaluation to Jackie and asked her to submit a detailed plan for evaluating the project in a month. He also told her that the evaluation plan would need to be submitted to the funding agency and filed in the grants office at the university.

After Ray left her office, Jackie worried about how to approach this task. She had never written an evaluation plan before. Jackie thought that she and the subject matter experts she was working with had been making good decisions in designing the instruction for the target audience and establishing the goals and objectives of the in-service workshops. However, because they were just getting started, Jackie did not feel ready to think about measuring outcomes of the teacher in-service workshops.

Concerned, she remembered reading a little bit about evaluation in the grant proposal. She pulled out the proposal and reread the section on project evaluation that Ray had written for the grant (see Figure 8–1).

Jackie read the section several times, trying to make sense of it. However, she did not have a background in quality. The most that she understood was that the "quality system" was supposed to provide a standard for evaluating and continuously improving AMTE's operations. There was no information in the section about how this was to occur. She pondered this for a few days and finally wrote down some thoughts (see Figure 8–2).

**FIGURE 8–2**   Jackie's Evaluation Planning Notes.

*Evaluation Planning Notes*

According to the grant proposal, the mission of the center is to

> "improve significantly the educational experiences and opportunities of students preparing for careers in manufacturing and distribution by keeping teacher enhancement as a major focus."

Tie evaluation to mission.

Answer the following questions:

Why evaluate?

Evaluate what?

How should the evaluation be conducted?

Who should be involved?

When should it be done?

# Conducting a Meta-Evaluation

The AMTE project had been operating for a year and a half. Ray shared with Jackie a letter that he had received from the funding agency regarding an upcoming meeting. The funding agency would be sending out a six-member team to review the project's progress and impact. This was a routine practice on large grants to ensure that the money was spent as intended and that the project was meeting its goals, as well as having its intended impact.

According to Ray, this meeting was very important. On conclusion of the review, the six-member team would report the success of the project to key administrators at the university and the funding agency. The review team had asked to meet with Ron Bentley, the dean of the school, and Bruce Stingel, the vice president for academic affairs.

Since the beginning of the grant, Ray and Jackie had talked about the importance of a good plan for project evaluation. Ray and Jackie knew that if they had a good evaluation plan they could accurately measure the impact of the project and identify areas where the project could be improved to increase impact. The upcoming review session would examine how well AMTE had achieved its goals and how goal attainment had been measured and reported. Ray told Jackie, "Well, that evaluation plan is going to be important now. We will get to show the agency and the university administration what we are all about. I know you did a good job on the plan." Jackie appreciated Ray's vote of confidence but didn't feel quite so confident herself. She did not feel comfortable having a lot of people review her work. Furthermore, the stakes seemed high. If she did a good job, it would reflect well on everyone, and they would have a better chance of securing additional funded projects in the future. If she did a poor job, it would not bode well for the institution and future projects.

As the meeting kicked off, Ray and Jackie became acquainted with the review team. The team included four post-secondary educators with a background in science, engineering, and technology and two engineering practitioners from industry. Each person on the review team was responsible for reviewing and documenting a different aspect of the project. Hank Lundstrom, an engineering technology professor, was the lead team member. Hank's job was to assess Jackie's evaluation plan. Hank had served on accreditation teams in the past, which gave him more experience in evaluation than his fellow team members.

During the two-day meeting, Hank spent the entire first day with Jackie. At the beginning of the meeting, Hank explained to Jackie that the team would be reviewing the project's progress and impact. He went on to explain that the impact of the project would be assessed using data gathered from the project evaluation plan. According to Hank, the value of data gathered would be directly related to the evaluation plan methodology, and his job was to document this. The team would then get back together, report their findings, evaluate the project, write a report, and present it to the dean, the vice president, and the program officers at the funding agency.

Jackie shared the AMTE evaluation plan in detail over the course of the first day (see Figure 8–3). During the time they spent together, Hank asked a lot of questions and listened intently as Jackie explained the evaluation plan. Hank had a very factual and impersonal manner throughout the meeting. He did not comment much on the information that Jackie shared, making it hard for Jackie to determine whether or not he thought it was a good plan. By the end of their meeting, Hank had detailed what he had learned from Jackie about the AMTE evaluation plan in a summary report. He thanked Jackie for her time and let her know that he would be sharing his summary with the rest of the team in order for them to write an evaluation report. As Hank walked away, he felt confident that he had enough information to start on his review.

**FIGURE 8–3**    Jackie's Evaluation Plan—Summary of Key Points.

*Overview*

The purpose of the grant is to improve the educational opportunities and experiences available to students through faculty development. Therefore, the evaluation plan is structured toward that end. The workshop was developed based on given instructional objectives and learning outcomes (an example from a workshop on Programmable Logic Controllers is in Appendix A). The evaluation plan consistently measures these objectives using the following instruments: an Implementation Survey, a Pre/Posttest, and a Reaction Survey (examples in Appendices B through D). Although each instrument is measuring the same set of constructs (i.e., the objectives), each instrument has a different purpose as described next.

**FIGURE 8–3** *Continued*

---

*Instrument #1—Implementation Survey*

The purpose of the implementation survey (Appendix B) is to measure the extent to which faculty transferred knowledge and skills gained in the workshop to their students.

Workshops are held in the summer with the goal of implementation occurring during the coming academic year. Therefore, the implementation survey is administered, 9 to 11 months later, to the faculty who attended a workshop. The implementation survey is used formatively and summatively. The survey instrument consists of closed- and open-ended items. Data collected via the closed-ended items are summarized and used to report impact and outcomes. The follow-up open-ended questions are used to obtain qualitative feedback from participants with regard to factors that facilitated or prohibited transfer.

*Instrument #2—Pre/Posttest*

Given that the implementation survey intends to measure transfer of knowledge and skills, project personnel determined that it is important to have a measure of knowledge and skills gained in workshops. A pretest and posttest (Appendix C) are being used to measure pre-workshop and post-workshop knowledge. The pretest is administered to the attendees at the beginning of each workshop, and the posttest is administered at the end of each workshop. Content validity has been established for the pretest and posttest by directly relating the test items to the instructional objectives and learning outcomes established for the workshop and the instructional materials used in the workshop. Objectives are indicated on the test in parentheses after the question stem.

Because it would not be possible for a faculty member to transfer knowledge and skills to their students that they have not yet mastered themselves, the pretest and posttest data are used in several ways:

(a) Formative evaluation with the learners (teachers who attend the workshops) to determine content requiring remediation for each learner to facilitate additional knowledge and skills gain and subsequent implementation.

(b) Formative evaluation of the workshop instruction and materials by looking at group trends in learning using an item-by-objective analysis. Objectives not mastered by the group as a whole are indicative of areas in the workshop and instructional materials that may require improvement.

(c) Summative evaluation of knowledge and skills acquired in the workshop by quantifying accurate measures of incoming knowledge, outgoing knowledge, and knowledge gain. Gain scores are converted to a standardized $t$-score and reported by significance levels.

(d) Summative evaluation of transfer. The data are also used to accurately correlate and report knowledge and skills acquired in the workshop with implementation. If a teacher who attended the workshop already possesses knowledge or skill in a given subject, and subsequently reports transfer of that subject on the implementation survey, then transfer cannot necessarily be attributed to knowledge and skill acquired in the workshop.

*Instrument #3—Reaction Survey*

AMTE also uses a reaction survey (Appendix D) at the end of each workshop. The purpose of the reaction survey is to gather immediate quantitative and qualitative feedback from teacher participants. Because there are several workshops that take place over the course of a summer, formative feedback and suggestions for improvement gathered on the reaction surveys from the first workshops are used to improve the workshops that occur later in the summer. In addition, the three years of funding provided for three cycles of workshops. The information has also been used to make improvements year to year. The nature of the feedback is described next.

**FIGURE 8-3**    *Continued*

The reaction survey asks participants to rate both their expectations and their experiences for each instructional objective according to (a) clear identification of the instructional purpose of the workshop, (b) knowledge and skills gained, and (c) usability of the instructional materials.

Expectations are compared to experiences to determine objectives where the instructional experience did not meet expectations. Although the closed-ended questions are useful for quantifying group reactions, they do not provide insight into suggested areas for improvement. Follow-up open-ended questions are used to provide suggestions for improvement. The information collected via the reaction survey is also used summatively at the end of each year.

# Preliminary Analysis Questions

Part A: Questions Related to the Evaluation Plan
1. What are the main evaluation questions Jackie appears to be addressing?
2. What are the strengths and weaknesses of the plan for addressing the questions?
3. Given the goals stated in the ATME proposal, are these questions sufficient? If not, what other questions would you add?

Part B: Questions Related to Instrumentation
1. How appropriate are the instruments for the goals of the evaluation?
2. Are the evaluation questions answered in enough detail, or are other instruments needed? What is your rationale?
3. What, if anything, would you change about the instruments and why?

# Implications for ID Practice

1. What is meta-evaluation? How is it important to instructional design?
2. In what kinds of situations is it appropriate to conduct a meta-evaluation? What are the challenges and advantages to conducting a meta-evaluation?
3. How do issues related to measurement instruments affect the practice of instructional design?
4. Evaluation is sometimes compared to quality management. How does this comparison apply in instructional design?

# APPENDIX 8–A

# Workshop

## Introduction to Programmable Logic Controllers

**Instructional Goal:**

This workshop will help you develop knowledge and skills in interfacing and programming PLCs. You will learn how to integrate hydraulics and pneumatic applications in teaching PLCs.

**Instructional Objectives and Learning Outcomes:**

1. Interfacing input and output (I/O) devices to a PLC
   Interface and test inputs and output devices to a PLC from a given schematic
2. Program a relay logic application using the A-B 6200 software
   Program rungs using the A-B 6200 software
   Program rungs for pneumatic applications
   Design and program a motor control application
3. Program the timer and counter applications
   Program the three basic types of timers
   Program a counter
   Use timers to control cylinder movement
   Use a counter to count machine cycles
   Design a time-driven sequence
4. Data manipulation applications (thumbwheel switch application)
   Use the move and convert instruction for controlling a thumbwheel switch
5. Math functions (simulated packaging applications)
   Program the multiply function for a packaging application
6. Interface and program a rung sequence application
   Program a three-event–driven sequence
   Program a four-event–driven sequence
   Program a six-event–driven sequence
7. Output sequencer instructions (time driven)
   Program the PLC using the output sequencer instruction
8. Input and output sequencer instructional (event driven)
   Program the PLC for an input sequence driving an output sequencer
9. Interfacing and programming a pneumatic robot
   Test the interfacing of the PHD pneumatic robot with a simple test program to determine if it operates properly
   Program the PHD pneumatic robot to run using the output sequencer instruction
   Design and program the PHD robot to be event driven using an input sequencer driving an output sequencer

# APPENDIX 8-B

# Implementation Survey

**AMTE Implementation Survey**

PROGRAMMABLE LOGIC CONTROLLERS

AMTE is interested in knowing how you implemented the knowledge, skills, and materials you acquired in the Programmable Logic Controllers workshop into your curriculum. We need your feedback for purposes of reporting results and for making improvements to this project. The information you share with us will be used to improve our work. The information will not be used to evaluate any one individual, institution, or community.

Another aspect of this project is focused on studying trends in staff development and characteristics of effective staff development. The data being collected here require that we be able to link reactions to pretest and posttest scores and implementation. In order for us to accurately do so, we are asking for the last four digits of your social security number on all evaluation activities in which you are participating. Thank you for taking the time to share complete information with us.

Last four digits of your social security number _____

| The following are content areas covered in the MCATE PLC workshop. Please indicate if you implemented each content area into your curriculum as a result of the workshop; provide the course title and number and the # of students enrolled. | Implemented into curriculum | | |
|---|---|---|---|
| | I implemented this into my curriculum | Course Title and Number | # of Students Enrolled |
| Interfacing input and output (I/O) devices to a PLC. | | | |
| Programming a relay logic application using the A-B 6200 software. | | | |
| Programming the timer and counter applications. | | | |
| Data manipulation applications (thumbwheel switch). | | | |

| Math functions (simulated packaging). | | | |
|---|---|---|---|
| Interfacing and programming a rung sequencing application. | | | |
| Output sequencer instructions (time driven). | | | |
| Input and output sequencer instructions (event driven). | | | |
| Interfacing and programming a pneumatic robot. | | | |

1. Previous workshop participants have identified facilitators and barriers to implementation. Please indicate which of the following were facilitators or barriers to implementation of the content presented in the workshop into your curriculum.

Facilitator          Barrier

_____          _____          a. Content knowledge gained in the workshop

_____          _____          b. Content skills gained in the workshop

_____          _____          c. Skill in teaching the content

_____          _____          d. Instructional materials acquired in the workshop

_____          _____          e. Time

_____          _____          f. Money

_____          _____          g. Administrative support

_____          _____          h. Change of assignment

_____          _____          i. Other, please specify _____

If you checked barriers above, please explain briefly.

_____
_____
_____
_____
_____
_____

*Thank you for the time you took to provide us with complete information. Please return the survey in the enclosed, self-addressed and stamped envelope.*

# APPENDIX 8–C

# Pretest/Posttest

---

**Name**_____

**SSN Last Four Digits**_____

### Programmable Logic Controllers Pretest and Posttest

Instructions: This test is given to determine the knowledge gained in the workshop. Please leave the question blank if you do not know the answer. NOTE: Numbers in parentheses refer to the related course objectives.

1. The success of PLCs used in industry over PCs for control is:   (1)
   A. Opto-isolation-Isolation
   B. Terminals for connection of input and output devices
   C. Indication (lights or LEDs) of signal condition
   D  Signal conditioning (control of 120 VAC and other voltages by low PC voltages)

2. Inputs such as limit switches and pushbuttons are wired to the input module:   (1)
   A. Normally open
   B. Normally closed
   C. Normally open and normally closed depending on the circuit

3. Outputs are wired to the output module:   (1)
   A. In parallel
   B. In series
   C. With one output to one output terminal

4. How many output devices can be programmed in one rung?   (2)
   A. One
   B. Two
   C. Two or more in series only
   D. Two or more in parallel only

5. Output devices can only be used once as an output in a program.   (2)
   True            False

6. Inputs devices can be used several times in a program.   (2)
   True            False

7. An address on an output device can be assigned to an input contact symbol.    (2)

True                    False

8. This is a *start stop rung*, which is very common to almost all programs. Identify the error in the program by listing the address with the error.    (2)

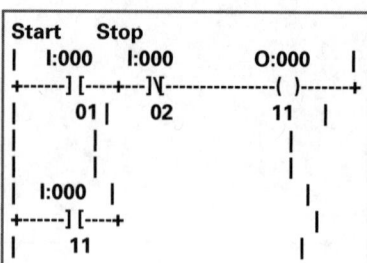

```
Start    Stop
|   I:000    I:000           O:000    |
+------] [----+---]\[----------------( )-------+
|      01 |      02            11   |
|          |                         |
|          |                         |
|   I:000  |                         |
+------] [----+                       |
|      11                            |
```

9. Use Figure Appendix 8–1. What address goes at contact X if O:000/14 comes on when the timer times out?_____    (3)

10. Use Figure Appendix 8–1. A counter (CTU) in the A-B PLC can count to a maximum of:    (3)
    A. 999
    B. 1000
    C. 32,767
    D. 65,535

## FIGURE APPENDIX 8–1

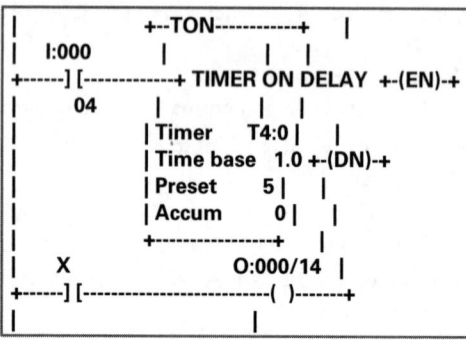

```
|                 +--TON------------+   |
|   I:000         |            |  |    |
+------] [------------+ TIMER ON DELAY +-(EN)-+
|     04          |            |  |
|                 | Timer    T4:0 |  |
|                 | Time base  1.0 +-(DN)-+
|                 | Preset      5 |  |
|                 | Accum       0 |  |
|                 +-----------------+   |
|    X                      O:000/14  |
+------] [-------------------------( )-------+
|                                    |
```

11. When a timer rung is true, the timer begins to increment the AC value at a rate specified by the time base. When the rung goes false, the timer resets the AC value to:    (3)
    A. TON
    B. TOF
    C. RTR
    D. RTO

12. When the timer goes false, the AC value is retained at: (3)
    A. TON
    B. TOF
    C. RTR
    D. RTO

13. Each time the rung goes true, the AC value is decremented to: (3)
    A. CTU
    B. CTD
    C. CTR

14. Which bit is set if AC > 32,767? (3)
    A. DN
    B. TT
    C. EN
    D. OV

15. Which instruction is used to compare two values in memory? (4)
    A. ADD
    B. SUB
    C. EQUAL
    D. MOVE
    E. CONVERT

16. The multiply instruction uses ___ memory location(s). (5)
    A. One
    B. Two
    C. Three
    D. Four

17. What type of addressing is used to keep the rungs in order with the sequence application, because outputs cannot be used more than once in a program? (6)
    A. Absolute
    B. Indirect
    C. Relative

18. Use Figure Appendix 8–2. An output sequencer program should have the first step as zeros for the T home position so no solenoids are activated when the PLC is put into the run mode. (7)
    True                    False

19. Use Figure Appendix 8–2. The sequencer uses a data table to control the outputs. To move from one step to the next step on the data table, the output sequencer must: (7)
    A. Be held high
    B. Pulsed
    C. In the run mode
    D. Activated with an external instruction

20. Use Figure Appendix 8–2. A zero in the Mask word will enable (allows bits to work) ____
    bits.                                                                          (7)

    True                    False

**FIGURE APPENDIX 8–2**

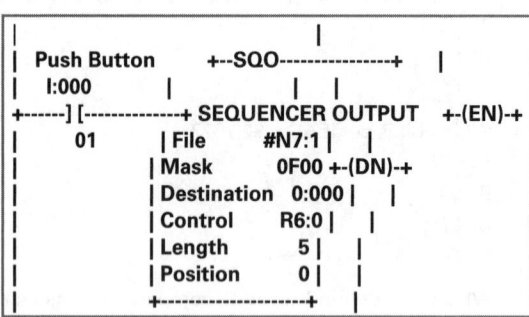

21. An input sequencer used to examine the sensors can drive the output sequencer to
    advance to the next step in the sequence. To keep them synchronized (on the same
    step):                                                                         (8)

    A. They must use separate control files
    B. They must share the control file
    C. They must use the same data table

22. The PHD Pneumatic Robot is a five-axis robot plus a gripper. There are six solenoids to
    control each movement. Each axis will have a limit switch at each end of the cylinders
    to detect position. If each of the five axes has two limit switches each, how many limit
    switches will be closed when the robot is at home?                             (9)

    A. 10
    B. 5
    C. 2
    D. None

23. It is possible for the robot to move and during the moves all limit switches could be off
    (open) for a moment.                                                           (9)

    True                    False

24. Using the output sequencer (SQO) allows outputs to used in a program as many times T
    as needed, which is unlike rung type programs where an output can only be used once
    in a program.                                                                  (9)

    True                    False

25. Design a continuous cycle reciprocation application for a pneumatic cylinder using a
    two-position, four-way, double solenoid valve (no springs). A start button should cause
    the circuit to start, and a stop button will stop the reciprocation of the rod. The cylinder

should stop retracting when the stop button is pressed. Use two limit switches as shown in Figure Appendix 8–3.        (9)

## FIGURE APPENDIX 8–3

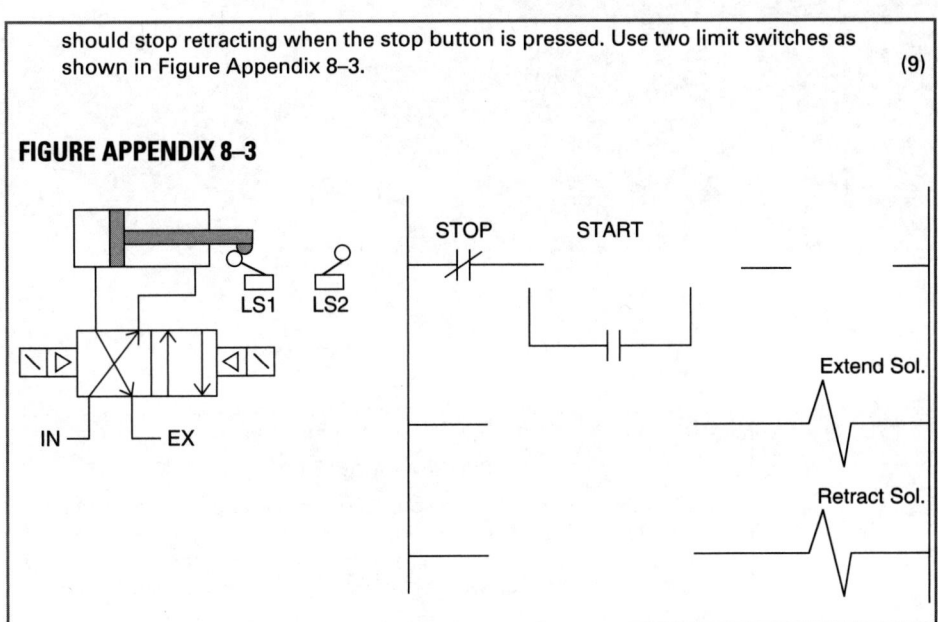

# APPENDIX 8–D

# Reaction Survey

**Reaction Survey**

PROGRAMMABLE LOGIC CONTROLLERS

AMTE is interested in receiving your feedback for purposes of reporting results and for making improvements to this project. Please provide us with honest, thoughtful and complete feedback to assist us in doing so. The information you share with us will be used to improve our work. The information will not be used to evaluate any one individual, institution, or community.

Another aspect of this project is focused on studying trends in staff development and characteristics of effective staff development. The data being collected here require that we be able to link reactions to pretest and posttest scores and implementation. In order for us to accurately do so, we are asking for the last four digits of your social security number on all evaluation activities in which you are participating. Thank you.

Last four digits of your social security number: _____

| Please rate the following aspects of the workshop according to your experiences. | What You Experienced | | | | |
|---|---|---|---|---|---|
| | Strongly Disagree | Disagree | Somewhat | Agree | Strongly Agree |
| **I gained skills and knowledge to enhance student learning in the following areas.** | | | | | |
| Interfacing input and output (I/O) devices to a PLC. | | | | | |
| Programming a relay logic application using the A-B 6200 software. | | | | | |
| Programming the timer and counter applications. | | | | | |
| Data manipulation applications (thumbwheel switch). | | | | | |
| Math functions (simulated packaging). | | | | | |

| | | | | | |
|---|---|---|---|---|---|
| Interfacing and programming a rung sequencing application. | | | | | |
| Output sequencer instructions (time driven). | | | | | |
| Input and output sequencer instructions (event driven). | | | | | |
| Interfacing and programming a pneumatic robot. | | | | | |

1. If you rated any of the sections above as "Disagree" or "Strongly Disagree," please explain your rating so that we can improve our professional development workshops.
2. What was the most useful/beneficial aspect of this workshop?
3. Before attending, how did you think this workshop would best help you update your curriculum?
4. Now that the workshop has concluded, how do you think that this workshop has helped you update your curriculum?
5. Before attending, how did you think this workshop would best help you update your teaching and content?
6. Now that the workshop has concluded, how do you think that this workshop has helped you update your teaching and content?
7. One of our goals was to provide instructional materials that you could readily use in the classroom. Will you be able to use the materials provided you?

   Yes                    No

   If your answer is No, how can the instructional materials be improved so that you could readily use them?

# Jennie Davenport and Pedro Lopez
## Converting a Powerful Workshop to an Online Format

*by Simon Hooper and Aaron Doering*

Jennie Davenport was beginning to wonder if she was making any progress in resolving the instructional design challenges in the project she had been assigned to coordinate. Both Jennie, a project manager with eduLearning Systems (eLS), and Pedro Lopez, a professor of learning sciences at Midwestern State University, had been recruited by Professor Clark Essex, a renowned sexual health expert at the university, to design an online version of his very successful "Man-to-Man" (M2M) HIV/AIDS prevention workshop. This workshop had been designed to improve sexual health for gay and bisexual men and had been delivered face-to-face at cities around the United States on a monthly basis for the past five years. This particular target audience had been shown to be at high risk: specifically, target audience members were in danger of becoming infected with HIV/AIDS though sexual contact with infected partners.

This danger had continued to increase with the use of the Internet as an anonymous communication medium and the meeting place of choice for many gay and bisexual men. HIV/AIDS infection rates were higher for men who used the Internet to find partners than for men who met their partners using more traditional approaches such as gay bars.

Several hypotheses had been proposed for the elevated risk of using the Internet as a meeting medium. Some who used the Internet to find partners were unaware of the health issues involved in engaging in unsafe sex. Others may have chosen to ignore potential dangers because of a wide range of intervening variables such as the effects of alcohol or drug use, pressure from partners to engage in high-risk sexual behavior, or internalized homonegativity (i.e., negative attitudes toward homosexuality that obstruct many gay men in the coming-out process). A third explanation is that the Internet simply improved "dating efficiency." It was faster to meet partners by using the Internet, resulting in an increase in the frequency of sexual contact.

Professor Essex had recently received substantial funding from the National Health Foundation (NHF), a government agency, to design and develop a highly interactive multimedia version of the M2M workshop that would be available via the Internet (IM2M). Although Essex was an expert on contemporary HIV/AIDS education initiatives, he candidly acknowledged that he did not understand what should (or could) be done to deliver his workshop successfully via the Internet. However, he was eager for the project to fully incorporate "state-of-the-art" web technologies, and was delighted that Pedro had agreed to participate in the project.

The timeline written into the NHF grant called for the project to be designed, developed, and evaluated over a two-year period. The first nine months were to be used for brainstorming and developing three levels of prototype. Product development would be conducted during the following six months, and during the last nine months the project would be evaluated using a randomized controlled study to compare the effectiveness of the face-to-face and online versions of the workshop. The project proposal called for the online version to follow the 10 components of the sexual health model: talking about sex, culture and sexual identity, sexual anatomy and functioning, sexual health care and safer sex, challenges to sexual health, body image, masturbation and fantasy, positive sexuality, intimacy and relationships, and spirituality.

The NHF project proposal was written primarily by Professor Essex, but with significant input on the instructional design approach from Pedro. Before joining the faculty, Pedro had worked for eight years as a project manager at an educational software development company that relied heavily on a "learning by doing" approach to instructional design. He was currently writing a book with the working title of *Authentic Pedagogy and the Use of Participatory Design in Instructional Design*, and his numerous research articles were considered to be "cutting edge" and had received enthusiastic critical review. He was delighted to have the opportunity to work on the design of the online version of the workshop as he relished opportunities to put his theories into practice.

Following notification of funding from NHF, Professor Essex contracted with eLS to develop the online environment after hearing positive reports about the company from a senior colleague working in human resources at the university. The colleague recommended eLS after working with the company on the development of an online version of a training program to help the university meet the requirements of the Health Insurance Portability and Accountability Act (HIPAA). eLS was an e-learning software company that prided itself, as its advertising said, on "designing and developing instructionally sound, cost-effective education and training solutions to improve performance" and on delivering these solutions on time and within budget. Indeed, eLS had won several prestigious awards in recent years for developing training applications. Some of the company's successes included the design and development of a multimedia application used to improve the performance of human resource managers at a large computer corporation and a cultural diversity training product used by a Fortune 500 company. According to eLS, the cultural diversity training was credited with raising awareness for 92% of participants, and with changing behavior of 84%.

Jennie, one of the most successful project managers at eLS, had previously coordinated two projects and had developed several learning objects that were integrated routinely into other e-learning products. Her charge was to work with Pedro to translate the face-to-face workshop into an online environment. Moreover, as project manager, it was Jennie who was ultimately responsible for the success or failure of the project. Given this level of accountability, she was highly motivated to identify clear project goals, to use these goals to establish criteria for project evaluation, to verify changes in behavior, and to determine the success of the project.

## Man-to-Man Workshop

The face-to-face version of the Man-to-Man workshop was presented to approximately 50 to 60 participants who traveled to a single location and met for approximately 16 hours over a two-day period. The workshops were facilitated by faculty from the departments of counseling psychology and human sexuality and from the university's medical school. All workshop presenters had received extensive sexual health workshop training and held advanced degrees in their fields.

The workshop curriculum included the 10 components of the sexual health model and used diverse instructional strategies such as lectures, games, opportunities for individual reflection, and discussions in both small- and large-group settings. The instructional strategies made use of a broad range of instructional media such as video clips, still images, and slideshow presentations. Workshop participants were recruited through local print and electronic media. For example, advertisements had appeared in *Leather and Lace,* a publication focusing on the local gay, lesbian, bisexual, and transgender community; *City Guide,* a local entertainment newspaper; and on local community electronic bulletin boards. Workshops were open to all participants who identified themselves as being gay or bisexual.

The face-to-face workshop had been shown to be highly effective in reducing the incidence of high-risk behavior. In fact, in an evaluation comparing workshop participants with a control group who viewed print and video sexual-health materials, data showed that incidents of risk behavior among the experimental group decreased by 32% after six months, and 27% one year later. In contrast, risk behavior among the control group decreased by 12% after six months and 8% a year later. Evaluation data pointed to a range of reasons to account for the success of the workshop. Many participants mentioned that the small-group experiences were particularly powerful: Within supportive small groups, participants were challenged to grapple with various issues that promoted heightened self-analysis, and this process seemed to have had a transformative effect on the attitudes and behaviors of the participants.

In addition, Professor Essex stressed the importance of using "hot cognitions" (i.e., use of sensual and/or erotic stimuli such as photos and movies) in certain phases of the face-to-face workshops. Cognitive behavioral therapists use the term hot cognitions to indicate that emotional stimulation is often crucial to the therapy process. Using hot cognitions may affect decision making and behavior more than techniques in nonaroused educational contexts. Moreover, Professor Essex maintained that research had demonstrated that the use of sexually explicit media in such settings gradually reduced participants' discomfort and shame while simultaneously facilitating positive behavior change. Counseling services were offered on-site for participants whose reactions to the workshop experiences made them feel especially uncomfortable.

## From M2M to IM2M: How Do We Get There?

Although Jennie and Pedro had only a few brief conversations about the Man to Man project, both were already beginning to see that they had quite different ideas about how to translate M2M to IM2M. Both were focused on achieving the same goal, but they were having difficulty agreeing how the face-to-face workshop could be translated to an online environment.

"I think that our design approach for this project is important because it addresses an issue that is likely to become increasingly common in the next few years," said Pedro. "As Internet use continues to expand, more and more people will want to learn how to develop an online format for a face-to-face workshop or class."

"Absolutely," agreed Jennie, "and I've already been involved in leading a couple of such projects. As you know, I was the project manager for the HIPAA training modules. My team members and I were asked to convert a classroom-based training module about patients' privacy into an online experience. The modules were completed by employees at the university and the project was very successful: We documented a 100% completion rate! I really think that I can apply what I've learned in that project to the Man-to-Man project."

"So, how did you approach designing the online version?" asked Pedro.

"Well," began Jennie, "it was clear that the original classroom-based HIPAA workshop was quite effective, so we assumed that customizing the content to specific cultural groups and including learning checks would further increase the effectiveness of the intervention while allowing us to reach a larger online audience. The online setting was the perfect environment for customizing content and guaranteeing that learning was taking place. Because much of the content was already in place from the live training, we were able to focus on the customization and learning checks to further improve the training and make it more appealing."

"Well, I haven't seen that workshop, but from how you describe it, it seems to be primarily about delivering information," said Pedro. "But in the Man-to-Man workshop, we're looking at very different learning outcomes. This project is not just about the delivery of information—it's much more about behavior change, and that has more to do with modifying people's opinions and values than it does with learning content. I mean, look at what people know about smoking—everyone recognizes that smoking is bad for their health, but such knowledge doesn't cause people to quit. The same is true here; we're not just trying to inform people about safe sex techniques. Our job is to change people's beliefs about themselves. By doing so, people will begin to make effective choices. I'm not so sure that we can take the existing content and reproduce it online with only minor changes in delivery."

"I see what you mean," noted Jennie. "I certainly agree that the Man-to-Man workshop is more than just about delivering information, but so was the HIPAA workshop—not only were the employees required to learn information about HIPAA, the training was also designed for them to perform a range of tasks related to the correct application of HIPAA requirements. In the classroom-based version of the workshop, the trainers had incorporated a lot of question-and-answer sessions and group discussions, and we managed to translate these to the online environment.

"In fact," said Jennie—trying to sound as upbeat as possible, although she was pretty sure she wasn't convincing Pedro—"we required participants to post comments for each discussion thread, and the result was that we obtained 100% participation in the online discussion forums, which was much higher than was ever the case in the classroom version of the training!"

"Although there might be some similarities in terms of the usefulness of online discussion forums," responded Pedro, "I don't think an online discussion forum is realistic for the Man-to-Man project. An online workshop isn't like an online class—workshop participants attend voluntarily, so we can't require them to submit responses to a forum."

Just as Jennie feared, Pedro's comments confirmed her suspicions that she and Pedro were not getting any closer to agreement on the overall design plan for the IM2M, let alone getting to the point of planning a detailed design.

"Also," Pedro continued, "I don't believe we can recreate the small-group experience online because we can't reproduce the empathy of a face-to-face discussion in an online discussion forum. The media associated with each environment differ greatly, and the experiences made possible by the face-to-face environment cannot be replicated. Physical proximity makes a huge difference when it comes to discussing important personal matters. Being physically close to another person produces a powerful affective response that may be impossible to recreate on the Internet."

"Do you really think so?" asked Jennie. "More and more people are routinely using social media to meet and date. People frequently discuss their most personal problems in online settings. It wasn't that long ago that we didn't even have a word for *blog*, and now you can find a threaded discussion or a blog on just about any topic of interest. If these men use the Internet regularly to meet with other men, surely they will also be willing to engage in discussions about their personal lives. Of course, we may have to tweak the format somewhat from the face-to-face version, but I have no doubt at all that this is not only possible, but highly practical."

"Well, it *is* true that people seem to discuss almost any topic on the Internet these days," mused Pedro, "but I'm still not clear on how we can translate the face-to-face interactions to the Internet environment so that we can achieve the same outcomes that Professor Essex has been achieving. For example, you know how Professor Essex uses what he calls 'hot cognitions' in the face-to-face workshop—how are we going to handle these in an online environment? Shouldn't we be concerned about the possible ethical and legal implications of hot cognitions? I mean, could the university or eLS be found liable if it can be proven that an individual who committed a sex crime did so after being aroused as a result of completing the Internet materials?"

Jennie appreciated that Pedro had raised some important points that had also been nagging at her. However, she wasn't about to mention this to Pedro at this point: She thought it better to wait until they had more time to come up with some potential ways to move forward. Besides, hearing Pedro mention Professor Essex reminded Jennie that she had a meeting with him in about 30 minutes and that she needed to finish her meeting with Pedro.

"You've brought up some really important issues," responded Jennie. "However, I have a meeting with Professor Essex shortly, so we'll have to finish for now. What about this as a way to move forward? Why don't both of us give some thought to how we might structure the online version of M2M over the next week and come back with some more detailed ideas for a proposed design? I'm sure that we can work out something that will meet the challenges that we have discussed."

"Sounds good to me," responded Pedro, "but I certainly think we have our work cut out for us."

Jennie had met with Professor Essex only once before to clarify some details about the timeline and budget and to agree on how they would work together over the course of the project. Based on her experience on other projects, Jennie knew that some clients did not realize that their involvement would be necessary as design and development proceeded, and she believed strongly in having a clear agreement on mutual responsibilities from the very beginning of a project. However, although much of their first meeting went well, she was surprised to find that Professor Essex seemed unwilling to work with her on the development of detailed measures of effectiveness for the online version of Man-to-Man. She had come prepared having read the NHF proposal that he had developed, which included project goals written according to NHF requirements. Although they were written clearly (see Figure 9–1), she thought Professor Essex needed to identify more detailed measures that she could use to establish evaluation criteria that would be applied during the online workshop to assess changes in participants' behaviors.

"If the goals were good enough for NHF, surely they should be good enough for eLS to work with," Jennie recalled him saying. Unfortunately, or fortunately, Jennie wasn't sure which; their meeting time was up before they could get into more detail about the need for more measurable goals. She hadn't really expected such resistance and had been somewhat taken aback by Professor Essex's reaction at their initial meeting. In any event, she had persuaded Professor Essex to meet again today. Since their first meeting, she had thought through how she would present her arguments for the need for more detailed measures and was hopeful, if not exactly confident, that she could convince him of the need for what she was requesting.

As she walked toward her car after her meeting with Professor Essex, Jennie reflected on her day. It was very important to her that the project be completed to a high standard, on time, and within budget, but Jennie already knew that this project would be unlike any of the previous projects she had coordinated. Would she and Pedro be able to come to agreement on the design issues they had discussed? Could they translate the face-to-face workshop to an online format while maintaining its power and effectiveness? Given Professor

**FIGURE 9–1**    Project Goal and Objectives Submitted to the National Health Foundation.

**Project Goal**

Our project goal, which will guide all design and development activities, is to broaden the impact of an HIV/AIDS prevention face-to-face workshop by adapting it to an online environment. The result will be an Internet-delivered sexual-health intervention for gay and bisexual men who use the Internet to connect with other men.

**Project Objectives**

The objectives of the project are as follows:

- To develop an HIV/AIDS prevention workshop for gay and bisexual men for delivery over the Internet.
- To use the 10 components of the sexual health model as the basis for the Internet-delivered workshop.
- To incorporate contemporary principles of e-learning and distance education into the online workshop.

Essex's attitude, would she even be able to measure its effectiveness? And what about the legal and ethical issues that Pedro had raised? "I think Pedro was right," she thought to herself as she drove off campus. "We do have our work cut out for us."

# Preliminary Analysis Questions

1. Pedro presents a number of challenges to Jennie regarding the translation of a face-to-face workshop to an online environment. Evaluate the validity of the challenges in the context of this project.
2. Given the differences between Pedro and Jennie's approaches to designing interactive online experiences, propose how they might proceed in their discussions and work.
3. Professor Essex depended strongly on hot cognitions for the success of his face-to-face workshops. To what extent can these be incorporated into the workshop's online workshop?
4. Consider the project goal and objectives from the perspectives of Professor Essex and Jennie Davenport. Develop a list of criteria that can be used to measure success.

# Implications for ID Practice

1. Consider the potential and limitations of designing Internet versus face-to-face workshops on sensitive content.
2. Discuss the risks and benefits associated with encouraging Internet communication (synchronous or asynchronous) when the topic is emotionally laden.
3. How does instructional design for behavior change differ from design for knowledge acquisition? Describe differences in terms of goals, strategies, and evaluation.

# CASE STUDY 10

# John Falkin

## Designing an Online Graduate Seminar

*by Thomas Michael Power*

John Falkin, an instructional designer at Rolling Hills University, was on unfamiliar terrain and definitely outside his comfort zone. When faced with challenges in the past, he had always been able to rely on his training and past experiences to help him sort things out. This time, although he was excited about the prospects of going beyond what had become routine, he was wondering if this was beyond his skill set.

John was an Instructional Designer at Rolling Hills University (RHU), a fairly large university located in central Canada, with about 35,000 undergraduate and 4,500 graduate students enrolled. The university was becoming increasingly involved in developing online learning courses in many programs but did not yet have the infrastructure to support faculty and expand to a large scale. John had been hired three years ago as part of a growing multi-faculty support team at the Teaching and Learning Center (TLC) with the mandate to expand RHU's online learning offerings. Thus far, John had worked exclusively on high-enrollment courses at the undergraduate level, designing asynchronous, discussion-based courses that attracted hundreds of students per term.

This term, John had been approached by his boss, Roy Barrow, the RHU Teaching and Learning Center Coordinator, about an issue he had recently been made aware of: "John, I'm glad you could come by. I just got off the phone with Dr. Jan Fellows, the Chair of the Graduate Studies Program over at the School of Social Work. She told me the school is having trouble maintaining enrollment levels in one of their graduate programs. She said that the program itself is sound but that potential students are highly mobile and spread all across the country; there simply aren't enough students who can come to campus to take the program." Jan also told him that, unless enrollments increased, they would have to shut down the program. So Jan invited Roy to a meeting with the Program Committee to discuss what might be done to make the program viable by offering it online. Roy asked John to join him at the upcoming meeting.

When John heard that the chair was considering taking the entire program online, he felt an instant sense of apprehension—he had never converted a graduate course to an online format, let alone an entire graduate program. He knew he could count on a junior, recently hired instructional designer, Bob Campbell, to pitch in despite the fact that he had been hired mainly to assist faculty who were migrating from an older Learning Management System to a newer one. There was also the tech team, but, given the potential magnitude of the task at hand with regard to the actual capabilities of the TLC team, resources would likely be stretched.

## Meeting with the Program Committee

At the meeting, besides Roy, John, and Jan Fellows, four other faculty members from the School of Social Work were present: Dr. Patricia Bello, Dr. Michael Hatty, Dr. Eliza Bainsbridge, and Dr. William Sears. These faculty taught the introductory courses in the program, and most likely their courses would be slotted for online delivery. There was also a graduate student member of the committee in attendance, Frank Jones.

Jan started out by explaining why they were meeting and then went on to describe the overall structure of the graduate program—its goals, components, and target population. She emphasized the specificity of graduate courses, or seminars as they were commonly designated. Turning to her colleagues, she said: "Here at RHU, up until now, we've mostly been involved in designing and delivering high-enrollment, undergraduate courses. But now, we need to start looking at the viability of graduate courses as potential targets for online learning." Turning to Roy and John, she added: "As you may know, a graduate seminar is quite different from an undergraduate course. Off the top of my head, I can think of three major differences, regardless of whether the seminar is on campus or online:

"First, enrollment numbers tend to be different between undergraduate and graduate courses, which often leads to different teaching strategies.

"Second, our faculty approach undergraduate courses differently than they do graduate courses. In the former, the lecture method is the norm (whether we like it or not), whereas in the latter, the seminar method is usually the norm.

"Third, when undergraduate courses are offered online, they typically require high-level, labor-intensive, front-end design, whereas graduate-level courses, in which content changes much more rapidly, do not.

"As a result of these differences, any decision we make must take into consideration the specific technological requirements of the seminar method and the ultimate viability of launching online courses for 15 to 25 students." In conclusion, Jan mentioned a worrisome trend she had observed: "Another thing we might want to keep in mind as we discuss our options is this: Over the years, there has been a gradual decline in the quality of students we are admitting, according to what I've witnessed and to what my colleagues have been telling me."

She described this as a threat to the program's credibility and expressed her hope that, by going online and opening up the program to a larger population of potential students, they could become more selective. Concluding, Jan reminded them all, "Inaction is not an option if we want to maintain our graduate program." She then invited Frank to say a word about how students felt about the current situation.

Looking around the room, Frank began: "I'm glad to have been invited to this important meeting. I'm confident that I represent my fellow students when I say our program is relevant, it is high quality, and it needs to be kept going. I really hope it will be taken online and become accessible to more students, because according to our statistics, all of the program graduates have found gainful employment in the field. As a matter of fact, a lot of students find a job before they even finish the program and they have to finish part-time, such as in my case. So going online will really make it easier for a lot of us."

Then Jan asked Roy, the TLC coordinator, to say a word about the design team. Roy explained how his team operated and what resources were available. He said: "Other programs here at RHU have achieved a significant measure of success by working with our team to integrate varying combinations of blended and online learning. For instance, ever since the Business School took their MBA program online, they have had higher enrollments and generally positive assessments as well as having achieved sustainable cost-effectiveness. So, rest assured that our team can support you in whatever course of action you decide to undertake."

John then spoke, explaining how the design process was actually conducted, emphasizing the kind of involvement faculty generally have to consider making for their project to be a success. He ended by saying, "It's often a lot of work upfront but, down the road, faculty usually recoup their time investment and more, leaving them with more time to invest elsewhere."

Patricia, an associate professor, jumped in. "I'm glad we're discussing this now, because there is a lot at stake here. I always look forward to starting work on my course, but I'm a little worried that I just won't have enough time to devote to it. I'm at a critical stage in my research just now, and it is taking up a lot of my time. So I'm concerned I won't be able to devote the time I should to redesign my course." Then she added, "I also have a question. Given the fact that this is a graduate-level course in which I'm constantly adding new material, how much redesign will it actually require?"

John responded, "You have a valid point; quality course design does take time and commitment but, depending on your course objectives and what you've already accomplished, the workload is usually manageable. At least many of your colleagues find it to be so."

Eliza, a young, recently hired academic, said she considered herself a "believer." "But as much as I'm convinced the future of university teaching is online, I am also convinced we, as faculty, have to be concerned about copyright and intellectual property issues that are far from being clear in our collective bargaining agreement. I'm fine with developing an online course, just so long as I maintain not only intellectual property, but copyright as well, on any materials I develop. So, before I agree to sign up, I want the university to sign off on that."

Michael, a full professor, said with a twinkle in his eye, "I think this all sounds great. As a former program director, I know full well that an increase in enrollments would not only save our program but would likely enhance its relevance in the eyes of our colleagues. The only downside," he said, "is that I, myself, am what you'd call computer illiterate.

**FIGURE 10–1**   Dr. Sears' Seminar Design Model.

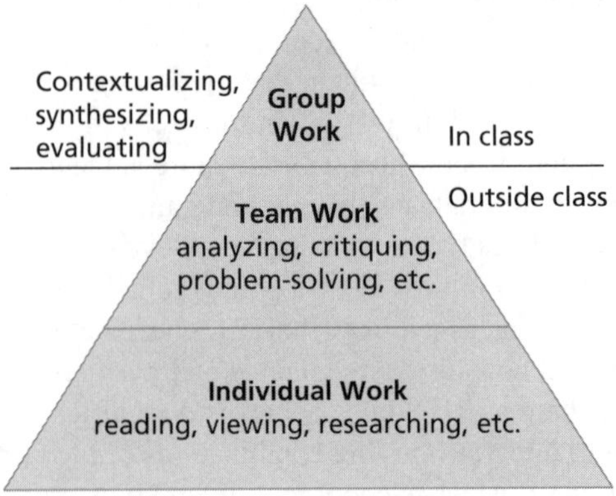

Basically, I'm a champion of hunt-and-peck!" He went on to explain that he only used his computer for e-mail and some occasional online navigating, adding that he was unaware of how an online course actually worked. "Besides," he said, "In our seminars, as Jan was saying, students interact spontaneously, exchanging viewpoints based on readings I hand out before class. Therefore, there is really not much need for computer stuff." He concluded by saying that, although he realized that outreach was necessary and that time was of the essence, he wondered "if it just might be a little premature to consider taking the entire program online."

The attention of the group then turned to William, also a full professor in the program. He began by providing a handout to his colleagues to explain his idea of a graduate seminar (see Figure 10–1). "Basically, like Michael, I have my graduate students do a lot of preparatory work before coming to class, which is to be expected. As they do this work, I expect them to take notes, write down ideas and questions and generally adopt a critical attitude towards what they are reading or viewing.

"I then require them to meet in teams of two or three before class and discuss their ideas, critiques, and questions so that, when we meet as a group in class, they have already resolved the minor issues. Then we can devote our time together to working on the major issues." Waxing philosophical, he said, "A course is more than just a collection of materials to be perused casually; it is an ancient and sacred covenant between the learned and the learner . . . a meeting of the minds." He emphasized the criticality of the pedagogical relationship—"the intellectual to and fro"—the Socratic approach to learning. He then paused thoughtfully and added: "This relationship must never be sacrificed simply for expediency's sake; on the contrary," he said, "we must never lose sight of this approach, and any use of technology should only serve that purpose and in no way detract from it."

After the meeting, John sat down at his desk and decided to collect his ideas so as to chart a course for this project over the next few months. He felt he first needed to jot down what he knew—the facts—as opposed to the lingering questions about what he did not know and go from there in trying to articulate possible courses of action (see Figures 10–2 and 10–3).

**FIGURE 10–2** Design-Related Facts.

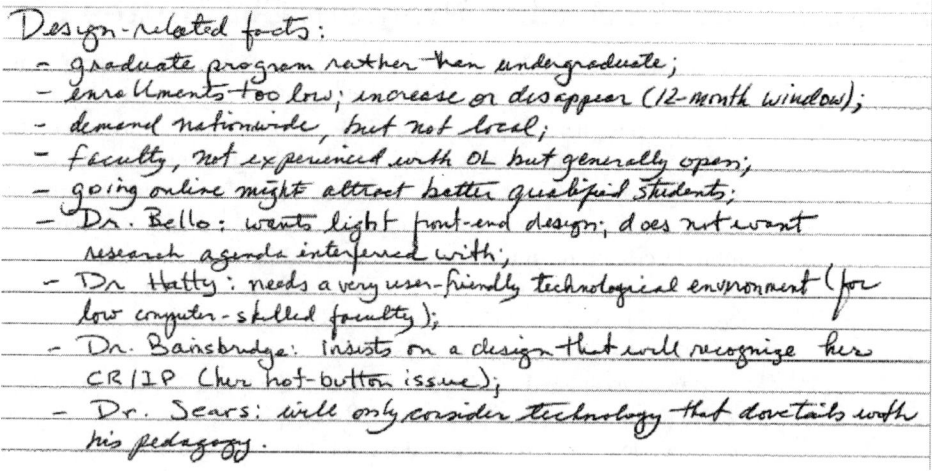

Design-related facts:
- graduate program rather than undergraduate;
- enrollments too low; increase or disappear (12-month window);
- demand nationwide, but not local;
- faculty, not experienced with OL but generally open;
- going online might attract better qualified students;
- Dr. Bello: wants light front-end design; does not want research agenda interfered with;
- Dr. Hatty: needs a very user-friendly technological environment (for low computer-skilled faculty);
- Dr. Bainsbridge: insists on a design that will recognize her CR/IP (her hot-button issue);
- Dr. Sears: will only consider technology that dovetails with his pedagogy.

**FIGURE 10–3** Design-Related Questions.

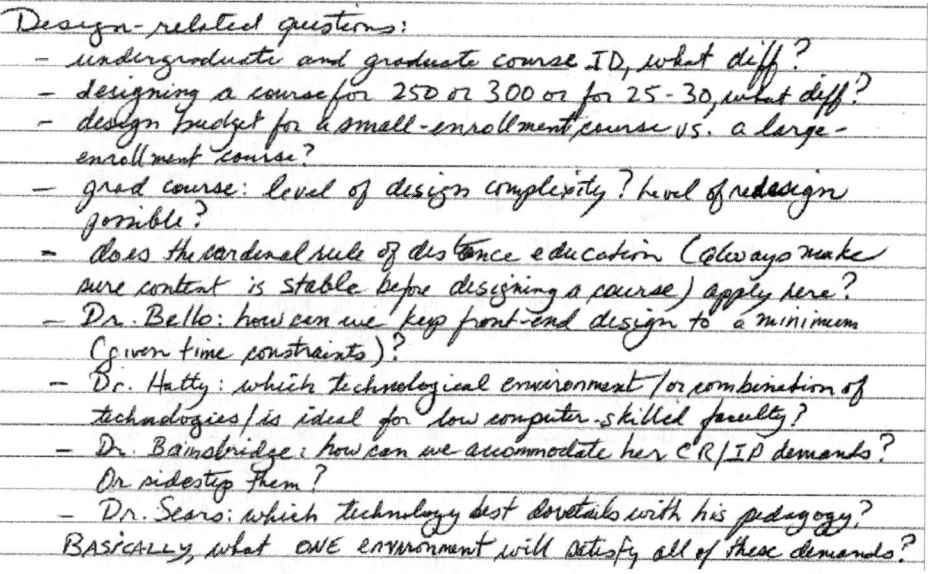

Design-related questions:
- undergraduate and graduate course ID, what diff?
- designing a course for 250 or 300 or for 25-30, what diff?
- design budget for a small-enrollment course vs. a large-enrollment course?
- grad course: level of design complexity? Level of redesign possible?
- does the cardinal rule of distance education (always make sure content is stable before designing a course) apply here?
- Dr. Bello: how can we keep front-end design to a minimum (given time constraints)?
- Dr. Hatty: which technological environment / or combination of technologies / is ideal for low computer-skilled faculty?
- Dr. Bainsbridge: how can we accommodate her CR/IP demands? Or sidestep them?
- Dr. Sears: which technology best dovetails with his pedagogy?
BASICALLY, what ONE environment will satisfy all of these demands?

John felt that these questions could keep him busy for a long time . . . but the clock was ticking.

A week later, Jan called Roy and said that she needed to meet with him and to ask John to come as well. Time was short and a solution had to be found before the end of the current term so that any design and development efforts that might be required could at least begin during the following term.

# Prepping for the Second Program Committee Meeting

Before meeting with Roy and Jan, John called Susan, a good friend and former colleague who was now a senior instructional designer at Northern Plains University (NPU). She was what designers liked to call a designer's designer, always up on the research, always looking for innovative ways to design and redesign courses, and always very upbeat about meeting challenges face-on. She had moved to NPU in order to enroll in a PhD program in instructional design and technology, hoping to eventually become a university professor. John described the situation to her and told her he had never designed a graduate-level course, let alone an entire graduate program. He said he felt doing so was quite different from what he was used to doing and, basically, that he was at a loss for ideas for the first time since becoming an ID. "Help!"

Susan explained that she had indeed designed several graduate courses and that, before doing so, she had been required to rethink the entire design process. "John, I won't try to tell you what you have to do. I don't know because I'm not in your shoes. But a few things do come to mind, so here goes. OK?"

"Yes, Susan, please—shoot!"

"OK, first," she said, "how much front-end design is enough? As you know, graduate courses are usually conducted as seminars and faculty are constantly changing content, depending on what's new and hot in the field. Do you think they could get their grad students to pitch in and help out with content refresh?"

John answered, "Good idea. It would be an excellent learning experience for them."

"Second, in on-campus seminars, there is always a lot of back-and-forth between faculty members and students. You said you have one faculty member in particular who is adamant about maintaining that, right? OK, so, here's my question: how can you best accommodate this professor? Should you try to convince him to just use the asynchronous design and delivery model as you've been doing with faculty teaching their online undergrad courses? Do you think that'll work? If not, what's the alternative?"

John was silent for a moment and then said, "No, I don't see that working at all. It'll never fly, especially with Dr. Sears."

Susan continued, "It sounds a lot to me like your faculty really don't want to lose contact with their students when engaging in online teaching. Are you hearing the same thing? If so, how can you accommodate that? What technology is out there that will allow them to stay in close touch with their students? I'm not sure what you'll find, but it's got to be affordable and robust."

John responded, "Well, I have my work cut out for me. Technology review, here I come."

"Anyway," Susan concluded, "these are just some of the thoughts that come to mind right now. I hope you find them useful."

After talking to Susan, John went online to his own ID community of practice websites to see what his colleagues were doing with graduate courses. He realized he was playing catch-up and had only a short amount of time to provide the Department of Social Work with a viable solution. He had to find that solution soon. Then he had to get Roy's sign-off before meeting with Jan.

## Meeting with Dr. Fellows

Jan started by referring back to the first meeting, saying a few words about her colleagues' reactions to the idea of going online and concluded by reiterating that the program would be shut down if nothing changed. Roy said that he and John had talked it over and thought they had a viable plan. "Since it's all John's, I'll let him present it."

John started by explaining that, after consulting with his colleagues and doing some online research, he thought he could provide a workable response to the points raised by all of the faculty members. After explaining his proposal to Jan, she decided to convene another meeting with the Program Committee members the following week as well as to invite the department chair, Dr. Rodriguez, to join them, because there would likely be workload issues to consider. The meeting was set for the following week, in the computer lab.

## Meeting of the Program Committee Members, the Department Chair, Roy, and John

John started the meeting by explaining that, since the last meeting, he had done quite a bit of research and had consulted some of his peers on the specificity of delivering graduate courses online. He then outlined what seemed to him to be the major considerations.

- RHU was primarily a research-based university
- Faculty were often hard pressed to devote enough time to designing (or redesigning) their courses
- Design-related resources were relatively scarce
- Graduate seminars required relatively small numbers of students
- Learning resources used in seminars had to be constantly updated
- Faculty expected high-level dialogue during seminars
- Administrators needed flexibility in scheduling courses, in light of actual enrollment levels

John then said, "So, given all of these considerations, this is what I think we should do. . . ."

## Preliminary Analysis Questions

1. If you were John and were faced with the challenges he is facing, describe the steps you would take to meet these challenges.
2. In this case, how important is the need for a faculty-friendly technological environment? How user friendly can a technology be and still do the job? How do we decide the balance between ease of use of a technology and its ability to support high-quality instruction?
3. Divide into groups and present a plan that will effectively address the needs and constraints that John has identified.

# Implications for ID Practice

1. Describe the advantages and limitations of moving a program online in order to address decreasing enrollments. Think critically about what taking a program online may mean to faculty, administrators, and support staff.
2. Discuss the instructional differences, if any, between an online graduate course and an online undergraduate course. How do time and human resource requirements differ between online graduate and undergraduate courses?
3. Research how copyright/intellectual issues are handled in university settings. What are the implications for online course development?
4. What advantages/disadvantages do you see to synchronous communications during course delivery? How can faculty determine the optimal mix?

# Malcolm Gibson

## Designing Authentic Online Experiences for Adult Learners

*by Joanna C. Dunlap*

## Dean's Conference Room, Bentley Hall, Craiger University—9:05 A.M.

"OK, let's go ahead and get started," directed Dr. Teresa Tsagas. "Does everyone have an agenda? As you know, the purpose of our work session today is to pull together all of the sections of the PTTP proposal, including the work that Malcolm has done. In fact, assuming all of you have already had a chance to look at the attachments Malcolm sent a couple of days ago, I'd like to go ahead and start with Malcolm, since his work is the core of the proposal. Malcolm, would you mind getting us started by walking us through your proposed certificate program structure, and then the online module?"

## Background

Craiger University is located in one of the top five technology states and ranks third in the number of high-technology companies. However, the information technology industry in the state is in crisis because there are not enough resident skilled employees to meet demand. Instead of continuing the practice of hiring people from out of state, a number of the state's information technology (IT) organizations have formed the Information Technology Consortium (ITC) with support from the state government. The mission of the consortium is to increase substantially the number of IT graduates over the next five years by funding programs that will increase the availability of highly qualified IT professionals. The ITC has released a *Preparing Tomorrow's Technology Professionals (PTTP)* Request for Proposals (RFP; see Appendix 11–A) that offers financial support to educational institutions that propose innovative methods for preparing an increased number of technology

113

professionals for the workplace. The ITC will award up to $2 million to each competitive educational institution during the first round of funding.

The School of Engineering at Craiger University has a computer science (CS) undergraduate program that the department chair, Dr. Teresa Tsagas, and the faculty believe could be easily repurposed for the PTTP initiative. According to the RFP, one of the possible program formats deemed appropriate for preparing IT professionals was online certificate and degree programs. The CS faculty had been thinking about making the computer science major available online for the past year and a half but hadn't moved forward because of a perceived lack of resources. The PTTP money could be the shot in the arm that the department needed to leap into online delivery.

## Initial Plan of Action

Dr. Tsagas and the CS faculty decided to propose a program that would make use of the existing face-to-face courses required for the CS major to offer four online certificate programs. Given this structure, people could take all four online certificates and apply them to the Bachelor of Science degree in computer science, or people not interested in a degree and just needing to update their knowledge and skills could take one certificate or a subset of certificates.

To create the certificates, the faculty divided the existing courses into the four categories depicted in Figure 11–1. In general, the faculty proposed that the CS curriculum be evenly distributed across the four certificates. Because each certificate would build on information gained in the previous certificate, they would be taken in sequence, from beginning to advanced. Each certificate program would be completed in 40 weeks, with each course lasting eight weeks. If a student applied the certificates to the BS in computer science, the major could be completed in two years.

One requirement of the RFP was to provide an example of the proposed approach to an online instructional module or course. To help the CS faculty address this requirement, Dr. Tsagas contacted Malcolm Gibson, a local instructional technologist with expertise in web-based course development. Because Malcolm is also an IT professional, Dr. Tsagas asked him to review and provide feedback on their proposed certificate program structure in light of the RFP.

After reviewing the RFP and Dr. Tsagas's proposal, Malcolm accepted the contract, hoping it would lead to more instructional design and online course development work, not only with the CS department but with Craiger University overall.

## Project Challenges

During Malcolm's first information-gathering meeting with Dr. Tsagas and the CS faculty, he realized that it was going to be a challenge for him to work on this project. For one thing, he didn't become involved in the project until late in the process. The CS faculty had

**FIGURE 11–1** Preliminary Certificate Structure.

| Certificate I: Fundamentals of Information Technology | |
| --- | --- |
| CS 145 | Calculus |
| CS 115 | Computing Fundamentals |
| CS 160 | Data Structures |
| CS 165 | Discrete Structures |
| CS 180 | Assembly Language |
| **Certificate II: Algorithms and Basic Languages** | |
| CS 150 | Advanced Calculus |
| CS 210 | Applied Linear Algebra |
| CS 225 | Algorithms |
| CS 215 | Differential Equations |
| CS 250 | Fundamentals of Programming Languages |
| **Certificate III: Operating Systems and Software Engineering** | |
| CS 245 | Operating Systems |
| CS 315 | Principle of Software Engineering |
| CS 260 | Theoretical Foundations of Computer Science |
| CS 265 | Numerical Analysis |
| CS 280 | Graph Theory |
| **Certificate IV: Advanced Computer Science** | |
| CS 390 | Applied Probability |
| CS 410 | Computer Architecture |
| CS 360 | Advanced Software Engineering |
| CS 482 | Ethical Decision Making in Computer Science |
| CS 475 | Software Development Project |

already been putting together information for various sections of the proposal, and the structure and content of the proposed program and curriculum were already determined. In addition, the proposal was due in six weeks. That didn't leave him a lot of time to develop the sample online module.

Malcolm was also very concerned about the faculty's proposed certificate structure because he didn't believe it would meet the goals of the PTTP initiative. Unlike other certificate programs, Craiger's proposed certificates were unable to stand on their own. The certificates relied on repurposing the same courses, in the same sequence, currently being delivered in the face-to-face program. The existing program appeared to Malcolm to be a sequence of isolated, decontextualized concepts and problems leading to a simplified capstone project completed in the final semester. If the current program were already "preparing tomorrow's technology professionals," there would be no need for the PTTP initiative.

Finally, Malcolm's expertise reflected the design of instruction that incorporates authentic, practice-based learning activities. A lot of the content for this project (e.g., computer programming) was procedural. Malcolm hadn't really designed instruction for rule-based content before and wasn't quite sure how to do it in a meaningful and relevant way for students online, which was a core requirement of the RFP. He was also concerned about his ability to develop a course that would be delivered in an accelerated, eight-week format. With as much diplomacy as he could muster, Malcolm expressed his concerns to Dr. Tsagas.

"Malcolm, I understand your concerns, and the fact that you have them reinforces my decision to hire you. If I'm hearing you correctly, your primary concerns are the structure of the certificate programs and the timeline?"

"Yes," responded Malcolm, "I guess that's accurate." *But*, he thought, *I really am worried about everything!*

"Well, I can't do anything about the timeline, but I would like to give you some lee-way to explore—and present back to us—different ways to structure the curriculum into certificate programs. We need all the help we can get if we want to present a competitive proposal to the ITC, so if you want to take a stab at it. . . . Would you like to propose a different structure to the faculty at the next work session?"

Malcolm agreed to develop a web-based module (one week of a proposed eight-week course) for inclusion in the proposal (and for stimulating further faculty buy-in for converting the CS courses to an online delivery format) and to propose a different structure for the certificate programs. Unfortunately, Malcolm had even less time to accomplish both tasks than he thought. Because the proposal was due in six weeks, he really had only four weeks to complete his task in order to be prepared to work with the CS faculty during their final session.

## Malcolm's Work

Based on Dr. Tsagas's request, the first thing Malcolm did was to reexamine the certificate plans of study that the faculty had constructed (review Figure 11–1). Based on his understanding of the marketplace and the requirements of the RFP, Malcolm generated an alternative certificate structure for the faculty to review (see Figure 11–2). Using the new structure, Malcolm decided to develop a module for the Programming with PHP and JavaScript course (a course he added to the Web Engineer Certificate). As a web developer, he was very familiar with the content and skills that students needed to learn in that course and, with only four weeks to develop an example good enough to help win the funding and future work at Craiger, he knew he wouldn't have time to work on any unfamiliar content.

For the next four weeks, Malcolm worked continuously in order to meet the deadline. Three days before the scheduled work session at Craiger, Malcolm sent his version of the certificate program curricular structure and the web-based module as attachments to Dr. Tsagas and the CS faculty for their review (review Figure 11–2 and see Appendix 11–B).

## Back in the Dean's Conference Room—9:06 A.M.

Malcolm stood up, walked over to the table in the front of the conference room, and projected a slide of his curriculum-restructuring memo for everyone to see.

"Hello again, everyone. Since you've already had a chance to review this, I don't want to spend too much time on it, if we don't need to. Maybe we could start with your comments and concerns."

**FIGURE 11–2**    Malcolm's Proposed Certificate Program.

**TO:** Dr. Teresa Tsagas

**FR:** Malcolm Gibson

**RE:** DRAFT—CS Certificates

Per your request, below is an alternative mapping of computer science curriculum to four certificate programs, organized by in-demand information technology positions. Each certificate stands alone—it's a vertical orientation as opposed to the original horizontal orientation. For example, in the Systems Engineer Certificate, the courses are sequenced from beginning to advanced—as opposed to the original structure of the certificates where the certificates themselves are structured from beginning to advanced. This structure, based on positions in the information technology field, better addresses the PTTP initiative because it is focused on preparing students for specific jobs in the workplace.

The challenge is that the current courses will not directly map to this alternative structure. As you see, the Data Structures course is now split out across all four certificates, but the content of each Data Structures course will be specific to the position students are being prepared for—i.e., network engineer or web engineer. Sorry, I didn't include course numbers because I am not that familiar with what is covered in each of your existing courses. But I am assuming that content from existing courses can be repurposed for use in these courses. I look forward to discussing this at our next meeting.

Systems Engineer Certificate
Fundamentals of Systems
Systems Algorithms and Data Structures
Programming Language: C/C++
Systems Architecture
Applied Systems Engineering

Network Engineer Certificate
Fundamentals of Networking
Network Algorithms and Data Structures
Programming Language: C/C++
Network Architecture
Applied Network Engineering

Database Engineer Certificate
Fundamentals of Databases
Database Algorithms and Data Structures
Programming Language: SQL
Database Architecture
Applied Database Engineering

Web Engineer Certificate
Fundamentals of the Web
Web Algorithms and Data Structures
Programming with PHP and JavaScript
Web Architecture
Applied Web Engineering

It was obvious that the faculty had read the materials and had looked at the online lesson. Over the next 15 to 20 minutes, Malcolm fielded a quick succession of questions. The faculty began by expressing their concerns about facilitating online instruction.

Dr. Will Jacobs started the discussion. "When I'm explaining programming concepts, I like to look at my students' faces to see if they're getting it. I can tell by looking at them if they don't understand what I'm presenting, and then I can try to say it in a different way. How will I know if the students get it in an online environment?"

"Can I jump in?" asked Dr. Judy Ruzic. "You know, some of the content in our courses is really challenging. I often see students before and after class, working together on different problems. Sometimes they form study groups. I just don't see how they can do this on the web."

"That reminds me. I don't know about the rest of you, but I am mostly worried about controlling and managing student activities in an online course. If I don't see them, how will I know they are doing their *own* work? Or doing any work at all?" asked Dr. Eli Anton.

"I'm less worried about that, Eli," said Dr. Angela Wang. "I'm worried mostly about keeping students engaged in the learning. I've seen some online courses that are just the syllabus and calendar online, with assigned readings and questions to answer in an online discussion area. Or the course is just an online textbook—either way, boring. There has got to be a better way of doing online courses, or I'm not particularly interested in participating."

Dr. Chris Newman picked up where Dr. Wang left off. "Angela's right. Besides being concerned about keeping students engaged, I really like 16-week-long courses because they give students time to reflect. If a course is condensed to 8 weeks *and* is online, how will students have time to reflect on what they are doing in class and on what they are learning?"

After Malcolm addressed the faculty's questions about online facilitation, Dr. Tsagas called for a 10-minute break before discussing Malcolm's proposed certificate structure. As the faculty filed out of the conference room, Malcolm reviewed his notes about the new structure. He knew from the quality of the faculty's questions about the online module that he would need to be sharp during the rest of the work session.

# Preliminary Analysis Questions

1. Why did Malcolm structure the certificates the way he did?
2. How do you think the faculty will react to Malcolm's proposed certificate structure?
3. Why did Malcolm design the module the way he did? How well do you think he did with his instructional strategy selection, given:
   - The goals of the PTTP initiative?
   - The nature of the content?
   - The accelerated delivery format?
   - The web-based delivery medium?
4. How do you think the CS faculty reacted to Malcolm's web-based module?
5. How would you conduct a formative evaluation on Malcolm's web-based module?

# Implications for ID Practice

1. Discuss the differences in design when incorporating authentic learning activities, time for reflection, and collaborative activities into online instruction versus face-to-face instruction.
2. Discuss the challenges and constraints involved when using the strategies outlined in question 1 in a course that will be delivered in an accelerated format.
3. Discuss the advantages and disadvantages of repurposing existing courses, as opposed to developing new courses for online delivery.

# APPENDIX 11—A

# Preparing Tomorrow's Technology Professionals Request for Proposals (RFP)

**Preparing Tomorrow's Technology Professionals**

**Request for Proposals**

In June of this year, the Association of Information Technology Professionals (AITP) released a study—*Building Our Information Technology Infrastructure*. This study stated that although the number of information technology (IT) professionals in the United States has stayed the same over the last two years (at approximately 10 million), industry is attempting to fill about one million new positions. To address the shortage of IT professionals in our state, the Information Technology Consortium (ITC) is working to ensure the availability of qualified IT professionals by providing financial support for educational institutions that will work with us to increase the number of IT graduates that enter the workplace.

**Program Description**

During this initial round of funding ($2 million is available), the ITC will consider awarding funds to educational institutions that propose projects that address one of the following needs:

- Programs that increase the number of students graduating from existing two- and four-year undergraduate programs
- Online certificate or degree programs
- Certification programs for professionals who need to update their technology knowledge and skills

To be competitive, the project must provide clear evidence that the new curriculum responds to changes in industry standards. New curriculum must prepare students for the IT industry, and learning activities must be relevant to the IT workplace.

**Proposal Contents**

All proposals must include:

- Cover sheet—title and type of project, contact information, date submitted
- Project summary (one page)
- Description of the program, curriculum, objectives, outcomes, audience, and delivery format

- Timeline showing when students involved in the proposed program will be ready to enter the workplace
- Data supporting the proposed curriculum's ability to address the needs of the information technology industry in the state
- Letters of support from the educational institution, the faculty, and industry partners
- Budget and project timeline
- Example of curriculum (e.g., if proposing an online program, provide an example of an online module or course).

# APPENDIX 11–B

# Module for Programming with PHP and JavaScript Course

Home  |  Syllabus  |  Collaboration  |  Projects

## Programming with PHP and JavaScript

### WEEK 2

### Overview

Much of the power of the Web lies in its ability for end-users to be able to provide data to a web application. This week you will start working with variables and forms in PHP. Forms allow users to enter data. Variables allow you to manipulate that data in your PHP scripts.

### Study Guide

**Variables**

The PHP book describes variables as containers for data. Variables are foundational to web programming (or any programming for that matter). When we think of data we normally think of lists of numbers coming from a database. Although this does correctly characterize data in the traditional sense, it is a very narrow definition. In the context of HTML, every word you type into a form, every checkbox you check (or don't check), every drop-down menu that you select an item from is data that can be stored in a variable. In fact, deciding to click one anchor (aka link) as opposed to another can be valuable data to a PHP application.

In PHP, variables can be identified by the dollar sign in front of them. Create this script and run it on the web server. Name it **vars.php**:

```
<html>
<head><title>Vars</title></head>
<body>
<?php
// Assign values to variables
$pi=3.14;
$pie="Apple";
$py="Pythagoras loves to eat $pie";
$two="The countdown finished...\"two\", \"one\", \"liftoff!\"";

// Print out the variables
print("1. PI is $pi<br>");
print("2. $pie is a fruit<br>");
print("3. $py<br>");
print("4. {$py}s<br>");
print("5. $two<br>");
print("6. \$two<br>");
?>
</body>
</html>
```

## HTML Forms and PHP

There are two things to keep in mind when using HTML forms with PHP:

1. The form tag must have an action attribute whose value is a PHP script that will process the form data:
   `<form action="process_form.php">`
   ("process_form.php" would be replaced with the name of your own PHP script)
2. Each field on the form should have a name. This name becomes a variable in the script that processes the form data:
   `<input type="text" name="age">`
   The name *age* can be accessed as the variable `$age` in the script that processes the data.

## PHP `print()` made easier

HTML forms (and HTML in general) has a lot of quotes. Since quotes in print statements must be preceded by a backslash, it can make for a pretty miserable time. Take this print statement:

```
<?php
print("<table border=\"1\"
cellpadding=\"10\"
bgcolor=\"#ffffff\">");
?>
```

To print out this simple table tag, there are a total of six quotes that have to be preceded by a backslash (As an aside, one nice thing about print statements is that they can span multiple lines as shown above. This can make your PHP much more readable). Here is a variant on the print statement that eliminates the quoting problem:

```
<?php
print <<<WOODCHUCK
<table border="1"
cellpadding="10"
bgcolor="#ffffff">
WOODCHUCK;
?>
```

In short, after the word **print** type in three less-than symbols and a word. I chose a goofy word to emphasize that you can use any word you like. On the following lines you put in all of the text, variables, quotes, etc. that you want to print out. To end the print statement you repeat the word and end it with a semicolon. If you have a lot of HTML to print out and you want to avoid placing a backslash before each quote, this is a good alternative.

There are some guidelines to follow if you use this type of print statement:

1. The first **print** line and the last line with the word should appear on their own lines.
2. The last line with the word must not be indented.
3. No spaces should follow either the first or last line.
4. Although it is not required by the language, convention says that the word that you choose should be entirely in uppercase.

## Readings / Surfings

## Deliverables

1. Add to the PHP script you created in Week 1. Tell the user what kind of browser they are using (hint, see the last page of Chapter 2).
2. Create a quiz form. The quiz should have at least one of each of the following:
   - Multiple choice question (using radio buttons)
   - Short answer question (using an input field of type *text*).
   - An essay question (using a *textarea*).
   Even though this quiz can be built entirely as HTML, name the file **quiz.php**. We will be adding PHP code to it later in the course.
3. Add a link to **index.html** that goes to your quiz.
4. When users press the submit button on the quiz, it should go to a php script that prints the answers that the user selected on the form.
5. A simple red "bar" can be done this way in HTML:

```
<table bgcolor="red" width="100"><tr><td> </td></tr></table>
```

   A. Create a script **bar.php** that simply prints a red bar exactly as shown above.
   B. Create a file **barform.html** that has a form that takes two values: A number for the width of the bar, and a name for the color of the bar. The action of the form should call **bar.php**. Change **bar.php** so that it uses the form fields (variables) for the color and width.
6. Add a link to **index.html** that goes to **barform.html**.

### Hacker's Challenge (aka, Optional Question)

1. Combine the contents of **barform.html** and **bar.php** into **bar.php**. That is, **bar.php** should contain the form followed by the code that prints the bar. Try entering several values for colors and widths to confirm that you can do it repetedly.

### Super Hacker's Challenge (aka, Boy, this is really optional)

1. Add another type of question to your quiz: a multiple choice question with more than one correct answer (e.g. Which of the following numbers are prime numbers: 1, 2, 3, 4, 5, 6, 7, 8). You will need to use an input field of type "select" with the *multiple* attribute. Creating the quiestion is not the hard part. The hard part is printing the user's answers.

## Collaboration/Discussion

1. Now that you've completed two weeks' worth of PHP, how confident are you feeling? Does PHP feel like an "in-town" horse and buggy or does it feel like a barely controlled stagecoach flung along by galloping clydesdales?
2. What would you like to do with forms in *your* work that isn't obvious based on what you've done this week?
3. **Macro View:** Talk a little about your problem-solving process. How are you getting your questions answered? What resources do you use? Have you tried using any Web resources?
4. **Micro View:** What about debugging? What is your routine when you seem to have most (or all) of the code in place and you are trying to get rid of a "parse" error?

# Helen Ginn

## Evaluating a New Driver Training Program for Teenagers

*by Molly M. Lane*

## The Client

Auto Safety is a privately held for-profit company that trains teenage drivers in accident avoidance skills. Recently, Angel Investors, a venture capital firm, approached Auto Safety with an offer to invest a significant amount of capital into the company based on a majority ownership. Angel Investors intends to expand the program to 160 additional locations.

To prepare for this business expansion, every aspect of the Auto Safety organization is being evaluated, including the training program itself. Angel Investors has hired Galloway Consulting, an instructional design consulting firm, to make recommendations regarding the feasibility of transitioning the classroom portion of the program to an online experience, and to review the current program evaluation for any changes considered appropriate.

Simon Deland is the chief investment officer of Angel Investors. Simon has a master's degree in business administration (MBA) and is a certified financial analyst (CFA). Simon is tasked with maintaining the integrity of the existing program, while structuring an expansion model that maintains or enhances the profitability of Auto Safety.

Helen Ginn is the owner of Galloway Consulting. Helen has a graduate degree in instructional design and more than 20 years of instructional design consulting experience. Although Helen has worked on projects involving all aspects of instructional design, she has particular expertise in evaluation. Helen has consulted for Fortune 100 companies, the military, and small business owners.

## Client Meeting

Helen received a memo from Simon a few days before their scheduled meeting (see Figure 12–1). Simon, wearing a crisply pressed white shirt with the sleeves rolled up, greets Helen in the lobby outside his office. As he extends his hand, he welcomes Helen, "I have been looking forward to this meeting. This project is very important to our company."

FIGURE 12–1 Simon's Memo.

<table>
<tr><td colspan="2" align="center">**MEMO**</td></tr>
<tr><td colspan="2">**ANGEL INVESTORS**</td></tr>
<tr><td>TO:</td><td>Helen Ginn, Galloway Consulting</td></tr>
<tr><td>CC:</td><td>John Oliver and Marcos Costa, Auto Safety</td></tr>
<tr><td>FROM:</td><td>Simon Deland, Angel Investors</td></tr>
<tr><td>DATE:</td><td>August 22</td></tr>
</table>

I recently crunched the numbers on several existing locations for the Auto Safety training program. I factored in instructional costs, travel, lodging, and other standard expenses associated with delivering the program. I think it points out a possible financial advantage to transitioning the classroom session to online.

I need your expertise on two issues: First, I would like you to give me your expert advice on the considerations associated with transitioning the classroom portion of the program to an online setting. Second, I would like your analysis of the current program evaluation along with any modifications you consider necessary to improve the evaluation of the program.

"I am ready to begin," says Helen as she follows Simon to his office. After they get seated, Helen opens the conversation with a question, "What was it about Auto Safety that got your firm's attention?"

Simon's response was quick and concise: "Auto Safety's approach to training is unique in the sense that it requires parental involvement throughout the training program. This is an established company with a good profit margin operating in a niche market with a consistent consumer base. We should be able to sustain a sizable profit throughout the expansion."

"I see," replies Helen. "In your memo you mentioned a possible advantage to transitioning the classroom portion of the program to an online format. I would like to talk about this in detail to better understand your motivation for moving the classroom session online. However, it would be great if you could start by giving me your perspective of Auto Safety's existing programs."

Simon leans back in his chair and begins to explain. "Auto Safety teaches teenagers how to react in an emergency situation. Most of the teenagers who go through the program have had some formal driving instruction or at least have spent several hours driving under their parent's supervision. The program introduces these new drivers to some techniques designed to improve their on-the-road driving skills, avoidance maneuvers, and their ability to recover from emergency situations.

"We inform parents how to perform as guides, and they sit in the passenger seat while the student practices each of the techniques taught. At the end of the program, each parent/student pair receives a workbook to use to track student progress at perfecting each of the techniques taught during the driving sessions. The course is divided into two parts, a 90-minute classroom session that usually takes place on a Thursday or Friday evening and a four-hour driving session that occurs on either Saturday or Sunday."

Helen looks up from her notes and asks, "How many students can participate in one of the programs?"

Simon responds, "Auto Safety uses the term *clinic* to indicate one full weekend of instruction. There are 40 students who participate in the clinic over any given weekend accompanied by their parents. All 40 of the parent/student pairs attend the same classroom event, and then each parent/student pair registers for one of the four sessions available during the weekend."

Simon perks up when he begins to describe the hands-on driving portion of the clinic. "The driving session is where the rubber literally meets the road," he states. "The first group of parent/student teams arrives before 8:00 A.M. in whatever car the student will be driving on a daily basis. Over the next four hours, the students receive a practical lesson on steering, braking, and staying alert for driving obstacles.

"At 8:00 A.M., there is a line of 10 cars. Students are behind the wheel and parents are in the passenger seat. The parents' role is to observe the instructor guiding the students in practicing the various techniques. Auto Safety believes that it is important to have the parents observe the instructor so that, one, they know what techniques their teenager is practicing, and, two, they can continue practicing these techniques with their teenager after the clinic has concluded."

Helen asks a follow-up question: "How many locations does Auto Safety serve?"

Simon responds, "Last year, Auto Safety had 200 locations and completed 1,300 clinics. Our goal is to expand to 160 new locations and add 860 clinics. I have spent a great deal of time examining the scalability of this program, and the majority of overhead increases are linked to three line items on the budget: instructor fees, lodging, and per diem expenses for the instructors, which together account for nearly 98% of the anticipated expense line item increases."

After a short pause, Simon leans forward and states, "The classroom session poses many logistical problems. When the program was first developed, there was an instructor delivering a presentation and there was substantial face-to-face interaction with students and parents. In its current format, the instructor relies on the use of a video presentation and has only intermittent interactions with the participants. Another major concern involves hiring new instructors for the expansion. The pool of individuals who are both available and competent enough to deliver appropriate instruction for the driving portion of the training program shrinks considerably for an additional Thursday or Friday evening classroom session."

Helen is puzzled. "Why do these classroom sessions affect the pool of instructors?"

Simon responds, "Most of Auto Safety's instructors have full-time jobs. Some of the instructors are law enforcement agents and can schedule a Friday off with reasonable notice. However, the vast majority of the instructors are teachers in the school system. It is very difficult to get a Friday off during the school year. Unfortunately, many of the host schools participate in sporting events on Friday evenings. Football and basketball are the most common. In addition, when you take into consideration not only the players but also the band members, cheerleaders, and other students involved in these events, most schools prefer Auto Safety to present the classroom portion on a Thursday. In many cases this requires instructors to travel on a Thursday to the location, present the classroom portion on Thursday night, and stay overnight, making them unavailable to work their full-time jobs on Friday. This additional lodging, per diem expense, and $150 daily rate of pay for Friday directly affect our profit margin."

Simon flips through a stack of papers and references a piece of paper. "I've been looking at the current and the projected expansion numbers. I figure we can save around 10% or more if we eliminate the classroom session and convert it to online delivery. But I don't know the costs of developing, delivering, and maintaining the online session to replace the classroom session. Plus, I imagine there are costs associated with monitoring students' completion of the online sessions. However, the figures look promising enough for me to want to investigate this further, which is where you come in. As I indicated in my memo, I'm hiring you for your expertise regarding the considerations I need to take into account in transitioning the classroom session into an online format. And on a separate but related note, you will recall I also want you to review Auto Safety's current evaluation program."

Helen considers this information and then asks, "Are there any other factors influencing your decision to consider transition to an online classroom?"

Simon nods and replies, "I also have to take into consideration the students who may not be signing up for the program because they cannot make the Thursday or Friday night sessions. Auto Safety has had many parents inquire about the program and then not sign up because their schedules do not allow them to come to the classroom portion of the training. More and more, Auto Safety is getting requests to send the video to the students. The major concerns for not transitioning the classroom session to an online format are finding ways to deal with the questions that arise in the classroom. And of course the cost issue, which brings us back to one of the reasons you are here today. What will something like this cost?"

Helen sets down her pen and looks across the table at Simon. "There are a variety of ways to engage the online learner. Of course I will need to get a complete understanding of the existing materials and clarify the learning objectives for the material. After conducting a thorough analysis of the program, I will be able to fine-tune the numbers and offer some different options if you choose to convert the classroom session to an online format. The next step for me is to meet with the Auto Safety team and gain their perspectives. I also need to observe one of the sessions. We should plan to set up a meeting time for the first part of next month. Why don't you look at your calendar and get back to me with a date and time?"

Simon smiles and responds, "I will get back to you by the end of the week. I look forward to our next meeting and to hearing what you come up with."

## Meeting with Auto Safety Team

Helen arrives at the meeting 10 minutes early and greets John Oliver and Marcos Costa, who are already seated at the table and ready to begin the interview. John Oliver is 70 years old and is the sole owner of Auto Safety. John developed the program and training materials based on a bestselling book he wrote on how to train new drivers. For the first several years of Auto Safety's existence, John was the only instructor and traveled nationally to deliver the training program. John had been a professional race-car driver before starting Auto Safety.

Marcos Costa has been the operations manager of Auto Safety for the past 10 years. Marcos runs the day-to-day operations with little oversight from John. Marcos is currently in charge of training new instructors, and he teaches the training program 40 weeks a year.

Helen begins the meeting by asking, "John, why don't we start with you telling me a little bit about your organization?"

John explains, "Auto Safety has been in existence for 25 years and has a strong reputation as one of the nation's leading providers of accident avoidance training for teenage drivers. About seven years ago, Auto Safety expanded programs to 21 states and began to hire contract instructors to facilitate the sessions. But we started to notice a lot of inconsistencies in the classroom delivery. Some instructors were very good at this, and some were not. To address the inconsistent delivery of the classroom training, Auto Safety hired a firm to create a professional video of this portion of the clinic. Instructors now use this video and a facilitator's guide to lead the classroom training."

"I would love to see your facilitator's guide for the classroom," Helen remarks.

John springs to his feet, hurries across the room, and removes a folder from the shelf. He hands the folder to Helen, who skims through it briefly and makes a few notations in her notebook before asking John to continue.

John states, "Currently, Auto Safety has 11 full-time employees and uses 50 contract employees to facilitate the classroom sessions and the hands-on driving sessions. Most of the instructors are teachers, commercial driver's education instructors, or law enforcement agents. Auto Safety trains instructors using a shadowing approach."

Helen says, "John, I'd like you to walk me through the program so I can gain a clear picture of your process and understand what you teach the students and parents about driving."

John hands Helen a document that describes the goals and content of the training program (see Figure 12–2). John explains, "The program involves two different training sessions: a classroom session and a hands-on driving session. During the classroom session, the instructor welcomes the students and their parents and provides them with an overview of the hands-on session. Then the instructor uses a video to explain how driving is a psychomotor skill that can be learned and refined through repetition. The video also describes what happens when things go wrong on the road."

John continues, "The video includes testimonials from parents who lost children in car accidents and teenage drivers who were convicted of manslaughter due to car accidents. Also included in the video are digital animations that illustrate some of the most common hazards that new drivers face. The instructor emphasizes to the teenagers how the decisions they make behind the wheel are serious, and how these decisions can have a lasting impact on their lives."

Helen looks up from taking notes and inquires, "I'm curious—how do the students and parents react to the classroom instruction and the use of the video?"

Marcos responds quickly, "I see a lot of the students zoning out during parts of the video presentation. This may be because the video was shot more than seven years ago. Basically we've been using the same material since then."

**FIGURE 12–2**   New Driver Training Program—Goals and Course Content.

| Auto Safety | New Driver Training Program |
| --- | --- |
| **PROGRAM GOAL** | After completing the New Driver Training Program, teenage drivers will be able to recognize, react, and recover from hazards to avoid accidents. |
| **COURSE CONTENT** | |
| *Classroom Training Session* | The following topics are introduced during the classroom training session, prior to hands-on training.<br><br>1. What is a new driver?<br>2. Driving as a psychomotor skill.<br>3. Teenage driver testimonials.<br>4. Parent testimonials.<br>5. Common hazards facing new drivers.<br>6. Possible distractions surrounding new drivers.<br>7. Driving accident testimonials.<br>8. How to deal with feedback from environment while driving.<br>9. Psychological factors involved with driving.<br>10. Speeding testimonial. |
| *Hands-on Driving Session* | The hands-on driving session includes a series of driving exercises that involve students steering, braking, recognizing, reacting, and recovering from emergency situations. |

Helen wonders about the students and asks, "Can you tell me a little more about the students and their level of engagement? Why do you think they're bored?"

It's John who chuckles and then goes on to explain, "Well, the actual materials are well designed and professional. The content in the video and workbook are not the problem. I just think these kids are on their cell phones or playing video games so much that they're bored whenever they have to sit and listen to someone for 15 minutes or more."

Helen responds, "That gives me a good sense of who your audience is. So what's working well about this program? How do you know it's effective?"

John replies emphatically, "We know our program is effective. I know that the feedback from our follow-up survey isn't always glowing, but I'm convinced our program is effective based on the fact that the number one objective of our program is for students to avoid car crashes. I feel confident that we accomplish this on a daily basis with our existing program. A recent study conducted by the Department of Highway Safety and Motor Vehicles compared a random sample of 600 male and female students ages 16 to 21 who had completed our accident avoidance program to a similar-sized random sample of a demographic of teenagers who had only completed traditional driver's education. Over a three-year period, the graduates of our program demonstrated a 77% reduction in crash rates over the other group. This initial pilot study provided such resounding results that the

Department of Transportation is funding a much larger statewide study this year. It is difficult to argue with hard data."

John's comment intrigues Helen. "The data are impressive and I'm interested in reading the study that you reference. But first, I'd like to go back to the classroom session again. Were there any problems when you reduced the role of the instructor to more of a facilitator for this video presentation?"

John responds, "From what I can tell, parents seem to like the classroom session. They've stated this both verbally and in writing in the program evaluations."

Helen sees this as an ideal time to gauge John's opinion on transitioning the classroom to an online experience. "John, have you given any thought to eliminating the instructor and video in favor of an online format?"

John says, "I disagree with changing the classroom session to an online course. If we eliminate the live instruction, we run the risk of damaging our reputation. I know Simon wants to head in that direction, but I just don't see how it's feasible."

Helen says, "Okay, John. You explained to me that it was difficult to find quality instructors who could deliver an effective 90-minute interactive presentation. This led you to create the video that essentially allows any instructor to hit play and then use a facilitator's guide to engage students in specific discussions. Why do you feel that having students or parents watch the same or very similar materials on their own computers would be any less effective or feasible than your current approach?"

John responds, "Well, one of my biggest concerns would be not knowing if they actually watched all of the training or if they turned it on and walked away to make themselves a sandwich."

Helen follows up. "John, I understand your concern. It's obviously essential that the students and parents be exposed to the classroom portion of your program. I think that before you completely rule out the online delivery, you should allow me to show you some recent examples of interactive, web-based instruction that incorporate a variety of approaches to maximize participation."

John explains, "Helen, I really appreciate your willingness to share this information. However, I've been doing this for a long time and I know that it would be really detrimental to remove the instructor from the course."

"In what ways do you see this being detrimental, John?"

John shakes his head. "I really think it may reduce the effectiveness of the program. You need a live person to explain some of the technical material in the video. I really don't think our program needs a technology component beyond the video. We know that most students enrolling in our training program are regularly connected to technology, but I don't think moving our program online will make it more effective."

Marcos shakes his head and says, "John, I hear what you are saying but I don't agree. I just think it's time for us to examine whether it makes sense to update our course materials and to embrace technology."

John reaches out for a water glass and the pitcher of water in the middle of the table and begins a loud lengthy pour. He raises his glass and takes a generous swallow before he responds: "We have been collecting evaluation data for years, and it seems to show that our students are bored and inattentive during the classroom training session. But the parents have continuously given the classroom training session high marks, and they're the ones paying for the course. However, they are our secondary audience, because the most important thing is to help these teens obtain the tools they need to be safe drivers on the road. I worry that students' poor attitudes toward the classroom instruction might have a negative impact on the benefits they get from our program."

Marcos jumps into the conversation. "I have another major concern. Currently, I train all of the new instructors and recertify our existing instructors by working with them for a weekend. This process currently takes about 40 weeks a year. My main concerns about the expansion of the business relate to how challenging, time consuming, and costly it will be to train additional instructors to facilitate the classroom training sessions. Angel Investors is looking to expand into many new territories, and this would create a lot of unknowns for us."

Helen probes for additional information. "What do you mean by this?"

Marcos says, "Well, our students are not excited about the classroom session any more. The classroom sessions increase scheduling and logistical issues, and they are costly to the company. I think putting the classroom part of our training program online can save us money and make us more efficient as a company in the long run."

"Thanks for that information, Marcos," Helen replies. "I'd like you to talk a little about these logistical issues and the costs."

"Sure," Marcos replies. "I'm in charge of scheduling instructors for each training clinic, and it can be a bit of a logistical nightmare. I have a network of contract instructors, but most of them have full-time jobs Monday through Friday. Whenever we have a course on Thursday, I have to scramble to find someone who is within driving distance of the training. Then there are additional costs because they normally drive home after the training is over and then back again for the hands-on training."

Helen asks, "How would the expansion affect the number of new instructors you would have to train?"

Marcos explains, "We would be hiring at least 100 new instructors when we expand."

Helen asks Marcos, "How would your role change when that happens?"

Marcos answers, "I would need to train multiple instructors in a setting. Likely we would have a training clinic made up entirely of instructors. We would rotate through stations as the instructor, assistant, parent, and student driver."

As the meeting draws to a close, Helen makes plans to observe a training session and to look at the evaluation data.

# Evaluation Data Review

Helen reviews the student driver evaluation data collected by Auto Safety. As Helen reviews the evaluation instrument (see Table 12–1), she considers the nature of the information being elicited.

**TABLE 12–1**    *Student Driver Evaluation Results (N = 1,995).*

**Student Driver Evaluation\***

| Learning | Strongly Disagree | | Disagree | | Neutral | | Agree | | Strongly Agree | |
|---|---|---|---|---|---|---|---|---|---|---|
| | *n* | % | *n* | % | *n* | % | *n* | % | *n* | % |
| I feel comfortable utilizing the shuffle turn method. | 0 | 0.0 | 0 | 0.0 | 338 | 16.9 | 155 | 7.8 | 1,502 | 75.3 |
| I feel in control with my hands at the 9 and 3 positions. | 55 | 2.8 | 77 | 3.9 | 566 | 28.4 | 897 | 45.0 | 400 | 20.1 |
| I can use my anti-locking brakes in an emergency. | 0 | 0.0 | 125 | 6.3 | 456 | 22.9 | 556 | 27.9 | 858 | 43.0 |
| I can simultaneously brake and steer. | 0 | 0.0 | 33 | 1.7 | 32 | 1.6 | 754 | 37.8 | 1,176 | 59.0 |
| I have better awareness of my vehicle's dynamics. | 125 | 6.3 | 344 | 17.2 | 395 | 19.8 | 580 | 29.1 | 551 | 27.6 |

| Satisfaction | Strongly Disagree | | Disagree | | Neutral | | Agree | | Strongly Agree | |
|---|---|---|---|---|---|---|---|---|---|---|
| | *n* | % | *n* | % | *n* | % | *n* | % | *n* | % |
| I would recommend the classroom course to a friend. | 1,097 | 55.0 | 213 | 10.7 | 37 | 1.9 | 195 | 9.8 | 453 | 22.7 |
| I would recommend the driving session to a friend. | 0 | 0.0 | 72 | 3.6 | 32 | 1.6 | 635 | 31.8 | 1,256 | 63.0 |

*\*NOTE:* Not all percentage totals equal 100 because of rounding decisions.

# Training Program Observation

Duke Ashland is an instructor with Auto Safety. Duke is a high school history teacher and football coach and has been a certified driver's education instructor for 14 years. He has worked as a contract instructor for Auto Safety for the past five years.

Helen attends the classroom training session and observes Duke delivering the instruction. Helen finds that some of the language in the video is outdated such as phrases like "tough noogies," "distractions when opening and closing a map," and "listening to your favorite CD while driving." Helen also realizes that there is only a brief mention of cell phones and no discussion concerning texting and driving or digital music players.

The parents seem to react emotionally to the testimonials, while the students appear to connect only with the most emotional and tragic ones. The video lasts a total of 50 minutes, but Duke stops it occasionally to engage the students and parents in discussions. The discussions are not particularly smooth; there are a number of awkward silences, and it is mostly the parents who respond to the questions.

At the end of the session, Helen asks Duke, "Was this a typical group of participants?"

Laughing, he counters, "Yeah. We have been to this school already this year, some of the students seem to have talked with their peers about the video, and they came with the mindset that this is boring."

The next day, Helen arrives at the school parking lot promptly at 7:30 A.M. to observe the hands-on training session. She listens as Duke begins the session with a brief tent talk. During this talk Duke outlines the agenda for the day and fields questions.

Duke explains, "Today we're going to go through a series of driving exercises that get progressively more challenging. At no time will you drive more than 15 miles per hour. Now let's head to the cars, buckle up, and learn our techniques. The goal is to make each of you more comfortable handling the automobile that you will be driving on a daily basis.

"The first exercise is pretty simple. You will have to put your front two tires in between two orange cones. There's one small problem. You will not be able to see your tires while you are doing the exercise. When you approach the cones, the cone on the right will first disappear out of your sight and then the cone on your left will disappear. The good news is that our brains are always working, capturing data from our environment, and today we're going to learn how to use that data to safely guide our automobiles. Your brain will allow you to do this task in the same way that every one of you can get up in the middle of the night and walk from the bed to the door of your room in the pitch black without knocking things over or walking into a lamp."

The next several hours seemed to fly by as Helen watched the students perform a variety of driving exercises. She witnessed the young drivers gripping their steering wheels as their engines roared. It was amusing to see the contrast between the faces of the parents and teens during the hard braking exercise.

Youthful grins of excited accomplishment contrasted with parents' furrowed brows as the tires marked the blacktop. But when the driving was finally over, most students and parents emerged from their cars with smiles on their faces and pride in their eyes. Duke called each student by name, and they walked forward to accept their certificates for completing the course, marking the end of the program.

As she strolled to her car, Helen reflected on what she had observed during the practice driving lesson. She believed that she had a solid understanding of both the classroom and driving portions of the program and felt confident that she would be able to present Simon with a comprehensive report on the feasibility of altering the classroom portion of the program. She also had several ideas for the course evaluation. As she drove away, she began to mentally develop a list of recommendations that she would need to give Simon.

# Preliminary Analysis Questions

1. How might Helen address John's reservations about developing an online version of the course?
2. Describe the factors that Helen must consider to evaluate the feasibility of converting the classroom video to an online experience.

3. Of what use is the current evaluation instrument in evaluating the effectiveness of Auto Safety's new driver training program? What are its limitations?
4. Outline an evaluation plan that Helen can present to Simon.

# Implications for ID Practice

1. What are some of the key considerations an instructional design professional should examine when converting a video to an interactive online experience when safety is a high concern?
2. What can an instructional design professional do to maintain the fidelity of a training program when it is scaled up for a significantly larger audience?
3. What approaches can an evaluator use when asked to develop an evaluation plan for stakeholders who disagree about current and future needs?

# Lindsey Jenkins

## Piloting Case-based Learning in a Blended Learning Nursing Curriculum

*by Xun Ge and Kun Huang*

As Lindsey Jenkins steps into her office, she realizes that she has worked for exactly one month at the Brooks Health Science Center School of Nursing (SON) as a faculty-rank instructional designer. Lindsey holds a PhD in instructional design and technology. Before joining SON, Lindsey had three years of experience as an instructional designer at another nursing institution and six years of college teaching experience.

Sitting in front of her computer, she looks at her Outlook calendar, and her eyes focus on a meeting event scheduled for 2:00 P.M. This is the first time she is going to host a meeting with two nursing professors about a course redesign pilot project. She feels a little bit anxious while anticipating and preparing for the meeting. With a deep breath, she tries to focus on the things she is going to discuss at the meeting. She is deep in thought as she reflects on what she has seen, heard, and experienced during her first month's work, which flickers across her mind like scenes from a movie.

## Initial Meeting with Dr. Barbara Miller, Associate Dean

On her second day of work, Lindsey met with Dr. Barbara Miller, the Associate Dean of Academic Affairs at SON. As Lindsey came into Barbara's office, Barbara stood up and greeted her. "Welcome aboard, Dr. Jenkins! We are very glad that you have joined SON." After some chatting, their conversation moved to the projects Lindsey would be working on.

"Let me give you some background information about SON," said Barbara. "There are five schools in the Brooks Health Science Center, and SON is the largest. We have

The authors thank Maribeth Moran, professor at the University of Oklahoma College of Nursing, for allowing us to adapt her nursing case for use in this text.

more than 1,000 students, including undergraduate, master's, and doctoral students. Each degree level has different tracks."

"The school is indeed quite large," Lindsey said. "I read from the school website that there are more than 100 faculty members."

"Yes," Barbara said, "and 70% of them are full-time faculty. They are the ones you will be mostly working with."

Barbara continued, "The main purpose in creating your position was the need for curriculum redesign at the school. Our school's percentile rank had traditionally been around 70 in NCLEX, you know, the National Council Licensure Examination."

"Yes," Lindsey said, "I'm familiar with NCLEX from my previous work."

"Okay, great," said Barbara, who then explained to Lindsey that in the past three years SON's performance in NCLEX had dropped, especially in the content area of physiological adaptation. "Physiological adaptation has been a weak area in our school's NCLEX performance. In the past three years, student performance has steadily decreased" (see Figure 13–1).

"The drop in performance on NCLEX was not surprising," said Barbara, "because our schoolwide student survey in the past couple of years also indicated a decrease in students' satisfaction with the quality of their education."

Barbara continued, "One of the main curriculum challenges facing us right now is to shift our focus to critical thinking. In recent years NCLEX has been placing an increasing emphasis on assessing students' critical thinking skills. Also, we have accreditations going

**FIGURE 13–1**   SON's NCLEX Test Report in the Past Three Years: Comparisons with Graduates from SON's Jurisdiction and with the National Population of Graduates from Similar Programs (Numbers Represent Percentile Ranks).

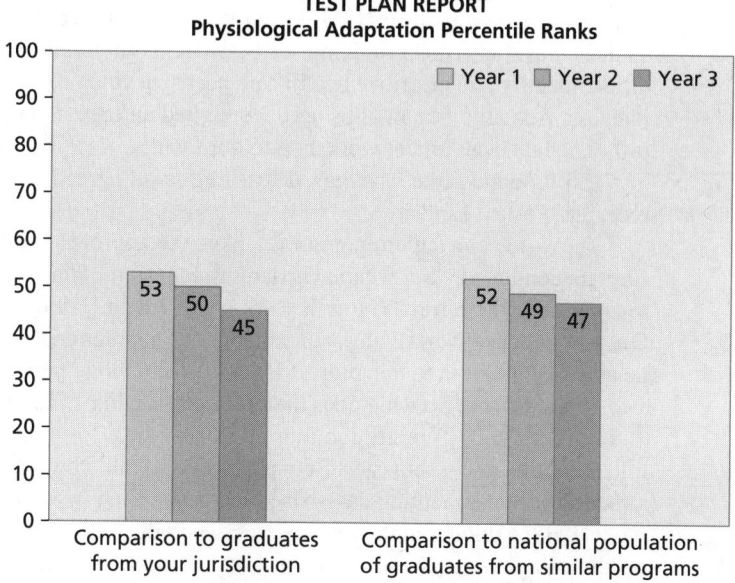

on at both SON and the overall Health Science Center—each calling for a curriculum to promote students' critical thinking skills. The dean and I, as well as the school curriculum committee, saw the synergy between improving students' performance in the board exam and meeting accreditation standards. We thought that by redesigning the school's core curriculum focusing on enhancing students' critical thinking, we could address both needs at the same time. That's why we hired you. Your training and expertise in education will help us with the curriculum redesign."

"Are you considering piloting the redesign in some courses before it is implemented more widely?" asked Lindsey.

Barbara replied, "Yes, in fact it was decided that two courses would be the pilot courses—Acute and Chronic Nursing I and II—since physiological adaptation topics are heavily addressed in the two courses. Based on what we learn from the pilot, we can roll the redesign to the rest of the undergraduate core courses."

"That sounds like a good plan," said Lindsey. "Let me just try to make sure that I understand the tasks clearly. The school is currently looking to redesign two courses with a focus on promoting students' critical thinking. After piloting these courses, we will turn our attention to the ultimate goal is to redesign the entire undergraduate core curriculum."

"That is correct," said Barbara. "About the two courses: Acute and Chronic I is offered to juniors in the spring semester. Professor Gina Smith teaches the course. Acute and Chronic II is a senior course taught in fall by Professor David Cunningham. Gina has already tried using case studies in Acute and Chronic I to promote critical thinking among students. As I recall, you're familiar with case-based learning?"

"Yes, I am," said Lindsey. "I worked with nursing faculty to write cases in my previous job, and we also developed the cases into several interactive learning objects for online modules."

"Great," Barbara said. "I have attended a couple of case-based learning workshops at some nursing conferences. I think real-world nursing case scenarios can really help our students develop critical thinking skills. Students should be able to assess a patient's condition, identify and prioritize health care needs, develop a care plan, and evaluate its effectiveness. Actually, two months ago, we invited an expert in case-based learning to give a professional development workshop to our faculty."

"So it sounds like case-based learning is an agreed-upon approach for curriculum redesign?" asked Lindsey.

"Yes—the curriculum committee likes the approach, and the dean supports it, too." Barbara continued, "So, for the curriculum redesign initiative, you will be the lead person to coordinate the effort. You will work closely with David and Gina on the pilot project. Oh, you will also work with Jason Huang, our instructional technology specialist. He will be able to contribute to this project from the technology perspective."

"I understand. So what does the timeline look like?" Lindsey asked.

Barbara said, "We are looking at a one-year pilot period. Right now we are in the middle of the spring semester. Between now and fall, you can do some planning and build a model for implementing case-based learning. Then in the following spring and fall, the model will be piloted in the two courses. The pilot will be evaluated, and we hope that the results will provide us with some insights for implementation at a larger scale."

"One thing is very important," Barbara added. "We are looking for evidence of improvement, which is what the accreditation bodies will look at, too. So the evaluation of the pilot courses is going to need some good planning. We hope that the findings will help us argue for adopting case-based learning across the entire core curriculum."

Lindsey came out of the meeting feeling both anxious and excited to start. She was excited that she had an opportunity to apply her knowledge and experience in this pilot project. At the same time, Lindsey felt a little concerned that she had been handed a project that was already under way with predetermined approaches.

## Gathering More Information

To learn more about the colleagues she would be collaborating closely with in the first year, Lindsey spent some time on the school website looking up information about the two professors. The school's online faculty profiles showed that Gina was an assistant professor in SON. She held a master of science degree in Nursing and a PhD degree in higher education. She joined SON two years ago and had been teaching Acute and Chronic Nursing I ever since. Before joining SON, she had more than 10 years of teaching experience in another school of nursing. David held a master of science degree in nursing and had been with SON for nearly 20 years. He had received several teaching awards throughout his tenure at SON.

In the following weeks Lindsey got to meet the two professors, both of whom agreed to give Lindsey access to their course websites. With Jason's help, Lindsey was able to access the two courses through the school's course management system. She found that both were large classes, with more than 120 students in each course. The course syllabi indicated that both courses were taught primarily online, but with some face-to-face sessions. The students met with the instructor only during the first class and the five exam sessions. During the rest of the semester, the students studied the course materials independently online.

The resources for both courses were well organized in content modules. Learning materials were mostly readings, PowerPoint, and narrated PowerPoint recorded by the two professors. Most modules had a quiz at the end. There was a forum in both courses, which was set for students to ask any course-related questions. Lindsey saw several students' posts asking questions about assignment requirements and deadlines.

Curious about how Gina had used cases in her course, Lindsey looked for cases and found one in a narrated PowerPoint. In several slides, Gina introduced a case scenario followed by a set of questions (see Figure 13–2). By looking at the case, Lindsey felt that the questions at the end of the case were not directly linked to the patient scenario, and virtually no critical thinking would be required to answer the questions. This reminded Lindsey of her past experiences with the nursing faculty in her previous job—the first drafts of cases that the faculty handed to her were very similar to what Lindsey saw here.

In the subsequent slides, Gina thoroughly explained the symptoms, treatment, and prevention of the disease presented in the case, and how nurses should take care of patients

**FIGURE 13–2** Gina's PowerPoint Slides on a Case Study.

### Case Study

- T.C. is a 7-year-old girl who was brought to the clinic where you work by her grandmother. Her grandmother states that she has "lost her appetite," complains of headache and abdominal pain, and that her urine "looks just like coke." On exam, you find that she is lethargic and appears unwell. Her vital signs are 136/98 98-116-28, with occasional crackles on chest auscultation. Her urinalysis reveals the following data:

### Case Study

- Color: reddish-brown
- Appearance: cloudy
- Odor: normal
- Sp. gravity: 1.035
- Protein: 3+
- Glucose: negative
- RBCs: too many to count
- WBCs: 10 per low power field
- Casts: 15

### Questions

1. What other information do you need to obtain from the child and her grandmother?
2. T.C. is diagnosed with poststreptococcal glomerulonephritis. Discuss the pathophysiology of this disease process, including the etiology.
3. What are the symptoms of glomerulonephritis?

### Questions-continued

4. What are some common treatment and drugs for treating poststreptococcal glomerulonephritis?
5. Discuss three ways nurses can help prevent the occurrence of glomerulonephritis.
6. Compare and contrast dietary restrictions of glomerulonephritis with those of nephrotic syndrome.
7. How would you care for a patient with poststreptococcal glomerulonephritis?

with the disease. She also stressed some common misconceptions in caring for the disease. In fact, Lindsey found that the most engaging part of Gina's narrated PowerPoint was her sharing of past experiences and the lessons she had learned as a nurse in caring for patients with the disease. Lindsey thought that it would be great to integrate Gina's experiences into the case scenario. For example, the patient could be presented with multiple symptoms, and students could be asked to assess the urgency of the symptoms, decide what to take care of first, and explain the rationale for their decisions.

Thinking that she would gain more insights into the current teaching of the courses, Lindsey requested from Barbara a copy of students' evaluations of the two courses from the past year (see Figure 13–3 for quantitative ratings). Lindsey also reviewed the students' comments in the course evaluations (see Figure 13–4 for representative examples of students' comments).

After doing research and preparation, Lindsey decided that she was ready to set up a meeting to start the course redesign pilot project. In her e-mail to David, Gina, and

**FIGURE 13–3**    Quantitative Summary of Course Evaluations of Acute and Chronic Nursing I and II.

| COURSE EVALUATION REPORT: N3134 ACUTE & CHRONIC NURSING I | | |
|---|---|---|
| TEACHER PERFORMANCE | AVERAGE | SCHOOL AVERAGE |
| 1. Knowledge of the subject matter | 3.8 | 3.6 |
| 2. Communication and explanation of subject matter | 3.4 | 3.2 |
| 3. Organization of course materials | 3.8 | 3.2 |
| 4. Encouragement of class interaction | 2.0 | 2.5 |
| 5. Stimulation of student interest in the subject matter | 2.1 | 2.9 |
| 6. Responsiveness to student inquiries | 2.5 | 3.0 |
| 7. Respect for students | 3.4 | 3.4 |
| 8. Overall rating of the instructor | 3.3 | 3.2 |
| COURSE EVALUATION REPORT: N4134 ACUTE & CHRONIC NURSING II | | |
| TEACHER PERFORMANCE | AVERAGE | SCHOOL AVERAGE |
| 1. Knowledge of the subject matter | 4.0 | 3.6 |
| 2. Communication and explanation of subject matter | 3.3 | 3.2 |
| 3. Organization of course materials | 3.3 | 3.2 |
| 4. Encouragement of class interaction | 2.3 | 2.5 |
| 5. Stimulation of student interest in the subject matter | 2.5 | 2.9 |
| 6. Responsiveness to student inquiries | 2.5 | 3.0 |
| 7. Respect for students | 3.6 | 3.4 |
| 8. Overall rating of the instructor | 3.2 | 3.2 |

Key:   1 = Poor   2 = Fair   3 = Good   4 = Excellent

**FIGURE 13–4**   Examples of Students' Comments in Course Evaluations of the Two Acute and Chronic Nursing Courses.

| COURSE EVALUATION REPORT |
| --- |
| **Question** |
| • What were the specific weak points of the course? |
| **Comment** |
| • I feel I needed more support. While the recorded lectures were easy to understand, and the tests were okay, I got stuck when practicing NCLEX questions. I feel this course did not prepare me for the board exam. |
| • We received a lot of information about acute and chronic diseases, but were not taught adequately how to apply the information in real situations. |
| • There was not much opportunity to actually talk to the professor to get my questions answered. Usually when I had a question when watching PowerPoint, I had to figure it out myself. |
| • The quizzes and exams often focused on trivia. It would be very helpful if they made more of an effort to reflect the boards. |
| • The online offering of this course made it hard for us students to interact with each other. But I learn best by studying together with other students. I had to form a study group with two other students to meet regularly. We learned quite a lot from each other. |

Jason, Lindsey indicated that the goal of the meeting was for all of them to review the current status of the two pilot courses and identify the needs or areas to be addressed by the project.

## The Meeting

Lindsey arrives at the meeting room early. She has brought along two articles on best practices in writing and teaching with cases in medical education to share with the two professors at the meeting. On entering the meeting room, she checks the display system to make sure that it works properly.

Gina arrives shortly. After greeting each other and some brief chatting, Lindsey asks, "So how is it going with the Acute and Chronic I class?"

"It's going quite well. We just had the first exam. Students seem to have done well," Gina replies.

Lindsey remarks, "That is great! I visited your course website and saw some cases in your narrated PowerPoint. I really liked the sharing of your own experience as a nurse. And I learned a few things myself!"

"I'm glad that you liked it, Lindsey. Yes, I have tried to incorporate at least one case in each narrated PowerPoint. I want the students to be able to relate the information for each disease type to some actual patient instead of simply memorizing all the symptoms, pathophysiology, drugs, and treatment. I think this process is very important to promote students' critical thinking."

"In addition to the cases in your PowerPoint, do you assign students other cases to work on?" asks Lindsey.

"Not at this time. That will be my next step. It takes time to write cases, and it's a steep learning curve for me, which is why I am very glad that you have joined us, Lindsey. With your help, I feel more confident in revising my course."

At this time David steps into the room. Lindsey welcomes him, saying that she and Gina were just talking about the cases in Acute and Chronic I. Then the three of them sit down at a table.

"Why don't we get started while waiting for Jason?" Lindsey says. "First, thank you for coming to this meeting. I thought that this would be a good time for us to sit down together and discuss the course redesign pilot project. I know that you attended the case-based learning workshop a while ago, and Gina has been using cases in her courses. As you know, I am new here. My charge is to work with you on the two pilot courses, and to evaluate the outcomes of these courses in improving students' critical thinking skills. I have been learning ever since I came on board. Your course website helped me a lot, but I still have some gaps to fill. Perhaps you can help orient me so that I can better understand the two courses. From there, we may be able to brainstorm some ideas for the project."

"That sounds like a good plan," says Gina. "I'd be happy to share with you any information about my Acute and Chronic course. I certainly appreciate your help in finding a good way to do case studies."

"Talking about the workshop," says David, looking at Lindsey, "I personally don't think it was very helpful. The speaker was not from the nursing or even medical field. The examples she gave at the workshop were not related to nursing. For business and social sciences, it is easier to do case studies because there are no right or wrong answers. But for nursing, it is different." He turns to Gina, "Gina, the cases might work better for your Acute and Chronic I. But for Acute and Chronic II, I have a lot to cover in each module. I still don't know which part I can give up for case studies, not to mention the time needed to develop those cases."

Lindsey responds, "I understand. Nursing is indeed different from some other disciplines. However, the model and the underlying principles for learning apply, regardless of discipline. Actually, I brought these two articles on using cases in medical education." She hands the two copies to David and Gina and continues, "The articles offer some great guidelines for writing cases and teaching with cases. One of the articles actually did a study, and the findings were very positive about case teaching. David, I can work with you and Gina on developing cases, but of course I will need to rely on your content expertise."

Turning to Gina, Lindsey asks, "Gina, for the cases you present in your narrated presentation, do students have a chance to work on them before getting your answers from the PowerPoint?"

"Yes," replies Gina, "I want to make sure that they have really worked on the cases before watching my PowerPoint. So for each module, I first assign readings and cases to students for them to work on. They have to submit their case responses by a deadline before I post my narrated PowerPoint with answers. I wish I could read all of their responses, but it is simply impossible for me to read or grade 126 of them. So I give them participation points for submitting the case responses, because otherwise many students would not really work on the cases."

Recalling students' comments that they had little opportunity to interact with each other, Lindsey asks, "Have you thought about letting students discuss cases or do some other online collaborative work?"

"Yes, I did try it before. I asked my students to post their answers to a discussion forum and encouraged them to discuss the case on the forum. But they didn't really discuss with each other. Instead, they only posted their answers, and that was it. So I dropped the discussion forum later on."

"Have you thought about using some tools like a wiki to have groups of students work on cases together?" asks Lindsey.

"A wiki?" David chuckles. "I keep on hearing about wikis. What exactly are they? Are they something like Wikipedia? I really don't like Wikipedia because it has very little credibility with me."

"Well, actually, both have similar characteristics, but think of it this way—both can be collaboratively edited by those with permissions. A course or content wiki allows a group of people to write and edit one single document at the same time."

Gina looks doubtful. "I actually tried wikis in the nursing research class the first semester I was here. I put students in groups to work on a research paper, and encouraged them to use a free wiki website to work on the paper together. But it didn't work very well. Most of the students ended up posting comments instead of really collaboratively writing and editing the paper. They tended to post comments like 'Great job!' or 'Here are some useful resources'—things of that nature. There is another issue related to the use of a wiki. Jason told me that since the wiki website was a free service, it did not have a service contract with SON. If the system goes down or if there's any technical issue, there will be no support available. So I kind of gave up using wikis at that point."

Jason, who has arrived a little late at the meeting, has been listening and keeping silent. As his name is mentioned, he smiles and nods at Gina, and then adds, "I have tried my best to provide technical support to the SON faculty, but sometimes I feel overwhelmed by the volume of questions and requests coming from the faculty. When I joined SON six years ago, the volume of support was not this high. But now, 70% of SON courses are either blended or completely online. It is hard to stay on top of everything. With the course management system alone I've got enough questions and requests for help. If each faculty member uses different free software, it is just not possible for me to answer all the questions, including questions as trivial as 'How do I create a page in wiki?' I wish I could provide all the IT support, but honestly it is just impossible."

Gina says, "I don't blame you, Jason. We've got to find a way to deal with these issues if we are going to encourage faculty to use technology in their teaching. . . . Now back to wikis. Even though I stopped using a wiki after my first attempt, I would love to give it a second try now that Lindsey might be able to help me use it as a tool for students to work on cases. Lindsey, if you can help me find out how to use wikis to facilitate students' discussion of cases, and especially how to assess students' contributions to a wiki, that would be wonderful."

"Absolutely," says Lindsey. "I'd be glad to. Let's arrange a time for another meeting."

"That will work. Thanks, Lindsey," says Gina.

David says, "Although I haven't tried case studies, I do value discussions and group work. I think it's a great way for our students to learn. In fact, before my courses went online, I used to do a lot of discussions in my class, and the students really liked it. However, based on my experience, I just think it'd be hard for students to discuss online, especially for a case. Each student may have a different answer, and the discussion may go nowhere when they aren't in one room talking face to face. I'm not a big fan of technology, and our current course management system has already given me enough headaches when we switched to it from another system two years ago. But, if you can find ways to give students the same opportunities to discuss and collaborate using the course management system or some other system, I'm willing to give it a try."

The meeting ends at 3 P.M., because David has to leave for another meeting. Based on the information she's been given, Lindsey now has a bigger picture of the pilot project. When she returns to her office, she plans to summarize her observations, list all the areas of needs to be addressed, and formulate an action plan for the next steps to be sent to the two professors and Jason.

# Preliminary Analysis Questions

1. What issues have you observed in this case? How would those issues affect the implementation of case-based learning?
2. Develop a plan of action for Lindsey to assist faculty members in developing, implementing, and evaluating case instruction that makes optimal use of the case-based approach.
3. How would you explain to David about the educational benefits of the case-based learning approach and the use of collaborative tools, given his current understanding?
4. What can Lindsey recommend to the dean regarding the technology constraints and challenges that Jason highlighted in the meeting?
5. What considerations should Lindsey be weighing for the pilot evaluation in Gina and David's courses?

# Implications for ID Practice

1. How would you encourage students to use technology effectively for collaboration to solve the problems presented by cases? Provide some specific examples.
2. What are the challenges of promoting new approaches to teaching and learning in an existing curriculum, especially in an online learning environment?
3. What are the core elements that need to be included in the evaluation of the case-based learning approach to assess students' critical thinking?

# Mark Jones and Sue Gulick

## Meeting Challenges in the Design and Delivery of a University-wide First-year Experience Course

*by M. J. Bishop and Allison Gulati*

## August, Year 1

"So . . . I have asked you both here today to see if you would be willing to continue serving as co-chairs of the task force working on the first-year experience initiative," Provost Callahan said as he started the meeting on that August afternoon. Mark and Sue glanced at each other, each knowing what the other was thinking. They had been at this task since March, and it was already very clear this was going to be an uphill battle.

Over the 6 years since Mark Jones had started as an assistant professor of instructional design at Bay Crest University (BCU), he had been asked to serve on various task forces and accreditation self-study committees associated with enhancing the first-year experience for incoming undergraduate students. Although this had seemed odd to many of Mark's graduate-only College of Education colleagues, given that he did not teach undergraduate students, it was actually very much in line with his research related to using distance instructional technologies to facilitate students' social and academic transition to college. That research had been well received by the field, and recently he had been promoted to associate professor.

Similarly, Sue Gulick's master's degree in student affairs with a concentration in leadership development made her uniquely suited to be involved in campus initiatives focused on core competency development for students, particularly over the first year. During her master's program she had taken a number of instructional design courses and had even consulted on several design projects. Since coming to BCU 10 years earlier, she had risen through the ranks in student affairs and had recently become an associate dean of students. Co-leading this first-year experience initiative was a perfect fit with her new responsibilities in the Student Affairs Office.

But Mark and Sue had already been through the wringer on this task and, although neither was likely to shy away from a challenge, it was beginning to look like the idea of a shared first-year experience that combined both curricular topics (such as writing, critical thinking, and information literacy) and co-curricular topics (such as planning and preparation, multicultural awareness, leadership, civic responsibility, and wellness/ healthy choices) within the context of an interdisciplinary or theme-oriented academic course was something that would never happen at BCU. They had accomplished far less leading this initiative in the previous spring semester than they had hoped.

# Background

Bay Crest University is a highly selective, research-intensive university with approximately 4,300 undergraduates and 2,000 graduate students. The university admits about 1,200 first-year students each fall semester. Although entering students do not commit to a major until their sophomore year, first-year students are required, on enrollment, to choose among Bay Crest's three undergraduate colleges (engineering, business, and arts and sciences). Once there, students are often routed into highly structured, college-specific programs and requirements instead of having the flexibility to "test the waters" by taking courses in a variety of content areas. This disciplinary tracking also means that, other than the English 101 and 102 composition courses all undergraduates are required to take, there are few opportunities for shared intellectual experiences among students from different colleges.

Recognizing the need to provide some additional support for enrolled students' academic and social transitions to college, the university created the First-year Experience Office (FYEO) within its Student Affairs Office 10 years ago. Since being established, FYEO programs for all newly admitted students had included:

- a May mailing of information about orientation and first-year programming (see Figure 14–1)

**FIGURE 14–1**    May Orientation Mailing.

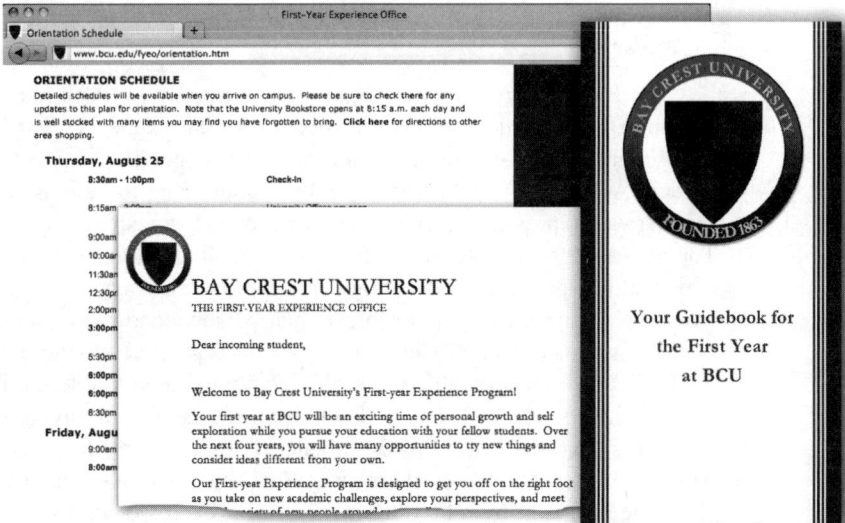

**FIGURE 14–2** Pre-orientation Summer Programs.

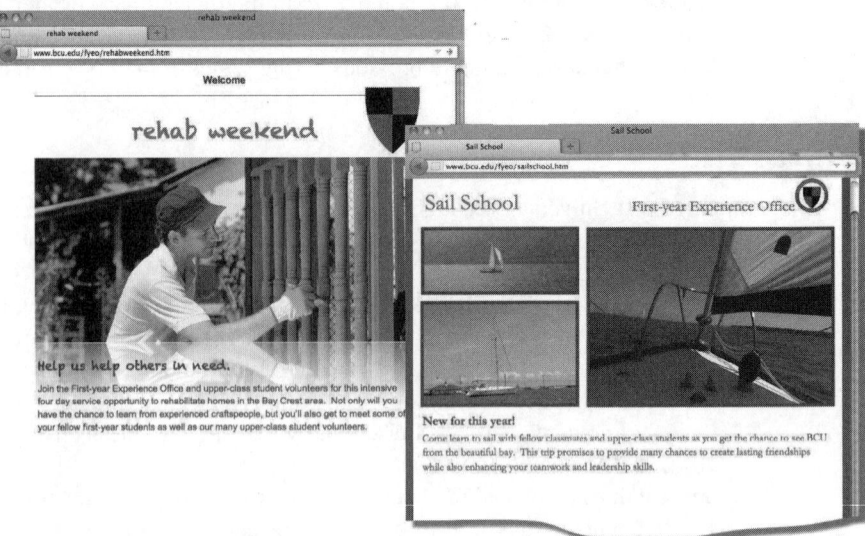

- summer online synchronous conversations covering topics from the course request process to move-in day logistics
- theme-based pre-orientation weekend programs such as "Rehab Weekend" and "Sail School" (see Figure 14–2)
- a summer shared reading that explored multiple perspectives, ideas, backgrounds, or cultures, and provided opportunities to engage in follow-up on-campus discussions; and
- a required four-day orientation program the weekend before fall semester classes began.

The FYEO's programming also included a required seminar of weekly two-hour meetings that extended orientation four weeks into students' first semester on campus. This seminar was co-facilitated by a peer leader (upper-class student) and a member of the Student Affairs staff, with a few faculty volunteering to help as well. The focus of the seminar was to provide information to help students transition into their new environment. Topics ranged from exploring students' individual identity development to exploring ways they could be proactive in creating curricular and co-curricular experiences at BCU that would help them identify and achieve their personal and professional goals after graduation. The summer reading selection was also incorporated into these discussions. Although the FYEO had not been able to get the faculty to agree to count this seminar for course credit, students who failed to attend these meetings risked having their spring semester course registrations delayed by 30 minutes. Because course registration at BCU was done online, a 30-minute delay could mean getting shut out of a section offered at a more desirable time or taught by a favorite instructor or, even worse, missing out altogether on a course required for one's major.

The FYEO also offered several programs over the year to support new students during their transition to college on topics such as study habits, library skills, working in teams, leadership, multicultural awareness, and making healthy choices. However, these topics were rarely contextualized within academic conversations as part of courses. Although the faculty largely understood the need for discussing concerns that arise when young incoming students discover the freedom of college life, most believed these issues were best handled by Student Affairs staff—out of sight (and mind) of most faculty members. Besides, like many highly selective institutions, BCU's remarkably low 3% to 5% attrition rate between the first and second year of college (as compared to national averages that hovered around 30% to 35%) meant the school did not appear to have any major *retention* issues around students' transition to college.

That said, as in many similar institutions across the country, there was mounting evidence to suggest that current incoming BCU students needed additional support to handle the academic and social pressures they were experiencing. Midyear surveys collected annually by Student Affairs indicated that current first-year students were increasingly feeling "overwhelmed," and the student emotional health ratings were at their lowest levels in the 15 years the surveys had been administered. Many respondents reported lacking the basic life skills and mechanisms for coping with the substantial increase in responsibility and stress. At the same time, faculty complained about the growing numbers of students skipping their classes and performing poorly on course assignments. As "Thirsty Thursday" devolved into "Wet Wednesday" and then "Tuesday Boozeday," the number of hospitalizations due to alcohol poisoning among BCU students, particularly those in their first year, was rising steadily each year. According to the results of the annual Student Affairs survey, current students were reportedly spending more hours each week partying than studying, and many suspected that students' academic performance would also begin suffering as a direct result. Although first-year student retention had not been an issue for BCU in the past, the recent surveys conducted by Students Affairs indicated that it might well become an issue in the near future.

Further, faculty had begun expressing concerns that BCU first-year students were increasingly preoccupied with decisions about selecting a major and focusing as quickly as possible on a career specialty, rather than valuing the opportunities the college presented for becoming a well-rounded educated person. In fact, as part of a recent coastal states accreditation self-study, BCU had opted to explore the extent to which their transition-to-college programs were helping incoming students adjust academically to college, as well as meeting their personal and social needs. The self-study report had recommended that, in addition to other components of a revised first-year experience (such as improved advising, special-interest housing, and academic initiatives in the residence halls), the institution should create a "shared academic experience for first-year students that might also help them develop closer mentoring relationships with faculty."

That said, there was also evidence to suggest that the faculty still had not agreed that this shared intellectual experience should take the form of a course to be added to the curriculum. In fact, the same coastal states accreditation self study committee had recommended against that approach, citing the practical barrier of adding another required course to students' already overloaded academic programs as well as BCU's long-standing preference for maintaining a program of more flexible, discipline-specific requirements, instead of adopting a core curriculum. Further, it was unclear exactly what the learning outcomes for a first-year course should be. It had been difficult even to come to agreement among the colleges on what term should be used to describe desired first-year outcomes (e.g., improved communication skills, technology and information skills, multicultural/ global awareness, and teamwork/collaboration skills). Should they be called learning objectives? Competencies? Understandings? Knowledge? Common skills? Orientations?

# Year 1

At its January meeting, BCU's Board of Trustees urged Provost Callahan to make the implementation of an enhanced first-year experience among the top priorities for the new calendar year. To this end, Provost Callahan asked Mark and Sue to co-chair a "First-year Working Group" made up of six key Student Affairs staff and 20 volunteer faculty as well as the associate deans from each of the three undergraduate colleges: Peggy Smith from Arts and Sciences, Hank Levitt from Business, and Eli Strauss from Engineering. By May, the group was to select a "reasonable" number of curricular and co-curricular outcomes for the first year, identify key elements of an enhanced first-year experience, and describe how objectives for first-year students might be assessed.

The group commenced with a March 4th retreat that began with the provost giving the working group their charge and encouraging them to think creatively about how BCU might develop a truly extraordinary first-year experience for its students. "Although I don't want you to lose sight of the recommendations of previous committees, I don't want you to repeat their efforts, either. I'd really like you to think outside the box on this."

When the provost had left the room, Hank began, "Well, anything we do is going to need to be aligned with our business college professional accreditation standards."

"That's true for us as well," Eli interrupted. "We just received the new engineering standards, and we've been struggling with how we're going to fit them into the curricula for most of our programs. They're already jammed full of courses!"

Sue noted, "I've reviewed the standards for business and the new engineering standards. The good news is that both sets of standards appear to be well aligned with what the previous reports recommended as suggested outcomes for an enhanced first-year experience—at least the academic skills."

"If that's the case, then why do we need to do more in the first year?" Hank asked. "We just finished revising the first-year business course to make sure it addresses those standards and, although there may still be a few things to tweak here and there, it seems to be going pretty well. Plus, all the discussions are contextualized within a business frame-work, which better prepares our first-year students for their business majors."

"Does your course help students learn to make healthy choices? Or develop multicultural awareness?" Sue asked.

"But aren't those topics better left to professionals who have been trained to address them with our students?" Peggy interjected.

"All I know is we're going to need a lot of help if we're going to be expected to address those sorts of 'soft skills' in our courses," said Eli with air quotes to punctuate his concern. "Plus, I'm not convinced the classroom is the best place to have those sorts of discussions." Turning to Peggy, Eli asked, "Does your college have an accreditation body you have to answer to?"

"There's no single accreditation organization for the entire college," Peggy responded. "I believe chemistry or biology might have something, but I'm sure theatre and philosophy don't. I'll have to check." After a short pause she added, "I have to say that getting faculty from all the diverse disciplines in our college to agree on a set of common learning outcomes won't be an easy task. They just don't speak the same language about these sorts of things."

After almost 90 minutes of discussion of desired first-year learning outcomes, Mark capitalized on a lull in the conversation to jump in. "Maybe we should try to avoid getting bogged down in a discussion of what the common outcomes might be—even though I think we are actually closer to agreement on those than may be apparent on the surface." Looking at his watch he suggested, "In the time we have remaining, how about if we set aside the outcomes discussion and try to start envisioning what an enhanced first-year experience at BCU might look like?"

"That's another thing that concerns me about all this," Peggy worried aloud. "We have approximately 1,200 new students arriving each fall. Whether this is a course or a seminar or some sort of experiential activity, in order to keep the students engaged and the discussion meaningful, it sounds like we're talking about small groups of students . . . say, around 20? And now we're talking about those groups being co-facilitated by both a faculty and staff member? That's 60 faculty and 60 staff!"

"Yeah, I don't see how we can make that work without significant additional hiring," Hank agreed. "Not to mention the facilities resources that will be required as well."

Mark asked, "Well . . . since we're brainstorming, is it possible there are existing courses or projects that could be dropped in order to accommodate the personnel demand?"

"Whew . . . I don't know about that," Eli responded. "What I can tell you is that I believe faculty course loads and enrollments within those courses have been slowly increasing over the past several years while we've been in this faculty hiring freeze. At the same time, folks aren't rewarded for teaching overloads: as you know, the coin of the realm is research and publications. To be honest, I'm not sure how we could persuade faculty to get involved in an enhanced first-year experience. I don't even know if there are any incentives we could offer to make it attractive."

Over the next several weeks the group met five more times to hear reports from each of the colleges and key offices within Student Affairs about what currently existed in terms of "formal" first-year experiences on campus and the various "wish lists" each had for what a revised experience might include. Although it appeared to Mark and Sue that some common themes were emerging around ideas such as communication skills, technology and information literacy skills, teamwork and collaboration, intercultural awareness, career exploration, academic integrity, problem solving, time management, and critical thinking, when the time came to draft the report for the provost, it was clear there was less consensus around these ideas than the pair had thought. "I know I missed the last meeting," Hank wrote in his e-mailed reply to the first draft of the report, "but I don't believe we specifically agreed on these outcomes as being the ones we want to tackle."

And, although the group did come to consensus fairly quickly on the need for tighter coordination of curricular/co-curricular activities between the colleges and Student Affairs, there was little agreement around what the key elements of a comprehensive first-year experience might be. "I really like the idea of forming learning communities within the residences in which students spend part of their first year working on an interdisciplinary project, but who on the faculty is going to be willing to do that?" one of the faculty from Arts and Sciences asked in his response to the draft. A business faculty member on the committee was far more direct: "If you don't remove the discussion of pre-major cross-disciplinary advising of first-year students from the report, then please remove my name from the list of contributors." By May, Mark and Sue were left with little to report in terms of the group's decisions about desired first-year outcomes or key elements of an enhanced first-year experience, much less any direction on how the desired first-year outcomes might be assessed. The group's primary recommendation in their one-page report was to reconvene a similarly constituted group in the fall to explore these topics further.

## Returning to August, Year 1

Sensing Mark's and Sue's hesitation after asking them if they would be willing to continue serving as co-chairs of the first-year initiative, Provost Callahan quickly added, "I gather from your report that you accomplished less in the spring than you had hoped?"

"Yes," Mark replied. "We had lots of good discussions and heard many really terrific ideas, which we were prepared to present in our report. But, frankly, as soon as we put some of those desired outcomes and key elements down on paper, folks backed off. I'm not sure what happened there, exactly."

"Well, to me it feels like the faculty just can't see the forest for the trees," Provost Callahan observed. "It's easy to get bogged down in the logistics of something like this . . . some of which are much bigger problems than others. What if we tried to eliminate some of those barriers by reducing the scale a bit? Instead of trying to tackle all aspects of an enhanced first-year experience, how about if we just start with a credit-bearing course or project or activity or something that we pilot next fall with around 200 undergraduate students? Once faculty see how successful it is, they'll *want* to get on board. Then we'll be able to talk about eventually scaling it up to include all incoming students."

"Well, it certainly seems like piloting something like this with just one-sixth of the incoming students should be a fairly benign request to make of the colleges," Mark noted.

"Okay . . . but if we're going to ask incoming students to participate in this experiment," Sue argued, "then it has to count for *something*—their English requirement, or the Arts and Sciences freshman seminar, or an elective, or something else toward their program requirements. It can't be just something extra we're asking them to do."

"I agree," said Provost Callahan. "I'm sure we can find a way to make that happen for these students."

# Fall Semester, Year 1

After having said yes to continuing as co-chairs of the first-year initiative, Mark and Sue worked with the provost to craft a call for faculty participation that was sent out via e-mail early in the fall semester. The hope was to recruit two faculty participants from each of the three undergraduate colleges; however, only three faculty members responded in total. When the co-chairs proactively recruited volunteers, they heard repeatedly that, although the common first-year course was a "good idea," it was unlikely to offer anything more than the current individual college initiatives underway. In some cases the co-chairs were told by prospective recruits that they were being actively encouraged by their department chairs *not* to participate in the initiative. Other concerns revolved around the project's long-term sustainability. One business faculty member responded, "Although I get that running the pilot is likely possible, what evidence do you have that the provost and the administration are really committed to an effort of this size in the long run?" He added, "I don't want to waste my time working on the pilot if it isn't ever really going to be possible to scale it up to the entire entering class."

During the fall semester Mark and Sue also learned about two additional initiatives that had been started out of the university's strategic plan implementation. The deputy provost, Cathy Lebanon, started working in September with the undergraduate college and associate deans of Student Affairs in an effort to synthesize the myriad campus-wide documents addressing student learning outcomes. Her goal was to come to some consensus around a shared set of competencies the university hoped students would have acquired by the time they graduated. Additionally, in October, the university's Director of Student Writing, Gary Dolin, e-mailed Mark to say he had been charged by the Student Writing Committee and the provost to conduct a study of writing across the curriculum; he included a copy of his project plan in the e-mail. When Gary and Mark met to discuss the synergy between these two projects, Gary added that there had been some discussion within his committee about whether the old model of requiring two writing courses in the first year (English 101 and English 102) was still the most effective way to improve students' writing and communication skills. Gary told Mark that it was looking as if his group's report would likely recommend the second required writing course be refocused on applied writing in the disciplines and that it be offered later in students' academic programs, perhaps in their sophomore or junior years.

# Spring, Year 2

Despite Mark's and Sue's efforts during the fall semester to recruit volunteers, by the start of the spring semester of year 2, the design team was still made up of just two members of the engineering faculty (well-respected full professors with many years at the institution), one member of the business faculty (a new non–tenure-track clinical professor with administrative duties as well), one member of the arts and sciences faculty (a part-time, non–tenure-track professor from the philosophy department whose primary responsibility was really administrative, in the faculty development area), the director of the First-year Experience Office, the director of Student Leadership Development, and the two co-chairs, Mark and Sue.

Shortly after the start of the spring semester, the co-chairs met with the provost to request permission to put off the pilot course until the fall semester of year 3. They explained that the additional time would be necessary in order to build a program that the larger campus community would see as having added value for incoming students.

"It's fairly clear to us that we need to do a lot more work garnering buy-in from the faculty in all three undergraduate colleges before we can have a successful pilot," Mark began. "At the very least, it would be nice to have guarantees that whatever we design will actually *count* for something for the students involved in the pilot. As Sue mentioned in our last meeting, this cannot be just an add-on for the students who participate."

"The other big issue we're hearing from both faculty and staff," Sue added, "is that folks don't believe the institution is really committed to this in terms of resources. Before we can make any progress on the design of an enhanced first-year experience, it's going to be necessary to come up with a clear plan for how this whole thing can be sustainable over time."

Sue continued, "We have also learned there is a lot of good work going on right now within other working groups and initiatives on campus, such as the shared set of competencies and the student writing initiatives, that we believe should come first and be near completion before we begin designing an enhanced first-year experience."

After some additional discussion, the provost agreed to the extension, but it was clear that there was not likely to be another. "I understand why this is going to take a bit more time, and I agree that it makes sense for some of these other components to be in place before your group moves forward with your planning. But we will be implementing *something* by next fall."

# Preliminary Analysis Questions

1. What are the obstacles that need to be overcome in order to gain widespread support for an enhanced first-year experience at Bay Crest University?
2. What strategies would you suggest for overcoming each of the obstacles you have identified in question 1?
3. Assuming the pilot is successful, how would you suggest scaling up the first-year initiative to involve all 1,200 incoming students at Bay Crest University each year?

# Implications for ID Practice

1. What are the organizational characteristics unique to higher education settings that can affect the success of a wide-scale curricular innovation?
2. In a higher education setting, what role should an instructional designer be expected to play with regard to "selling" the project and garnering "buy-in" from key stakeholders for instructional interventions, and what strategies might he/she employ?
3. How can instructional designers ensure quality is maintained when a wide-scale curriculum project is scaled up in a higher education setting?

# Pat Kelsoe and Jean Fallon

## Implementing Innovation within an Established Curriculum

*by Carol S. Kamin and Brent G. Wilson*

## Background

State Medical University trains physicians, nurses, and health professionals in a variety of specialties. The training of physicians is fairly traditional, with two years of basic science instruction followed by third- and fourth-year clinical experiences. The primary teaching strategy for clinical experiences has been apprenticeships in hospital settings. However, because of a changing health care environment, fewer than 5% of all pediatric interactions result in hospitalization, and hospital stays have been greatly shortened. Therefore, increasing numbers of medical students complete their required rotations in pediatrics offices around the state.

The pediatrics department is considered to be among the top 10 in the country, with a strong history of pediatric research. There are many older faculty members known to be excellent teachers and mentors. The chair of the department noted, "The faculty on this campus wrote the textbook on pediatrics." All medical students are required to take the pediatric clerkship in their third year. Thus, the pediatrics department gets between 15 and 18 new third-year students every six weeks, year-round.

Dr. Jean Fallon is eager to begin a new project that will use technology to change how the pediatric clerkship is taught. She has called a planning meeting to brainstorm ideas, so that she can apply for a pilot grant through a recently released request for proposals (RFP) from the office of the president.

## Meet the Characters

*Jean Fallon—clerkship director and primary subject matter expert (SME):* A physician in academic medicine, Dr. Jean Fallon recently switched her focus from laboratory research to educational research when she became the director of medical student education in pediatrics. After working for a year on a National Institutes of Health grant, she returned the award, at some risk to her tenure prospects, in order to assume these new responsibilities. The promotion and tenure guidelines recently changed to allow faculty to be promoted based on educational scholarship, and Jean wanted to take advantage of this opportunity. Colleagues have told her that she has given up a "sure thing" and has switched to an unproven track for promotion. Her mentors and section head have advised her to work on her interest in educational research after she is tenured. Nevertheless, she is enthusiastic and interested in initiating and evaluating innovative teaching methods. She is also ambitious and wants to make a difference in pediatric medical education nationally, as well as locally.

The pediatrics course in the third year of medical school is the only direct experience all medical students are sure to have caring for children. Physical examination courses and other generic skills are taught with an adult emphasis. As clerkship director, Jean is interested in adopting the recently created national pediatrics curriculum that stresses field experience, but she wants some standardization of this learning experience. She believes that, as practicing physicians, students will need the lifelong skills inherent in independent learning, problem-based learning, and electronic information retrieval. She is open to innovative instructional solutions.

When asked to name the one thing she wants medical students to know when they complete the clerkship, Jean's reply was, "To look at an infant or a child and know if his or her condition is urgent."

*Pat Kelsoe—medical educator:* A doctoral-level instructional designer, Dr. Pat Kelsoe is a brand-new assistant professor in pediatrics accustomed to collaborating on development teams. She has been an instructional designer for the past six years, with all of her experience in academic medicine. She helped two other medical schools transition to problem-based learning. She worked full-time while she completed her doctoral degree in instructional technology a year ago. "I dragged my family across the country to accept this position; there's no way I'm going to take this job lightly," emphasized Pat.

There was no job description for Pat's position when she interviewed, so she asked the chair what success would look like in five years. His response was, "I want the department to have a national reputation as a center for scholarly research in pediatric medical education." After she accepted the position, the chair confided, "The medical educator position is a new one for our department; some of the old guard were opposed to it."

To prepare for the planning meeting, Pat asked for past course materials and evaluations for the pediatric clerkship. She received 45 pages of qualitative comments from an open-ended student survey. After conducting a content analysis, she found that the strengths of the course appeared to be the teaching that was conducted primarily by pediatric residents. The primary weakness appeared to be the lack of course organization. The students who were dispersed to clinical sites seemed to enjoy the experience but felt somewhat isolated from their peers and unsure of the intended learning outcomes. They were not sure they were getting what they needed from the course or how it compared with what their peers at other sites were getting.

*Sam McConnell—senior colleague:* Dr. Sam McConnell, a senior faculty leader, was also asked to attend the planning meeting to discuss potential changes to the pediatric clerkship. Sam thought the new clerkship director had the potential to be a star, given the research she was doing, and was upset that she did not wait until after she was tenured to take this educational position. He has heard some of the grumbling from other faculty members about the medical educator position, and he, too, wonders why she was hired and what she will do to help the department's already excellent teachers.

Sam gets outstanding evaluations of his teaching, but he thinks one is either born a good teacher or not. He gives lectures on Wednesday afternoons and has students and residents in his clinics. As far as Sam is concerned, seeing patients is the only way to learn medicine. Most pediatrics faculty members prefer to teach residents who are going to be pediatricians. He's one of the few senior faculty members who teaches medical students, but he does it because he is committed to recruiting the best students possible for pediatrics. Sam is always disappointed when he gets a student who shows absolutely no interest in specializing in pediatrics.

Sam wonders why this group is meeting. The clerkship gets good reviews, and the department has highly qualified applicants for its residency program. "If it's not broken, don't fix it" is his view. There is constant pressure to produce revenue by getting large grants and seeing more patients. Sam believes that this is the only way to keep a medical school department afloat in a volatile health care environment. Pediatricians love to teach, but as far as Sam is concerned, teaching does not generate significant revenue for the department.

*Harry Lipsitz—department chair:* Though he has received a lot of heat from some senior faculty members for creating a medical educator position and appointing a junior faculty member as clerkship director, Harry is excited about the potential of these young professors. He sees that there are many research questions to be asked in pediatric education and is anxious for his department to be a leader in this area. He believes that he has two very talented and hard-working faculty members who share his vision for the clerkship. Harry is concerned, however, about their overriding interest in technology. He recalls a colleague who took a sabbatical to create an educational software program. This colleague worked hard on the project, but nothing ever came of it. Harry fears educational technology initiatives could take a lot of time and money without a productive result.

Harry thinks that his most important job is to get these two junior faculty members promoted under the new evaluation system. They will be two of the first faculty members to attempt to secure tenure under these new guidelines. Although he knows that educational innovations are a risky venture for untenured medical professors, he believes these two could conduct some interesting studies and obtain some useful research findings with the potential to inform innovative approaches to medical education.

# The Planning Meeting

Faculty members begin arriving in the department conference room. After several minutes of friendly banter, Jean begins the discussion:

Jean: Thank you all for making the meeting. I know it's a busy time of year, but I want to get this project off the ground. There are a lot of great things already in place with the clerkship, but there seems to be some room for trying out new ideas. The president's office just came out with a grant program, and I thought we are strongly positioned to compete for some of that money.

Sam: Always happy to take someone else's money!

Jean: That's right, and I think this project could be worth the investment. I've been thinking—our clerkship students often have great experiences out in the field, but they sometimes don't see any critical cases. It's a bit risky out there. Our students can get a great education, but we leave a lot to chance. So, I've been playing around with a possible solution. What if we developed a set of cases, such as digital case studies, covering some cases we think everyone should see—say, an urgent case of abuse? Then we'd be giving students something that's very close to real life, and we'd be able to guarantee they will actually encounter it during their clerkships.

Harry: You mean, show some video on the computer?

Jean: Show some video, either actors or real patients, depending on what we're thinking of. Give students a look at some symptoms and a situation, and let them ask questions, order tests, somehow leading to a diagnosis. Then we could give some feedback.

Harry: Wouldn't that be kind of expensive—putting all that up on the web?

Pat: Yes, a project like this could easily run up a budget. But I see the grant from the president's office as a way to get it started. It could lead to some new ways to think about the clerkship.

Sam: [shifting in his seat]: Hold on a second. Having directed the clerkship for 12 years before your arrival here, Jean, I have to say that it's one of the most respected in the country. Our students graduate well versed in pediatrics. We get a good number of them deciding to specialize in pediatrics after their rotations.

Jean: That's important; we want students to be attracted to our department. I'm just thinking—maybe some video cases could even increase the appeal through meaningful and active student engagement.

Harry: I'm still worried about the scope and cost of this kind of project.

Pat: Video production is getting cheaper and easier, but it's still a lot of work. I'm not sure about our in-house talent—we may have

|        |                                                                                                                                                                                                                                                                           |
|--------|-----------------------------------------------------------------------------------------------------------------------------------------------------------------------------------------------------------------------------------------------------------------------------|
|        | to contract out the work. And we'd need to develop some internal expertise.                                                                                                                                                                                                |
| Sam:   | That's just what I need, some fancy new technology to learn. I remember taking an HTML course once—never again!                                                                                                                                                            |
| Pat:   | I don't think faculty members should have to do all the authoring. We could get a couple of interns or part-time help to do most of the production. Your expertise, though, would be very helpful in determining how to approach a case, Sam.                               |
| Sam:   | I don't want to do *any* of the authoring. It will take far too much of my time, and time is money.                                                                                                                                                                        |
| Pat:   | Maybe I should clarify. We would have a team working on the case. The design and technical aspects would be handled by me and the interns. But we need experts to review the cases to ensure that they are realistic. This is what I mean when I say authoring.             |
| Sam:   | Oh, well, I could do that. Of course, you'd need some expert advice, since you're not a physician or pediatrician.                                                                                                                                                         |
| Harry: | Tell me more about your ideas for the video case.                                                                                                                                                                                                                          |
| Jean:  | Pat, why don't you share the ideas you were telling me about PBL, or problem-based learning?                                                                                                                                                                               |
| Pat:   | As you know, PBL is heavily used in medical schools, and digital cases are commonly presented on the web, though most of them are for individual students to work through on their own. Here is what Jean and I were talking about. We present a video case, with some footage and some background information—make it interactive, so that students can explore some information, order tests, and ask questions. That part is kind of standard, like an interactive case or a problem online. The part that I'm excited about is somehow connecting small groups of students and a faculty member online asynchronously, talking to each other about the case. Students won't be so isolated in their different field sites; they will be able to learn from each other. Research suggests that this type of active student engagement, fostered by case discussion is what makes this type of learning so robust. |
| Harry: | Wow, that sounds exciting. You're trying to get the best of both worlds—video on the computer, but then having people connect and talk about it from different locations.                                                                                                  |
| Jean:  | That's right. You get the benefit of field experience, but also some assurance that key learning experiences will be encountered and shared. That increases our confidence that they're all mastering similar content. Students would get the best of both worlds: the lectures on campus and the opportunity to stay connected throughout their distributed field experiences. |
| Harry: | Students do tend to feel isolated out there. Having some way to work together would be good.                                                                                                                                                                               |

# Preliminary Analysis Questions

1. In small groups, complete a role-play exercise and finish the meeting. Delineate specific design ideas that would address the concerns of all parties and satisfy the needs of the clerkship and the department.
2. Identify Sam's biases and preconceptions regarding this proposed new approach to pediatric education. Suggest strategies for addressing these biases and preconceptions from an instructional design perspective.
3. How should Jean deal with the chair's concerns as expressed in the meeting?

# Implications for ID Practice

1. What mistakes could innovators make if they were unaware of the political tensions arising from different cultures and habits within an organization? What steps can innovators take to ease these tensions?
2. Innovations typically happen within the normal constraints of an organization—limited time, money, and expertise. Add to that list desire or will. In the face of these serious constraints, what "magic" has to happen for innovations to succeed? Draw on your own experience in addressing this question.
3. Some innovations are resisted for fear of negative impacts on an institution's reputation, which may have been built on traditional practices or methods. How can a change advocate respond productively to those concerns? What steps can be taken to measure or assess ongoing perceptions of a program and its reputation—before and after an innovation is implemented?
4. Faculty are increasingly asked to do more production and development work within their teaching (with few additional resources). Although more work gets done, some faculty members complain that technology makes their jobs more demanding. Critique this perspective from multiple sides. Make some recommendations for the following stakeholders and consider ways to ease their transitions into new innovations:
   a. Administrative and technology professionals who select and implement new technologies to support teaching and learning
   b. Training professionals tasked with developing materials and resources for supporting new innovation
   c. Faculty or staff who are asked to adopt and implement the innovation
   d. Learners who are typically meant to benefit from the innovation (and who frequently subsidize the added costs through technology fees and membership subscriptions)

# Beth Owens

## Addressing Multiple Perspectives and Constraints in ID Practice

*by Michael L. Wray and Brent G. Wilson*

## Charge from the Dean

It's a rainy day as Beth Owens arrives to meet with Dean Carlton Jacobs. Stepping into the dean's suite, she laughs as she shakes the remaining water from her raincoat thinking to herself, "I always enjoy the rain, especially in the West. We don't get enough of it!" Beth has lived the past 10 years in Colorado, first as a stay-at-home mom, more recently completing a master's degree in instructional design at a nearby state university. Eight months ago, she accepted a faculty consulting position at State College, a four-year, open-enrollment college in the downtown metro area. State's academic programs are always changing, and faculty members appreciate the instructional design support that Beth provides. At any given time, Beth is consulting on 12 to 15 projects, with only an occasional need for in-depth analysis and evaluation. Technology leadership is a part of the job, but she sees her primary role as helping faculty members make the transition from traditional teaching methods to more student-centered teaching activities.

Dean Jacobs welcomes Beth into the office. "Thank you again for meeting with me. Your study of our programs is one of my highest priorities right now, and I know your findings will make a big difference to us." The School of Consumer Technology was recently divided into two schools because of the growth of the Information and Office Systems department. This left half of the remaining students in a wide array of service-oriented programs: cosmetology, fashion merchandising, hospitality management, and culinary arts. The dean is anxious to develop a growth plan for his remaining programs and to make improvements at all levels. His first goal is to review the culinary arts program, the smallest within the school.

"As you know," the dean continues, "Information and Office Systems was something of a cash cow for us, to some extent subsidizing our smaller programs. Now every program has to stand on its own two feet, both quality-wise and by the raw numbers. We're starting our analysis with culinary arts. The program is small but self-sustaining. We're having a few problems, which I'd like you to look at."

Beth is looking forward to jumping in on this project but just a little anxious about the prospects. In her eight months at State, she has heard occasional rumors about the program director of culinary arts. Chef Gerhard Reiner is known to be something of a taskmaster and disciplinarian. Beth turns to the dean. "I understand that Chef Reiner teaches both the introductory class and the upper-level culinary classes. His teaching and leadership must be important to the program."

The dean responds, "Yes, he's a major figure. Reiner gets very good teaching ratings, although you'll always find the occasional student who complains. He is well known within the school for being a challenging instructor. He maintains strict rules in his lab; any student can tell you that!"

"What kind of rules?" Beth is curious about this instructor. She doubts that this chef has even heard of such things as constructivist teaching methods.

The dean leans toward Beth. "I've had a couple of students in my office in tears, feeling overwhelmed by the demands of the program. They feel Chef Reiner is too strict. With enrollments more of an issue now, I don't want to lose any students unnecessarily. It's all about including all students and growing enrollments."

The dean leans back in his chair. "My problem is complicated. I want the program to produce quality graduates, but I also want to retain students and grow the program. I'd like you to figure out how we can be more inclusive, improve retention, and maintain a quality program at the same time!"

"Piece o' cake!" Beth jokingly replies. "Thanks for your time, Dean Jacobs. I think I would like to see the classroom and visit with Chef Reiner."

The dean smiles, "I'll give you much more than that. How about a personal tour and lunch in our student dining room?"

Beth agrees. "I think that would be wonderful. Please lead the way." Dean Jacobs shakes hands with Beth and escorts her from his office to the culinary labs.

## Tour and Lunch

Beth is eager to see the students in action. Dean Jacobs shows her the student culinary lab, where students are preparing the meal before service. She is impressed to see everyone in crisp uniforms, each busy and involved in food production. It is easy to see who is in charge. Chef Reiner, in his tall white hat, has an air of authority, his name clearly embroidered on his starched chef whites, with his culinary title and a patch from the school he attended prominent on his breast pocket. The students rush from their work areas, receiving instructions from the chef. She notices him sampling the students' work, tasting and checking temperatures.

Following the tour, the dean and Beth take a seat in a small dining room adjacent to the culinary lab. The room is filled with administrators and staff members who pay a small fee to attend the luncheon. The dean explains, "The restaurant serves meals three days per week, offering a sample of the students' accomplishments. It continues to be a popular event on the campus and attracts the general public." Beth smiles as she is served an inviting meal of roast chicken with a light cream sauce. "The plate is so elegant," Beth remarks. The garnish on the plate captures Beth's attention: roasted tomatoes pierced by rosemary stems. Beth sighs, "It smells wonderful." The dean nods in agreement as they both begin their meals.

During lunch, Beth begins to think about her approach toward advising the chef. From what she has heard, Reiner's approach to teaching can be old-fashioned and somewhat confrontational. She wants to introduce student-centered teaching principles but thinks it may be difficult to convince Chef Reiner of the related benefits.

Beth declines the dessert, although it does look delicious, a five-layer chocolate cake with a rich frosting and mint leaves—decadent, indeed. Beth keeps imagining how nice the dessert would have been as she watches other guests enjoy it. But she settles for coffee and enjoys the pleasant service by the students.

After the meal, Beth concludes her tour with the dean and is anxious to get a chance to meet Chef Reiner and talk to him about the course. She thanks Dean Jacobs for his time and shakes his hand firmly.

## Meeting the Chef

Beth knocks on Chef Reiner's door with a sense of anticipation. What is he like, really? As the door opens, Chef Reiner extends his hand, saying, "Good afternoon! I'm Gerhard Reiner. I've been looking forward to meeting you." Beth is relieved to see a tentative smile on his face. Stepping into the office, the two engage in conversation aimed at breaking the ice.

When Beth takes her seat, she is immediately impressed by the order of the room. The desk is clear, all items in their places. Beth's eyebrows rise as she notices that the books on the shelves are in order of height, smallest to the tallest, and the edges of the books are in line with the shelf. She smiles and thanks Chef Reiner for a great lunch. "It was a true pleasure," he returns. "I'm glad you had the chance to see the students working."

He gets to the point. "When the dean told me that you were coming, I immediately thought of how you could help us increase program enrollment. I'm looking forward to our work together. How can I help you get started?"

Beth reflects for a moment and responds, "Perhaps you could start by telling me about the successes the program has had. Tell me about your history with the college and what you consider the strengths of the program to be."

Chef Reiner begins a lengthy recital of his qualifications and the program's strengths. He has been at State College for five years, following a career as an executive chef for a major cruise line. He had also worked in fine dining in France and Germany. He speaks several languages and has had the opportunity to work with many fine chefs. He is also the president of the local chapter of the American Culinary Federation. His students have a chapter as well and participate in local competitions. The program's greatest accomplishment is the quality of the graduates. The previous dean had been concerned about the reputation of the program. They hired Chef Reiner to develop the prestige of the school and produce quality graduates capable of obtaining high-level chef positions throughout the metropolitan area.

"Since I arrived," Chef Reiner explains, "I have instituted a student dining room, which produces meals three days a week, as you saw today. Before that, we had no outlet for the student work; most of the food production was in the classroom only. I have found that students like to see the public enjoy the meals they create."

Beth smiles. "I certainly enjoyed it!"

Chef Reiner continues, "We have had problems with student professional standards, and I have worked hard to reverse that problem."

"What do you mean, 'professional standards'?" asks Beth.

"We are in a metropolitan area," Chef Reiner explains. "Our students don't like to wear uniforms and maintain hygiene standards. We have had problems with long hair, nail polish, jewelry, and body piercings, which are not part of a professional and sanitary kitchen."

"How have you solved that problem?" Beth asks. Chef Reiner shows her his culinary laboratory evaluation sheet (Figure 16–1). "Following each class, the students are evaluated on their appearance, quality of work, attendance, and so forth."

Beth studies the performance criteria and behavioral categories. Something in this grading sheet conflicts with her preferred approach. Beth ponders how effective a point

**FIGURE 16–1**  Chef Reiner's Behavioral Checklist for Student Performance.

| Timeliness | Production |
|---|---|
| On time | Listens well |
| Stays entire time | Tastes all food |
| No idle time | Takes direction well |
| | Displays knowledge |
| **Uniform** | Observes others, stays involved |
| | Respectful of speed, timeliness |
| Hat | Quality of food production |
| Clean whites | Respectful of waste and food cost |
| Black slacks | |
| Nonskid shoes | **Sanitation** |
| Closed-toe shoes | |
| Ironed | Aggressively cleans |
| | Cleans/sanitizes well |
| **Appearance** | |
| | **Teamwork** |
| Hair clean, pulled back | |
| Fingernails trimmed 1/4″ | Volunteers to work |
| Hands and nails clean | Is supportive of leader |
| Jewelry: two rings, watch, stud | Offers suggestions |
| earrings only | Provides constructive criticism |
| | |
| **Equipment** | |
| | |
| Chef's knife sharp | |
| Paring knife sharp | |
| Apron | |
| Kitchen towel | |

system like this would be. She sees the value of meaningful experiences, such as the student lunch, but wonders how such strict behavioral monitoring can be effective.

Beth looks up from the sheet. "Hmm. Neatness, organization, teamwork, ability to follow instructions. Does this work? How do the students respond to this evaluation?"

"It is quite effective," the chef explains. "Before our daily evaluations, I would get frustrated with student uniforms and professionalism in class. They would not behave professionally and respect uniform standards. I would give them low grades and they would get angry and not understand why they got bad grades. It is almost as if they expected to get an *A* for just being here."

Beth's mind is racing with ideas and conflicts as she asks, "How does the checklist evaluation change that?"

Chef Reiner is resolute in his response. "I get better performance from the students because the evaluations tell them what I expect. If they don't behave professionally, they can see how many points they will lose for not meeting standards. It is also less stressful on me."

"What do you mean?" Beth wants to understand what's going on in the chef's mind.

"At first, I would do the same as I was taught in culinary school. If a student didn't show up in uniform or behaved unprofessionally, I'd send him or her home, with a zero for the day."

Beth chuckles. "How did that go over?"

Smiling, Chef Reiner responds, "Not well at all! Students got frustrated, and I quickly realized I'd lose most of them. The daily evaluation gives them more immediate feedback on my expectations. They can choose to change their behavior on their own, knowing the penalty. I'd say the daily forms are less forceful than how things were before."

Beth is skeptical. "Less forceful?"

Chef Reiner explains: "Most students actually like getting a grade each day—and they don't blame me as much for their grades. At least they know where they stand. The bottom line is, my students now wear their uniforms and act like a team. I do have some who still don't respond, but overall it's much better."

Beth is trying to process this approach. "Do you think the evaluation is causing some students to drop out?"

Chef Reiner sighs, "No, they make this decision themselves. I view my role as preparing them for success in the industry. Kitchens require a distinct chain of authority and rules. The students need to learn how to survive in that environment while in school. If not, they won't succeed in business. I'd rather they fail here than later on the job."

Raising her eyebrows, Beth responds, "Are you saying, if they can't stand the heat, get out of the kitchen?"

"Exactly!" Chef Reiner continues, "I realized that these students had never learned to take school or work seriously and professionally, so I created a performance system that takes me out of the picture almost entirely. Instead of blaming me when they don't get the grade they want, they look at the point totals and see where they can change."

"Sounds as if it worked," Beth admits.

Chef Reiner continues with enthusiasm, "You wouldn't believe the difference. Before, I had students refusing to complete a cooking assignment, afraid it would wreck their nails. Nail polish, clothes, hairdo, whatever the excuse, I had students who were not doing the work.

Now, everyone shows up on time, in uniform, ready to work. And word has spread around campus. The students take a great deal of pride in their accomplishments. Employers see the difference, too. We have a 96% placement rate, with starting pay up 60% in five years."

Beth stands to leave. "You've given me a lot to think about. Let me get back to you with some notes and observations; then we'll figure out where to go from here."

"That sounds fine," answers Chef Reiner as he stands to see Beth out. "If I can be of further help, please feel free to ask." Beth shakes his hand and leaves the office with a lot to think about. "Maybe I should have had that dessert!" she muses, returning to her car, umbrella in hand. The rain is gone and the sun is shining again.

On the drive home, Beth continues to turn over these ideas in her mind. She is unsettled about the strict behaviorist approach used by the program, but it seems to be working. She had wanted to suggest more constructivist ideas but didn't quite see where they would fit. In fact, the situation is something of a challenge to Beth's beliefs about good teaching.

## Preliminary Analysis Questions

1. Identify the problem in this case from the viewpoint of each stakeholder: Dean Jacobs, Beth, and Chef Reiner.
2. What is causing the conflict within Beth? How do her preexisting ideas about constructivism and behaviorism relate to her observations of the program?
3. What suggestions do you have for Beth for how to deal with her perceived conflict between constructivist and behavioral approaches to instruction?
4. Beth has only begun her review of the culinary arts program. What further data should be gathered to address the dean's concerns and provide suggestions for improving the program?

## Implications for ID Practice

1. Constructivism and behaviorism are often presented as competing philosophies, yet many designers seek to include elements of both approaches in their practice. How can that be done while maintaining foundational cohesion in philosophy?
2. Professionals such as Beth develop their expertise by paying close attention to both theory and practice. What kinds of conflicts have you experienced between textbook approaches and everyday concerns of practice? How can instructional design professionals learn to respect both sources of knowledge and incorporate them successfully into their outlooks and practice?

# Camille Suarez

## Redesigning Curriculum for Hybrid Training in a Public Health Setting

*by Julie Jabaley and Laurie Brantley-Dias*

## Setting

Camille Suarez is near the end of earning a Master of Public Health (MPH) degree and has just begun her thesis defense in front of an audience composed of student colleagues and her committee. The defense is entitled *The Silver Tsunami*. Let's listen!

## Late April

"So," Camille continued as she pointed to her slide (Figure 17–1), "as many of you know from the 2006 Alliance for Aging Research 2006 report and especially from the work here at the State Center for Healthy Aging, or CHA, the silver tsunami refers to the phenomenon of 10,000 Americans turning 65 years old every day for the next two decades (Figure 17–1). You can do the math!"

She paused to let that sink in and glanced at her advisor and chair, Dr. Lee Robert, the executive director of CHA. He was smiling and appeared pleased with the way Camille began her defense.

Camille moved to the next slide and continued, "Research tells us that most older adults prefer to remain in their own homes and communities, but the support and adjustments they need to make this possible simply are not systematically integrated into eldercare in this country. As a result, interventions such as ElderSafe are being carefully researched and funded for scaled-up dissemination."

"The Center for Healthy Aging is a three-year-old, grant-funded organization situated within the College of Public Health here at the university." Referring to the slide, Camille went on to explain CHA's funding and mission (Figure 17–2).

**FIGURE 17–1**    The Silver Tsunami.

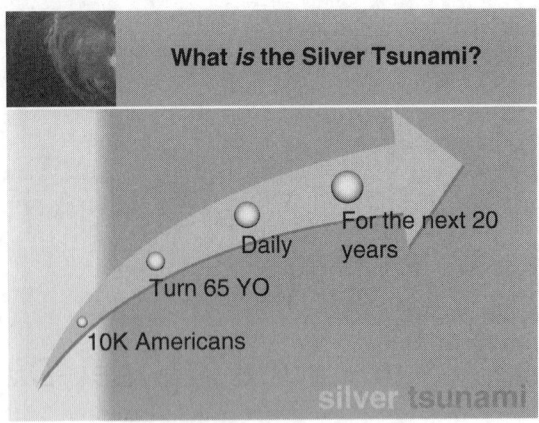

**FIGURE 17–2**    State Center for Healthy Aging.

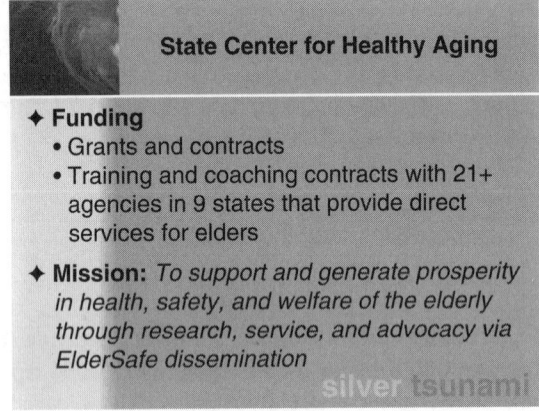

"Why is ElderSafe important? Camille asked, advancing to the next slide. "Besides the tsunami that will batter the public health system in coming years, many elder injuries are preventable. In fact, my elderly neighbor, Phyllis, who is still recovering from a broken hip after tripping on one of her treasured antique area rugs last summer, is one of the primary reasons I wanted to work with Dr. Robert on ElderSafe for my thesis research." She continued, pointing out facts concerning falls (Figure 17–3).

"Let me share a little about the ElderSafe intervention itself," said Camille. She moved to the next slide (Figure 17–4) to talk briefly through each point: "... and outreach workers, or OWs, go into the home to deliver ElderSafe. It's a modular intervention, and each module typically takes four weeks. The modules are health, nutrition, social community, and home safety."

**FIGURE 17–3**    Elder Injuries Due to Falls.

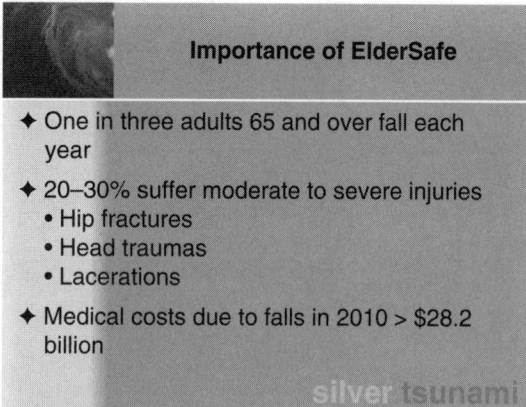

**FIGURE 17–4**    Description of ElderSafe.

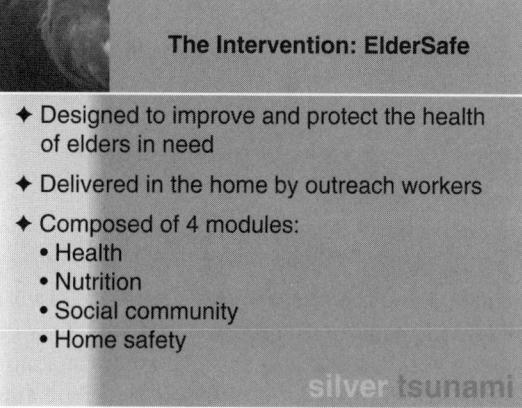

Continuing with her presentation, Camille explained how CHA was staffed. "In addition to the four faculty members and seven support, research, and administrative staff, we have six national trainers, who are wonderful!" Camille waved her hand in the direction of the three trainers present at her defense and smiled. "Our dissemination is based on a train-the-trainer model (Figure 17–5). So, our trainers typically travel to eldercare agencies around the country to train outreach workers and coaches, and they continue supporting the coaches by phone as they work to master the coaching process."

Camille pointed to the *Coaches* box on the slide. "The coaches coach. They coach the outreach workers within their agency. They monitor fidelity of the OWs in the field, usually by digital sound recordings of in-home visits with elders. The OWs, obviously, provide the direct services," finished Camille. "By the way, most of the agencies with whom CHA contracts use a traditional caseload management model to provide *many* different services around eldercare: ElderSafe is just one of them."

**FIGURE 17–5**   Dissemination Model.

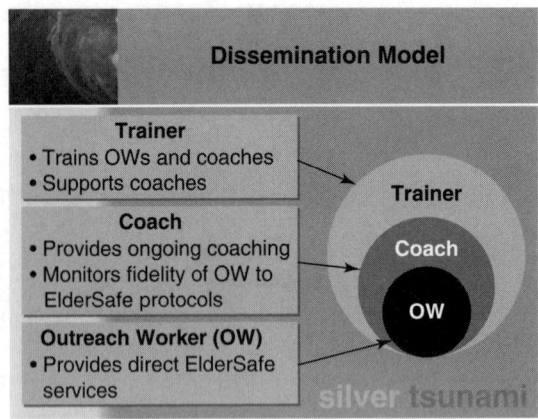

Camille went on to explain her research and present her data. The committee asked a few questions: Ned Simmons, the CHA director, asked about her methodology, and Dr. Robert asked what she learned most from her research. "Never get old!" she responded. Her defense finished with a few laughs.

# Early May

The next week, Camille was in Ned's office discussing ElderSafe. He was talking about the center's growing pains, especially as they related to ElderSafe, which was one of the center's biggest progams. "So, more and more of our agency contracts are becoming challenging for us in terms of ElderSafe fidelity. As you know, when agencies adopt a new initiative in name only, without fidelity to the ElderSafe protocol, it usually means a sharp decline in the positive results seen during the research phase, which translates into loss of momentum and possible loss of contracts for the center. That's really risky for us, because our intervention is already more expensive to implement than many of the typical services or interventions agencies provide. Based on your review so far of our train-the-trainer model and the ElderSafe curriculum, what do you think is going on?"

Camille paused, thinking about what she had reviewed and glancing at her notes. Because of Camille's Master of Science in Instructional Technology and now MPH, the center had recently hired her as project manager and instructional designer for a grant-funded project designed to revise the ElderSafe curriculum.

"Well, I've been analyzing the curriculum as you asked," Camille began, "to look for possible problem areas around fidelity. In some ways, the fact that ElderSafe is a behavior-based intervention may be a factor."

Ned cocked his head to the side with a questioning look, and Camille continued, "We both know that behavior change is among the most challenging problems in public health. Although we're dealing with population issues, it often ultimately boils down to individual behavior change: will teens use barrier methods to protect against sexually transmitted diseases and unwanted pregnancy? Will people exercise to help combat overweight and obesity? Will elders get rid of area rugs?"

"With ElderSafe, we're trying to help elders change behaviors and habits to keep them safe and healthy; however, there's another group whose behavior has to change, too: the OWs! The ElderSafe approach is unique in that it's a *behavioral* intervention. Our OWs, mostly social workers, don't generally have that type of background. We're trying to reshape elder behavior *and* social worker behavior! So, we get a lot of attention and interest because ElderSafe is evidence based—a real buzzword for funding in social services today—but we have difficulty with fidelity because our behavioral approach is somewhat foreign." She and Ned continued to discuss ElderSafe in this context for several more minutes.

This job was an exciting opportunity for Camille. Her favorite class in her MPH program had been a class about translating public health research into practice, and because of the challenges surfacing vis-à-vis scaled-up dissemination of ElderSafe, she was sure this job would pivot around similar issues. She'd been doing instructional design work in K–12 and higher education settings for more than 15 years, and her MPH was already expanding her content base, both with this job and with the two public health curricula she'd written as an intern with The Cancer Project. Additionally, Phyllis, her neighbor, wasn't recovering well from her injury—this reality made working at the center very personal for Camille. She didn't want her friend and neighbor to become a statistic. She thought of Phyllis, too, as she and Ned talked.

"Well, there's certainly a lot of important content that elderly people can benefit from," she continued with Ned. "And the OW materials seem to address the learning objectives, more or less."

"Sounds like there might be a 'but' . . ." Ned said.

"I see two main issues. First, ElderSafe was born out of research, and the center was funded to disseminate and study the intervention's dissemination and implementation, right?" Camille asked. Ned nodded. "So there's some solid content, as I said, and it's been validated through years of research before the establishment of the center, but in many ways the curriculum looks and feels as though it's still used for research. For example, the OW trainees are given a thick binder of training materials that contains a lot of unformatted text, making it difficult to locate the most important pages and quickly pick out the critical points for a given home visit. And second, the content knowledge that the trainers provide OWs is lecture oriented—we could liven it up a bit. I think by making some adjustments we could better prepare OWs, and we'd see a commensurate increase in fidelity."

Ned shook his head, smiling. "Yes, it is pretty dry stuff—even for me! The OW trainees have even nicknamed the binder 'Thickum'—probably not the most positive endorsement!"

Camille smiled, too, thinking to herself that "Thickum" was an understatement—the binder contained more than 750 pages! "There's another point," she said. "Now that the train-the-trainer model is in place and we're no longer delivering all of the training ourselves from the center, we have much less control over how well the external trainers deliver the content."

"Hmmm," Ned said. "We've been thinking that the curricular revisions you will work on might lead to the creation of 'ElderSafe Online' to reduce the face-to-face training time for OWs. This would decrease the cost of training, which may be deterring agencies from using ElderSafe in its current form. With the burgeoning aging population and the rising costs of medical care, our grant mandates are around prevention, which we know costs less than treatment, and innovation. Our grantor is particularly interested in technology-related innovations, but we were intentionally vague in outlining how technology might be integrated into our training model." Ned paused to contemplate this for a moment. "Maybe because of the fidelity issues, that thinking is erroneous. Maybe we shouldn't be thinking of reducing face-to-face time in favor of hybrid OW training."

Camille was thinking exactly the opposite. She was considering how the integration of technology through a combined online and face-to-face OW training might serve multiple purposes. She was thinking that if part of ElderSafe training were packaged as an asynchronous deliverable, then at least everyone would receive identical content for greater quality control and consistency. She was also reasoning that if the knowledge portion of the training were covered before OW trainees attended training, more time could be spent during the face-to-face time aligning OWs' thinking with behavioral methods and thus improving fidelity to the model.

"Well," Camille said, "our conversation gives me a lot to think about, and I'd like to begin with a thorough analysis of the current curriculum and performance of trained OWs. I plan to look holistically at ElderSafe, but I'd like to take a modular approach to the actual work, beginning with the Home Safety module—that's where I conducted my research, and it is the module I'm most familiar with. How does that sound?"

Ned agreed with Camille's plan of action, and she got started on a two-pronged analysis. First, she studied the ElderSafe dissemination model to think through whom she might interview, both internally and externally. With the help of the national trainers, she selected two OWs with different levels of experience and scheduled a couple of interviews within a few days. She completed the external interviews, as well as informal internal interviews with two of the national trainers at the center, over the next several weeks.

Second, Camille gathered a dozen audio recordings of actual in-home OW sessions. As she listened to the audio files over the next weeks, Camille was surprised by the variability in fidelity to ElderSafe protocols, or session outlines, and she recalled her conversation with Ned weeks earlier. Some of the OWs followed the outline fairly accurately and therefore hit the important learning points. Some of the OWs tried, but the content was more difficult for the elder. These situations required a lot of creativity from the OW, and some of them were better at coming up with sound learning approaches than others. In other cases, the OW neglected the protocol, and the session hardly resembled Elder-Safe at all.

During her analysis (Table 17–1), Camille noticed that some of the problems she had identified in the audio files also came up in the interviews, but new performance issues surfaced as well.

**TABLE 17–1**   *Learner Analysis: Outreach Worker Interview Summary*

| Interview Topic | OW 1 | OW 2 |
| --- | --- | --- |
| Experience in the field | 15 years<br>Mostly clinical work experiences until working with ElderSafe. | 2 years<br>Mostly social work including individual and group therapy as well as some program management. |
| Experience with ElderSafe | 2 ½ years<br>Certified OW training (4/10)<br>Certified Coach trainer (5/11)<br>Conducted 2 training sessions | 6 months<br>Has only completed the Home Safety and Nutrition modules |
| Comments on current ElderSafe training | All of the modules seem to work, but Home Safety and Health modules take longer for the OWs to complete.<br><br>The observation checklist that coaches use with OWs is too long. | The videos used in training were okay, but they didn't represent the settings the OW worked in.<br><br>Thought that the checklists for preparing a home visit were useful. |
| Performance problems after training | Some OWs take a long time to build rapport with the elder person(s).<br><br>Others had a hard time problem-solving when the elder person wouldn't use the materials or brought up safety issues that weren't the specific examples presented in the training. | OW didn't feel confident modeling for the elder person how to use the Home Safety Checklist to identify potential safety hazards in his home.<br><br>Persuading the elder to make changes to the home environment to improve safety was difficult. |

# Late May

Camille rapped lightly on Mia Mason's door. Mia, a senior national trainer with the center since its inception, was slated to be on the home safety project team by choice—home safety being her favorite module to train and support.

"Got a few minutes?" Camille asked. Mia spun around at her desk as she smiled and motioned Camille in. Camille continued, "I'm studying our train-the-trainer model and have a couple of questions. Do you have time to address these now or should I come back later?"

Mia responded, "Actually, your timing is great. I have an hour until my next appointment. Why don't you have a seat?"

Camille sat down and then checked her notes before she began. "First, I want to make sure I correctly understand something about the OW training. For each level—OW, coach, and trainer—there are certification criteria that must be met, right?"

Mia nodded, reaching into her file cabinet to extract a detailed certification document. She passed the document to Camille, and they briefly discussed the process. Mia explained that OWs attend training to become provisionally certified in ElderSafe delivery protocols.

**FIGURE 17–6**   Outreach Worker Fidelity Checklist for Certification.

### Outreach Worker Fidelity Checklist: Training

OW Staff _____          Session Date _____     Family # _____

Coach _____     Module _____     In-person or Recorded? _____

| Has materials ready | | | |
|---|---|---|---|
| Checklists | + | – | n/a |
| Training materials for elders | + | – | n/a |
| Supplies | + | – | n/a |
| Other materials | + | – | n/a |
| **Opens the session** | | | |
| Exchanges an appropriate initial greeting | + | – | n/a |
| States goals for the session | + | – | n/a |
| **Demonstrates appropriate demeanor** | | | |
| Sits facing client | + | – | n/a |
| Communicates empathy, warmth, understanding | + | – | n/a |
| Maintains an open posture | + | – | n/a |
| Has good eye contact | + | – | n/a |
| **Uses active listening techniques** | | | |
| Uses words/expressions (e.g., "uh-huh") to encourage the elder to talk | + | – | n/a |
| Uses open-ended questions | + | – | n/a |
| Uses reflecting statements | + | – | n/a |
| Uses summarizing statements | + | – | n/a |
| **Conducts assessments as needed** | | | |
| Conducts assessments as indicated in the outline | + | – | n/a |
| Explains the purpose of the assessments | + | – | n/a |
| Explains the process of the assessments | + | – | n/a |
| **Trains the elder** | | | |
| Uses the appropriate material to train the elder | + | – | n/a |
| Models steps and behaviors | + | – | n/a |
| Has elder practice an appropriate number of times | + | – | n/a |
| Balances explain vs. modeling behaviors and steps | + | – | n/a |
| Provides general, positive feedback | + | – | n/a |
| Provides specific, corrective feedback | + | – | n/a |
| **Addresses issues that arise during the session** | | | |
| Encourages the elder to ask questions and express concerns | + | – | n/a |
| Responds to elder questions and concerns | + | – | n/a |
| Uses problem solving approaches as appropriate | + | – | n/a |
| **Follows an appropriate closing sequence** | | | |
| Summarizes the session | + | – | n/a |
| Gives general positive feedback | + | – | n/a |
| Schedules meeting date/time for next week | + | – | n/a |

Items scored + _____

Percent correct = _____          Total items scored + or - _____

"Right," Camille said. "And this certification comes from a single role play per module and a written quiz, both of which happen during the face-to-face training."

Mia nodded, "And after that level, OWs begin field certification by audio recording one-on-one home visits with an elder. That's what you've been listening to. They typically conduct four home visits per module, each lasting one hour. An ElderSafe coach, the second tier of our model (Figure 17–5), listens to the audio-recorded sessions and conducts small group and individual meetings with OWs during their induction period. Full certification is achieved by reaching 85% mastery on criterion-based home visit checklists for each of the four modules" (Figure 17–6). Mia reviewed the rest of the document with Camille, highlighting the certification requirements for coaches and trainers as well.

"This is really helpful," Camille said. "Because I'm focusing on OW training, I haven't looked into our other levels of training yet, but I want to make sure that I keep the big picture in mind. But back to OWs: do trainees ever 'fail'?"

"Not often," Mia responded. "But there is certainly a range of performance. Coaches often have to do a lot of re-training."

"What does that look like?" Camille asked.

"Well, they go over the materials one on one. And coaches discuss the recorded sessions *a lot* over the phone. It takes quite a bit of time, but that's what it takes to get them certified."

"Hmmm. That does seem time consuming. Thanks for explaining all of this in more detail," Camille said. "By the way, in the last team meeting, we were talking about the different hazards that cause unintentional injury to elders. Do you know the underlying rationale for the order in which they are presented during the training and then during home visits with elders?" (Figure 17–7).

Mia cocked her head to the side and thought for a moment. "That's a good question. I can't recall, but I do remember there being some strong opinions about it when we designed the materials." They talked for a few more moments before Camille said goodbye and headed back to her office.

**FIGURE 17–7**   List of Hazard Categories.

## HOME-BASED HAZARDS FOR ELDERS

- Poisonous Solids and Liquids
- Sharp Objects
- Crush and Abrasion
- Fire and Electrical
- Fall, Trip, and Slip

# Over the Summer

Weekly project team meetings took place beginning in late June. The group approved overall project plans and timelines and plowed through substantive decisions related to curricular changes based on questions about the Home Safety module Camille included in each week's agenda. Near the end of summer, she felt the work was close to completion.

As an early August meeting concluded, Camille asked, "Are there any additional suggestions related to the Home Safety module?"

"It's not a suggestion, but I just remembered something," remarked Edie Sanchez, the associate director of curriculum. "About two years ago, the center consulted with two eldercare specialists who produced analyses of the ElderSafe curriculum. One consultant was a generalist, and the other had expertise in persons with intellectual disabilities, a core audience for the ElderSafe intervention." Surprised, Camille asked to see copies of the reports and promised to report back during the next meeting.

She looked around the table at the team. "Anything else for the good of the group?" Everyone smiled, but no one had anything more. "OK! Great meeting, everyone! Please look for minutes with action items for homework. As always, let me know if you're overwhelmed with your tasks and need help." The meeting adjourned, and Camille quickly went back to her office to check her e-mail for the SME reports from Edie (Figure 17–8).

**FIGURE 17–8**   Consultant Report.

---

**Summary Report**

**Project Name:** ElderSafe Curriculum Review for Elders with Limited Literacy

**Prepared For:** The Center for Healthy Aging

**Prepared By:** Elder Care Consulting

---

**Project Recommendations**

**Recommendation Highlights**

- Printed materials should be at the lowest reading level that will still convey the message.
- Provide information in short segments with an easy layout.
- Write all instructions in active voice.
- Explain meanings of difficult or unfamiliar words and provide examples.
- Provide realistic visual presentations using photographs and sketches.
- Supplement all written materials with auditory aids for those with reading problems.
- Use videos to demonstrate step-by-step procedures.
- Include interactions and reviews with elders to ensure that they comprehend and learn the material.

---

The SME reports, in fact, yielded some of the same information that had surfaced during the analysis stage, but also more specific ideas that Camille had not considered, many of which would truly enhance the intervention. However, the added work would probably jeopardize the timeline. For instance, the reading level of the elder materials was too high throughout, and the consultant made specific suggestions as to how to make them more accessible for low-literacy audiences or elders with intellectual disabilities. Camille was aware that the elder materials could use revision, especially having listened to several audio files of home visits, but with everything else going on, these tasks had fallen to the wayside in favor of revising the OW training curriculum.

Camille took out a copy of the elder materials (Figure 17–9) for the Home Safety module and some of the notes from her earlier interviews (Table 17–1). She began jotting down ideas based on the consultants' reports and what she was seeing with the added benefit of the SMEs' lenses. She made a note to pull out salient points from the latest National Assessment of Adult Literacy before the next project team meeting.

**FIGURE 17–9**   Example of Elder Materials.

**Home Safety for Seniors**

Your safety at home is of primary importance. Each year seniors report, on average, 2.3 million unintentional home injuries with falls being the leading cause.

As you age, some modifications or improvements in your home become necessary to create a safe environment that will enable you to function better and more comfortably thereby allowing you to maintain independent living. These changes don't have to cost a lot of money and most are fairly easy to do yourself or with a family member or caregiver. However, more significant home improvements (e.g., lowering kitchen countertops or installing ramps) will have an increased monetary cost and require assistance from a handyman or general contractor.

Here are some precautions that you can take. Keep this list and use it often to check the safety in your home.

- Install smoke detectors and carbon monoxide alarms. Check the batteries on these devices every six months.
- Ensure that the lighting inside and outside of your home is non-glare and sufficient for you to see your surroundings clearly.
- Keep a fire extinguisher in the kitchen.
- Replace outlets in the bathroom and other wet areas that don't have a ground fault circuit interrupter.
- Keep your floors clear of hazards such as electrical cords, boxes, and rugs.
- Replace faucet and handles with a single-lever mixing faucet.
- Install support grab bars in the tub and toilet areas.
- Store flammable liquids in a safe location.
- Equip your tub and shower with slip-resistant materials.
- Remove throw rugs from the kitchen.

For the next several weeks, project team meetings continued as the group tackled new issues raised by the consultants' analyses and tied up loose ends around other ongoing revisions. The timeline seemed less and less manageable as the project crept beyond the initial scope, particularly because of the revisions to the elder materials. Camille decided to chat with Ned to provide him with an update, something they did informally and without a specific schedule, although regularly.

"So, with the revisions to the existing curriculum taking a significantly larger portion of my time and the time of the project team, I'm concerned about our timeline," Camille finished, having just reviewed a progress report she'd prepared for Ned.

"I see," Ned said, looking over the report. "I also see that these are pretty substantive changes on the one hand. On the other hand, they're issues we've been talking about updating for almost three years, and we need to tighten up the curriculum." Camille nodded her head vigorously in agreement. "So, I see two possibilities, and they're not necessarily mutually exclusive: One, we can always ask for a one-year, no-cost extension of the grant. That buys us more time, and we haven't exhausted the funds, so we could keep you on for a second year. And two, we could do less. Our internal trainers are really thrilled by the changes so far, but we could scale back."

"Well," Camille said, "I didn't plan to talk about my job security today, but it's good to know that an extension is an option. In terms of the second idea, I'd hate to scale back. I'm thinking in a different direction, one that may help alleviate some of my anxiety about the timeline."

Ned raised his eyebrows in interest, but then looked at his watch. "Can you explain in 15 minutes or less? I've got a conference call coming up with a potential new contract in California."

Camille explained several things guiding her thoughts. She started by talking about the gaps she observed between trainees' performances during face-to-face training and their subsequent field performances. Then they discussed adult learning preferences and differentiation during face-to-face training. Finally, she shared some specific ideas about time efficiencies with regard to the project as a whole.

When she finished, Ned was nodding his head. "I like what I hear, but I want to make sure the faculty and the project team are in agreement."

"Can you come to the next project team meeting?" Camille asked. "I'd like to present this to the team, and there will likely be discussion before we can get consensus around this approach. The next meeting is on Tuesday, at 9:00, as always."

Ned agreed to attend the meeting, and Camille got right to work. Because the module they were currently working on was Home Safety, Camille had to come up with a method for teaching OWs about how to conduct a home safety inspection to determine the number of hazards in the home. The trick to the inspection was organization. ElderSafe had already defined five categories of hazards that research indicated were threats to elders living safely at home. The protocol called for counting the number of hazards in each category room by room (Figure 17–10).

Camille also wanted to use a series of interactive lessons to introduce and teach the related skills. She thought about integrating newer, more flexible technologies, but wondered if Ned and the team would be in agreement. Finally, she had to figure out ways to increase fidelity to the module. Wow! She had a lot of work to do before Tuesday.

**FIGURE 17–10**    Preventing Home Injury Tool (PHIT).

**Preventing Home Injury Tool (PHIT)**

Client's: _____

Home Visitor: _____    Timing:  ❑ Baseline

Location: _____                  ❑ Training

Date: _____                        ❑ Follow-up

| Hazard | No. of Hazards | Comments |
|---|---|---|
| **Fall, Trip, and Slip**<br>• Steps/stairs<br>• Area rugs<br>• Bathroom w/o bars<br>• Unlit hallways and paths | | |
| **Crush and Abrasion**<br>• Stacked items<br>• Items stored above eye level<br>• Heavy items | | |
| **Poisonous Solids and Liquids**<br>• Medications<br>• Alcoholic beverages<br>• Cleaning products<br>• Pesticides, herbicides, etc.<br>• Paints, solvents, etc. | | |
| **Fire and Electrical**<br>• Cooking areas<br>• Small electrical appliances<br>• Hair appliances | | |
| **Sharp Objects**<br>• Knives<br>• Kitchen tools<br>• Gardening tools | | |

# Preliminary Analysis Questions

1. Critique Camille's approach to her analysis of the training, materials, and learning environment, outlining specific aspects, if any, that need improvement.
2. Camille thought that technology could serve multiple purposes to address the problems identified at the beginning of the project. What technologies should she consider and why?
3. According to the SME reports, not all of the elder training materials were appropriate for every group within the target audience. What kinds of modifications should Camille recommend?
4. What are some instructional strategies that Camille could use to help the OWs demonstrate their proficiency in the ElderSafe protocols?
5. Why is Camille's project experiencing scope creep? How can she keep this from derailing the project?

# Implications for ID Practice

1. How can instructional designers increase the fidelity in a train-the-trainer program when multiple trainers are involved?
2. What factors should designers consider when determining how to sequence a series of related but non-sequential tasks?
3. What problems might instructional designers face when they assume the role of both project manager and instructional designer?

# Reference

Alliance for Aging Research. (2006). *Preparing for the silver tsunami.* Retrieved from http://72.32.160.218/content/article/detail/826

# Frank Tawl and Semra Senbetto*
## Designing Curriculum for Southeast Asian Trainers

*by Peggy A. Ertmer and Walter Dick*

About 10 years ago, the Singapore government, in cooperation with a major U.S. electronics corporation, began to plan the development of a training design center in Singapore, in which participants would be trained to design instruction using a systems approach. The hope was that Singapore would obtain the long-term capability to determine the need for, and then to develop, appropriate training programs for its workforce. At the time this decision was made, no instructional design (ID) training programs were being offered in Singapore, although various training institutes were in operation (e.g., the Teacher Training Institute, the National Training Center, and the Vocational Education Center), and numerous government employees provided training for local businesses. Although these employees served as trainers, they themselves had received little, if any, formal instruction in instructional design theory or practice; furthermore, they had never participated in a curriculum that used a systems approach to the design and development of training. Although Singaporean trainers often delivered instruction on specified content, they had no formal experience with, or knowledge of, adult learning principles or the use of interactive teaching strategies. The instruction they created typically depended on their own content expertise or was based upon instruction that had been imported from the United States and then adapted.

A pair of U.S. designers was hired to plan and develop a curriculum for preparing Singaporean instructional designers. One of these designers, Frank Tawl, was a university professor and a noted expert on the use of the systems approach for designing instruction. Frank had developed a number of courses at his U.S. university on ID topics and issues, and he felt fairly confident that these could be modified to fit the Singaporean learners' needs. Frank's teammate, Semra Senbetto, was a private consultant who had worked with Frank on a number of previous projects and was noted for her ability to recognize and address culturally relevant issues in situations involving learners from diverse backgrounds.

---

*Based in part on a 1991 article by Walter Dick, which appeared in *Performance Improvement Quarterly, 4*(1), "The Singapore project: A case study in instructional design," pp. 14–22. Note that information from the original case was altered in order to increase its educational value for our readers. Readers should not consider this case to be a true representation of the Singapore government.

As part of their front-end analysis, Frank and Semra conducted interviews to determine the current perceptions of professors at the national university, as well as training staffs at the Teacher Training Institute, the National Training Center, and the Vocational Education Center, regarding the proposed ID training curriculum. Among other things, they were interested in determining the following: What kinds of training experiences were currently in place at the existing training centers? What procedures did Singaporean trainers follow when designing new instruction and presenting training to their colleagues?

In these initial interviews, it became clear that the professors at the national university were supportive of whatever the U.S. designers thought best—teaching whatever content Frank and Semra thought was appropriate, as well as using whatever strategies the U.S. designers typically used. During follow-up interviews, they posed virtually no opposition to Frank's and Semra's ideas; after a suggestion was made, the professors would simply nod in agreement. Although Frank and Semra made a concerted effort to uncover any culturally sensitive issues that needed to be taken into consideration in the design of the curriculum, they identified none. If the Singaporean professors had any culturally related concerns, they didn't acknowledge them.

Additional interviews were held with potential learners of the ID curriculum—namely, the current trainers. Frank and Semra asked questions to determine the following: What did the Singaporean trainers already know about the design process? What beliefs did they hold that reflected potential acceptance of the systems approach and/or findings from current research regarding the teaching and learning process? What beliefs seemed contradictory to these current theories about teaching and learning? How motivated were they to participate in this new training program? Although, on the surface, these potential learners seemed to accept Frank's and Semra's ideas about interactive delivery strategies and alternative assessment measures, they were obviously unclear as to what was expected of them. They wondered how similar this training would be to the imported training they had become accustomed to modifying. Was this instruction going to be more or less effective with their students?

The Singaporean trainers indicated that they preferred lecture-based instruction and memory-based assessment measures. Interestingly, it was discovered during the interview process that Singaporean trainers had been modifying "imported" instruction by eliminating the built-in interactive activities and changing the assessment techniques to be more memory-based, as opposed to performance-based. The Singaporean trainers indicated that, although they "mostly" liked these training programs, they were concerned that their students would be uncomfortable performing in front of their peers and mentioned that losing face was something to be avoided at all costs. There was an additional concern that students over 40 years of age might not be sufficiently motivated to perform under the nontraditional conditions advocated by the imported programs. These students would be retiring when they turned 55 and mentioned that the time spent learning new skills, at their "mature" age, was "a real waste."

The majority of the trainers interviewed expressed little motivation to attend this new training when it became available. Those who were interviewed mentioned the following concerns:

- Additional time commitments involved in completing a degree program (all worked full-time)

- A need to learn a new way of designing and delivering training
- The lack of job advancement, salary compensation, or other rewards or recognition being tied to the completion of the program
- A lack of confidence in convincing clients to let them use these new skills

If these concerns were adequately addressed, the trainers indicated, they would perhaps participate.

Frank and Semra decided to observe a few training programs currently being offered by the National Training Center. Additional time was spent with the instructors of these courses to determine how their training courses had been developed. In essence, the observations supported what had been suggested in the interviews. Singaporean trainers were accustomed to presenting and attending instructor-led training. They did not like being put on the spot (performing or responding in front of their peers); they liked assessment measures that provided a quick indication of how much they had learned. Also noted was the fact that they used very few media during instruction and did not engage in either needs analysis or formative evaluation procedures when developing instruction. It was difficult, if not impossible, to determine whether any of the training being offered was making a difference on the job.

In contrast to the opinions and preferences mentioned by the Singaporean trainers, the Singapore government strongly supported a move to more "modern" training—it was more than eager to imitate the U.S. approach to the systematic design of instruction. Although Frank and Semra agreed that appropriate teaching methods, such as simulations, role plays, and case studies, should be used when such methods supported the instructional objectives of the ID curriculum, they were concerned about motivating the learners to engage in these activities.

Frank and Semra realized that the typical ID competencies needed to be included in a way that fit the needs of the Singaporean students. Some modifications to a typical ID curriculum would be required. Finally, the question of who should teach the new courses, U.S. or Singaporean trainers, needed to be addressed. There did not seem to be any easy answers to the many questions facing this experienced design team.

As Frank and Semra labored to design a blueprint for the ID curriculum, including the identification of the strategies and approaches that should be used, they were faced with a number of difficult decisions:

- How to help the Singaporean trainers master factual information and develop intellectual skills and positive attitudes regarding the systems approach to ID
- How to motivate the Singaporean trainers to use effective learning strategies, including interactive techniques, if and when appropriate
- How to design and evaluate performance-based assessment measures (e.g., project-based assessments, simulations, role plays)
- How to teach the trainers to use mediated instruction effectively
- How to get buy-in for the use of needs assessment and formative evaluation methods
- How to build the trainers confidence to respond and perform in front of peers when appropriate
- How to motivate the older employees
- How to build confidence to work effectively with clients

## Preliminary Analysis Questions

1. Make recommendations for the design decisions facing Frank and Semra.
2. Discuss the trainers' rationale for modifying existing programs. How can their concerns be addressed? Can you suggest modifications that are culturally sensitive?
3. Discuss the previous training experiences of the students in the new design program. What will their expectations be for the new curriculum? What kind of adjustments will they have to make? How can you facilitate this?
4. Provide a recommendation and rationale for selecting instructor(s) for these courses. How much should the instructor(s) be involved in decisions affecting classroom instructional strategies and assessment techniques?
5. Consider evaluation as a sensitive issue in this case. How should the effectiveness of the methods, materials, activities, and media be evaluated? How should the students be assessed?

## Implications for ID Practice

1. Describe how an instructional designer might deal with issues related to the use of interactive instructional strategies in contexts where such strategies are not common and might not be welcomed. Provide specific examples of adopting culturally sensitive methods.
2. Describe strategies for meeting the needs of older employees, as well as students who work full-time.
3. Describe the importance of conducting learner analysis in culturally diverse settings. What specific characteristics should be addressed?
4. Outline strategies for promoting needs analysis and formative evaluation techniques.

# PART II
## Case Studies

Section 3: Corporate Audience/Context

# Abby Carlin

## Documenting Processes in a Manufacturing Setting

*by Monica W. Tracey*

Just a few short months ago, while sitting in her final graduate instructional design course, Abby Carlin, a master's student in instructional technology, believed that she had found her life's profession. However, now that she had graduated and was standing in the middle of the floor of the Fritz David Manufacturing (FDM) steel stamping plant, she began to have doubts. FDM, a company that manufactures large steel car parts, had hired Learning Together Through Training, Inc. (LT3), the instructional design firm where Abby's former instructor, Dr. Joyce Abbott, was vice president of design. The contract was for the design and delivery of training on the use of steel blanker machines. These were large, 60-year-old machines used to stamp out car parts from flattened steel. Abby, who had never been in a manufacturing plant before, received a call from Dr. Abbott, asking her to come work with her on this project. "Abby, you will be perfect for the job," she explained, "and this will be a great experience for you." These words gave a nervous Abby little comfort as she approached her first real instructional design job. Abby wanted to make sure she followed all of the necessary steps and completed the project successfully.

Abby's main contact, Andrew Thomas, the plant manager, met with Abby while Dr. Abbott was wrapping up another project. Watching him approach, Abby recalled what Dr. Abbott had told her. "You will have to approach Andrew carefully," she had warned. "He is somewhat anxious about the training process, since he has never had a reason to use it before. Most of his senior employees have been working these machines for the past 30 years, and he has never had to train anyone. However, now that they are all retiring because of the incentives offered by FDM, he is faced with hiring new employees who have no idea how to operate this equipment. Andrew is just beginning to realize how much help he needs in this transition. That's why he's called us. He knows something must be done to keep production on track."

Andrew approached, holding out his hand. "Welcome to FDM," he said. "Why don't we go to the break room to talk?" They headed toward the break room located on the plant floor, and, after settling down with a cup of coffee, Andrew laid it on the line.

"This is the situation," he began. "Over the next 90 days, I have three shifts of employees retiring and being replaced by young, inexperienced operators. All of my guys have been with me for 30 years and have never needed any training to operate this equipment. The way I see it, the only way to learn how to use this equipment is while you're using it, and we've always had a new guy follow an old guy. But this time it's different, since there are so many new guys. We have to figure out a way to get them trained so I don't lose productivity."

"I'd like to begin by asking a few questions, if I could," Abby said.

"Fire away," Andrew replied.

"First of all, can you tell me a little bit more about the plant floor where the blanker machines are located?" Abby asked. Pulling out a notebook, Abby began to take notes.

"I'll take you on a tour in a minute, but, for the most part, it's a typical plant. All employees are required to wear safety equipment, goggles, hard hats, earplugs, and hard-toed shoes. The noise levels are pretty high down there, so there isn't much talking, and the lighting is bad. If the employees need to talk, they use this break room." He pointed to the wall, where a large bulletin board was filled with papers. "There's a board over there. They all know to check it for messages and announcements at the beginning and end of every shift."

"Can you tell me more about the current employees who operate the machines?" Abby then asked.

Andrew replied, "For the most part, my guys are ready to retire. They are a good group of men, but, once they knew they were leaving, that was it. They aren't really interested in training the new guys. The problem is, they are the only ones who know how to operate the equipment. I came in as the foreman from another plant. Abby, I don't even know how to operate a blanker machine the entire way through. I have watched, but a lot goes on there that I just can't understand. We also don't have anything in writing on how to operate them."

"Can you tell me about the new employees you have hired?" Abby asked.

Andrew said, "For the most part, the new guys don't have a clue how to operate the blanker machines. Some have been in plants before; we even have a few transfers from other departments at FDM. They don't know what they have to do, even though all of them want to be here. We've had many applications, and we were able to pick the best of the best, which was great. The pay is good. We offer a lot of overtime, and this is known as a great plant to be in."

"Is it possible for me to meet one of the retiring employees now?" Abby asked.

Andrew, pleased with Abby's eagerness to learn more about the plant, replied, "Sure, let's go down to the floor now." The first stop was the safety area, where Abby received a pair of safety goggles, earplugs, and a hard hat. After putting on all of the equipment, she had difficulty hearing Andrew as he directed her to the stairway to the floor. Everything sounded muffled and looked darker because of the safety glasses.

The first stop on the tour for Abby and Andrew was the blanker machine operated by "Big Jon." She glanced at his name on his hard hat and began, "Hi, my name is Abby Carlin, and I am in charge of training the new employees to operate these machines. I was wondering if I could ask you a few questions." Big Jon stared and shrugged. Andrew signaled to Abby that he couldn't hear her. "My first lesson learned," Abby said to herself. "It's instinct to talk to the worker to get information, but I can see that's not going to work here." Abby decided to observe what Jon was doing. "I'm going to have to come back and really watch him," she thought to herself, "but he's moving so fast I'm going to have a hard time writing down what he's doing." Andrew signaled that it was time to move on.

An hour later they finished their tour of the plant floor. As Abby took off her safety gear, she commented, "Well, Andrew, that was an eye opener. This is going to be a bigger job than I first realized. I'd like to come back tomorrow to observe Jon and try to document the process."

"That's not a problem," Andrew told her. "Keep your safety glasses, earplugs, and hard hat, and, when you come in tomorrow, stop by my office and I will give you the proper identification to get on the floor."

As she was walking to her car, Abby recalled that one of the things Andrew had mentioned was that the only way the new workers could really learn how to operate the equipment was by using it. "Where do I begin?" she thought on her way back to LT3 headquarters.

The following day, Abby was back at the plant, watching Jon as he operated one of the blanker stamping machines. She tried to write down the steps he was taking, but had difficulty seeing the buttons he was pushing. In fact, she had problems seeing at all with the poor lighting and the safety glasses. Abby also felt frustrated, since she couldn't talk to Jon as he worked, and he showed no interest in slowing down or demonstrating the steps for her. "I can see now how the trainees need to learn on this equipment, but I can't even write down the steps they need to follow, let alone create classroom training here on the plant floor," she thought. "I can't believe I have to train everyone while keeping up production. Boy, do I need to talk with Dr. Abbott." Abby left the plant after stopping by Andrew's office, where he reiterated the tight deadline. "Don't forget, Abby, we need three shifts of employees trained in 90 days," he reminded her.

"You can count on us," she assured him. As she made her way to the parking lot, she wished she felt as confident as she had sounded.

On her drive to LT3, Abby had a comforting thought. "I think the blanker operators hold the key to making this training a success. I must figure out a way to document the steps they take in operating the equipment and how to talk to them where they can hear me. Then, I have to figure out a way to train the new employees on the equipment. I'm sure I can do this. I just need to figure it out."

A short time later, while in conversation with Dr. Abbott, Abby began to feel more confident. Dr. Abbott said, "The most important thing for you to do, Abby, is to think outside of the box. I brought you in on this project because you didn't seem to be stuck in a certain design or delivery mode. Let's take a minute and list what we know and all of the needs and constraints we have to work with. Once you write down what you know, that will help you define our needs and constraints. Then we can develop our plan. Let's begin with our list." Dr. Abbott wrote the words "Our Needs" on one sheet of flip chart paper and used a second one to write "Our Constraints." "Let's begin here," said Dr. Abbott, pointing at the first flip chart.

## Preliminary Analysis Questions

1. What should be included on the two lists that Abby and Joyce are creating?
2. How can Abby work with the current employees to document the steps of operating the blanker stamping equipment?

3. What did Abby observe on the plant floor that can inform the training design?
4. Given the constraints in the case, what instructional strategies can be used to deliver the training?

# Implications for ID Practice

1. How can designers perform a task analysis in situations where it is difficult to capture and document task components?
2. Manufacturing environments tend to require a range of cognitive, procedural, and psychomotor skills of their employees. What are some ID approaches that extend beyond the ADDIE model in these settings?
3. How can instructional designers gather task information from subject matter experts who are unable or unwilling to provide all the required information?

# CASE STUDY 20

# Iris Daniels

## Cross-Cultural Challenges in Designing Instruction

*by Timothy W. Spannaus and Toni Stokes Jones*

## Prototype Review Meeting

Finally, the project was coming together! Iris Daniels and her team had just agreed to create a prototype and present it to the seven-member consortium of software users. The prototype would show both the instructional and technical approaches of the web-based training software that they wanted to see developed. Iris was hopeful that the prototype would be positively received by all of the consortium members and would enable development to proceed. Iris had worked for Jim Huggins on many projects with their client, Hill Industries, and knew the importance of prototyping to communicate design, instructional approach, or feasibility. But getting to this prototype had taken longer than anyone had expected. This was Iris's first time working with an international team and, in addition to having to reach consensus regarding the prototype, she had to learn the corporate cultures of the organizations that made up the consortium.

## Two Years Ago: Initial WBT Design

Hill Industries depended on a complex suite of manufacturing management software products used by thousands of engineers and product designers within Hill and its suppliers. The software was developed by a French software developer, Lapin. For years, all of the training on the software had been in the classroom, led by a trainer. Several years ago, Hill Industries joined a consortium of large companies from several countries. About two years ago, the consortium members began to push Lapin to offer web-based training (WBT) for the software. That request fit with Lapin's business strategy, so they began developing the WBT.

The initial version Lapin produced had disappointed some members of the seven-member consortium, especially the U.S. Americans. The WBT was attractively designed and very well written, especially considering that the developers were all working in a second language. However, it was not very interactive. For example, a lesson about designing a piston consisted of descriptions for the learner to read, followed by step-by-step exercises to be completed using the software. Because the lessons were not written in an interactive authoring system but in a word processor, there was no feedback. In fact, the learner could do anything or nothing in the exercise, and the lesson did not respond at all. Learners had little control; they could only access a menu or click "Next" or "Back."

## WBT Review Meeting

The Lapin development team had demonstrated the WBT at a consortium meeting. The consortium members were happy to have something with which to work. However, the U.S. Americans pushed for more interactive designs and wanted to include simulations, case studies, and feedback to help learners improve their performance. Still, Lapin believed that there were technical constraints, beginning with the requirement that the WBT run on a wide variety of browsers and platforms, from workstations to smart phones, sharply limiting what development tools would work. The consortium members agreed that the technical issues would work themselves out over time, as the development tools improved. Far more difficult, it seemed, were the expectations of which training approach made sense for the users. The design that Lapin had produced was one with which it was comfortable. The U.S. Americans, influenced by their instructional design training, were expecting something more task-oriented and interactive.

Iris began the discussion by raising questions about practice, feedback, and transfer. The blank stares from the French and German participants were a surprise to the U.S. Americans. Jonathan Naik, a U.S. engineer from another large Lapin software customer, described some of the WBT with which he was familiar. "In the past, we have demonstrated the procedure, then had the learner practice it, decreasing the amount of help and reinforcement as he or she continued to practice."

"Are you sure that's what learners want or expect now?" was the polite but incredulous response from Jacqueline Colbert, the lead training developer from Lapin. She had never used such a design and wasn't quite sure what to think of it. "I think they might want a theory section, and then a problem to work on, don't you? Maybe we could run a screen capture video to demonstrate the task. That would take care of it." For the rest of the afternoon, the consortium talked through various design approaches, without coming to any agreement. Not only could they not agree, but it seemed that, though everyone was speaking English, they were not communicating.

Iris and Jacqueline left the meeting together, talking about the design of Lapin's WBT. Back in Jacqueline's office, Iris showed her some web-based training her company had developed for other large clients. "We have always tried to avoid any long sections where the learner is just reading," Iris explained. "We've used a couple of case studies, walking the learner through the first one. The learner is always doing something, maybe clicking or filling in a field to respond to a question or problem, but it's always related to the task or procedure. That way, from the beginning, the learner is practicing."

Jacqueline went through a portion of Iris's demo, and then responded, "To me this seems as if it might work, though I think some users would think it's too simple. I'd still like to have a theory section to explain what it is we want the learner to do, and why."

When the user consortium met again the next morning, there were two agenda items— one on design, the other on technical standards. They decided to start with design. Dieter Hoffman, the engineering representative from a German aircraft company, asked if he could speak. Dieter rarely spoke at the consortium meetings but was always well prepared and worth listening to whenever he did speak. He plugged his laptop into the projector and began what appeared to be a prepared presentation. Very thorough and nuanced, he restated everyone's positions on the design, including both theoretical and practical viewpoints. He observed, as no one else had, that instructional design language and thinking pervaded U.S. but not French, training. Indeed, French universities generally do not have anything like instructional design in their programs. "So yesterday's discussion," Dieter observed, "did not move us forward, but only around each other."

As the meeting continued, Iris observed that some of the things she had said to Jacqueline in their private conversation yesterday were coming out in the meeting. Jacqueline shared with the group that, after some consideration of the U.S. approach to having practice and feedback as part of the WBT, she felt it was appropriate. The consortium didn't come to any agreement on design, but at least they understood each other's positions a little better, thanks to Dieter.

The afternoon session dealt with technical standards, about which there was little disagreement. The only reasonable way to achieve the cross-platform compatibility necessary was to adopt HTML5 as a standard, avoid plug-ins, and use only the major web browsers. The decision not to use plug-ins took a while to sort through, but the objective was that the WBT should run the same on the Windows and Mac platforms and several varieties of smart phones and tablets. Plug-ins might not exist for all those platforms, or they might not work identically. With a little better understanding on design and agreement on technology, the consortium members headed home from the meeting, agreeing to meet again in three months in the United States.

# Back in the Office

Once back in the office, Iris debriefed with Jim Huggins about the plans for meeting with Hill Industries in a day or so. Jim thought the technical decisions made at the consortium meeting were good, but the design decision (or lack of it) baffled him. Then, when Iris talked about the way the meetings went, a thought struck him. "OK, let me see if I understand. During discussions in the meeting, you and Jacqueline didn't seem to connect. She basically used the meeting to report on what she had decided. Discussion seemed to go nowhere."

"Right," Iris replied. "Then, when we talked outside the meeting, we had a good exchange of ideas. However, the next morning, she reported some of our discussion as her ideas."

"Got it," Jim said. "So maybe what you want to do is make sure you have more one-on-one discussions with Jacqueline. You might also want to meet individually with the other French people, hash out ideas, then use the meetings as a forum where people can bring decisions to be ratified. I think we might find that different cultures view the purposes of meetings differently. As I recall from my business trip to France last year, the French are more comfortable making decisions outside of public meetings. The U.S. idea of coming to a meeting for the purpose of discussing and deciding is literally quite foreign to them." He smiled. "Meanwhile, why don't we prototype a short learning module that demonstrates our design ideas and that incorporates elements of the French approach? Let's talk it over with Hill and see if we can build something that will communicate our ideas better than the discussion did."

## A Meeting at Hill Industries

The next day, Jim and Iris met with Kimberly Mooney, their client at Hill Industries. Kimberly was the project leader of the group that trained the prospective users of the Lapin software. Kimberly thought the prototype would help communicate the design approach the U.S. Americans had in mind and would show that the technical approach the consortium agreed on would work. Jim agreed that they could show feasibility with the prototype, but it would be a challenge. After all, they needed to simulate a complex system, with just a browser and no plug-ins. Jim, Iris, and Kimberly agreed to create a prototype to demonstrate the design they wanted and to show that it could actually be done, given the technical constraints.

The design would need the following segments and would need to allow the user to modify an existing part with and without assistance:

- A theory section, which they called "logic," that explained the procedure and showed which functions of the software were used
- A demonstration, which used a screen capture video to show the procedure, with a voice-over narration; they decided to call this one "show me"
- A guided simulation, in which the learner completed all the steps in the procedure, with step-by-step prompts; they called this one "try it with a little help"
- An unguided simulation, in which the learner completed all the steps but without the prompts; they called this one "on your own"
- An assessment, in which the learner used the Lapin software to complete the procedure and then compare his or her result to the result in the lesson, using a checklist to highlight important measures of accuracy; they called this one "putting it all together"

"This is a good start," said Jim. "Now the hard part begins. Let's get to work developing our prototype."

## Preliminary Analysis Questions

1. How was the design process beginning with the initial design of the WBT to the proposed elements of the prototype influenced by the different backgrounds of the consortium members?
2. Evaluate Jim and Iris's approach to handling cultural differences among consortium members.
3. Critique the elements of the prototype proposed by Iris, Jim, and Kimberly. What would you add or eliminate, if anything?
4. What outcomes might Iris expect from the demonstration of the prototype?

## Implications for ID Practice

1. What steps should a designer take to prepare for working on a cross-cultural team?
2. Discuss the importance of bringing to the surface assumptions about teaching and learning among members of an instructional design team.
3. In what ways can the development of a prototype help or hinder further design and development work?

# Lynn Dixon

## Designing an Interactive Kiosk to Celebrate World Wetlands Day

*by Christie Nelson*

Lynn Dixon is an instructional designer at a small e-learning company in Sydney, Australia, called Telopea Learning. Telopea Learning creates online training for a variety of clients including banks, insurance companies, government departments, and the retail industry. It's a fast-paced working environment with tight deadlines. However, the company also encourages a fresh, lively atmosphere, with music playing, frequent company fun days, and sporting events. Lynn often wonders how she's meant to keep her clients happy while having all of that fun!

Lynn has been working at Telopea Learning for almost a year. She took this job after she moved to Australia from the United States, where she grew up. Although Lynn had very similar work experiences in the United States, she has discovered some interesting differences between U.S. and Australian workplace cultures. The Australians seem much more casual about things, whereas her American colleagues were very "by the book." Lynn has a master's degree in educational technology with a focus on instructional design. She was surprised to learn that not many of her colleagues at Telopea Learning had ID degrees; instead, many were hired in from other disciplines and had acquired their learning "on the job." As a result of her formal education and experience, Lynn was quickly regarded as one of their best designers and asked to take the lead on many projects.

## A New Project for Lynn

It's now 9:00 on Monday morning, and Lynn has been at her desk for a couple of hours. Coming in early allows her to get her to-do list organized and to make sure she's ready for the week ahead, before others get to work and start needing to talk with her, ask questions, troubleshoot issues, and so on. People are starting to arrive now, and the familiar hum of phones ringing, keyboards clicking, and conversation fills the large open-plan workspace. Lynn glances up and sees her colleague, Janette Parks, giving her a wave from across the room. Lynn recognizes the look on Janette's face—*she's going to ask me to do something*. Janette is the head of the sales team at Telopea Learning. It's an important role—Janette is the person who secures project work with new and existing clients for the company. Lynn finds herself wishing she could be more involved in these conversations, because there often seems to be a disconnect between what is sold to the client and what the company is capable of achieving within the time and budget allowed. It's a problem that Lynn often finds herself resolving. Janette is walking over to Lynn's desk now.

"We've got a really exciting new project kicking off this week, and I'm told you're going to be the lead on it," Janette begins excitedly. Lynn gets a nervous feeling in the pit of her stomach; she's already quite busy and wonders how she'll fit another project into her schedule. "It's working with the Marine Park on a touch-screen kiosk for The Aquarium in Cairns (see Figure 21–1) to celebrate World Wetlands Day." Lynn's interest picks up. Lately, she's been working on some really mundane projects, and the idea of doing something for a public institution is appealing. "We need to fly up there on Wednesday for a day trip to get things started. Can you run the kickoff meeting?"

Janette tells Lynn more of the project details. The Aquarium is building a new wetlands exhibit to enhance their already impressive collection of fish tanks and aquatic exhibits. The new exhibit will include visual displays, 25,000 liters of water, 800 fish, and a 3-meter-high waterfall, all designed to show the connection between the wetlands and the Great Barrier Reef. The team responsible for the exhibit is led by Laura Barton, who works within the government department responsible for The Aquarium. As a part of the

**FIGURE 21–1**  Map of Australia.

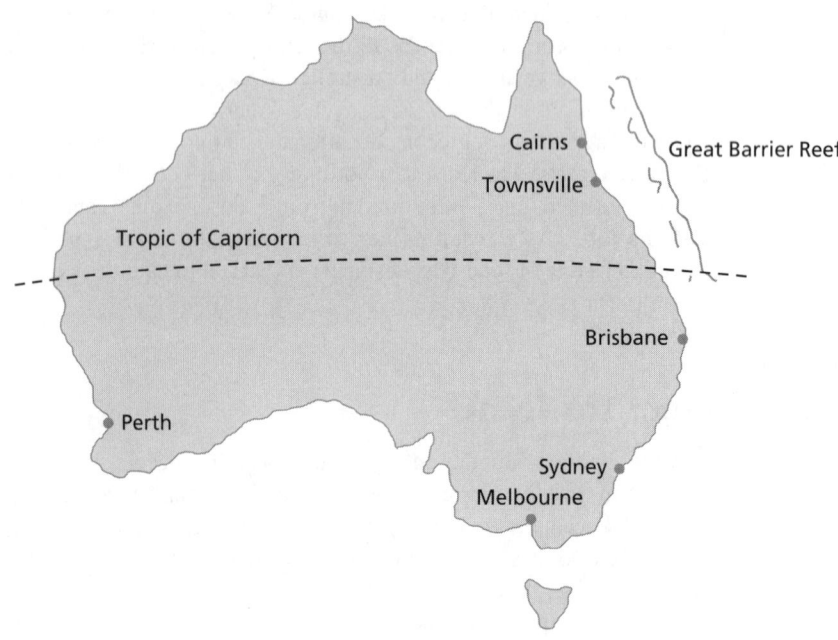

wetlands exhibit, Laura wants to develop a touch-screen kiosk to provide another way for visitors to explore and learn about the wetlands. Telopea Learning has been contracted to provide the software for the kiosk. Laura has engaged another provider to supply the necessary hardware.

For the first time in a while, Lynn is thrilled to be taking on a new project. This is the type of work she imagined herself doing when she was in graduate school. She spends the next day getting her other projects in order and doing some initial reading about touch-screen interfaces and instructional design. Lynn has only designed instruction for the traditional computer screen, so there are a lot of new factors to consider. On Tuesday night, she sets her alarm for 5 A.M. in order to make it to the airport on time for their early-morning flight to Cairns.

## A Visit to the Client Site

Lynn steps off the plane into the warm and humid Queensland sun on Wednesday morning. It's a refreshing feeling after leaving Sydney on a chilly morning. The change in climate she experiences is similar to traveling from New York to Florida or the Bahamas. Lynn is a bit chagrined that she finds Sydney winters cold after enduring harsh Chicago winters for the previous five years, but she does sometimes. Now she can feel the warm, wet air opening up her sinuses and rousing her out of her sleepy haze. She and Janette hail a cab and head over to The Aquarium. They get out of the cab and walk up the front steps, weaving their way through clusters of schoolchildren waiting excitedly to enter the building. Going through the front gates, Lynn sees a couple of friendly-looking people waiting for them by a large fish tank. Laura introduces herself and Ben Williams, the Education Manager at The Aquarium, and suggests they take a quick tour of The Aquarium before getting started. Lynn welcomes the chance to walk around and stretch her legs.

They step into a world of marine life and beautiful coral as they make their way through a maze of tunnels that go around, above, and through enormous tanks of water. They step into the construction area for the new wetlands exhibit. Ben shows Lynn and Janette where the kiosk will be in relation to the new waterfall and fish tank. Lynn is impressed, and excited that her work will be on display in such an amazing environment.

They leave the exhibit area and sit down in a meeting room. Lynn hands out the meeting agenda and some sample project documents (project plan, phases, etc.) to Laura and Ben. They begin by discussing their roles and responsibilities. Laura is the project sponsor—she works for the government and is busy with several other projects—so she wants to be involved only in major reviews and signoffs, not in the day-to-day running of the project. That involvement falls to Ben, who will coordinate directly with Lynn and also serve as the subject matter expert (SME). Ben will be available to answer Lynn's questions and will also do all preliminary reviews and provide feedback for the project deliverables. He will manage the project timeline on the client side and report progress back to Laura.

He's also a resident wetlands expert. Ben readily admits that he could talk about the wetlands for hours, if permitted. He hands some brochures, books, and posters to Lynn, and she wonders how she'll carry them all onto the plane back to Sydney. He also promises to provide more information electronically.

Ben then provides an overview of the general requirements for the kiosk software. The theme of the new exhibit is Connections—between the Great Barrier Reef, the wetlands, and the catchment areas. The various displays in the exhibit will demonstrate the relationships and interconnectedness among these three environments. Ben and Laura are hoping the kiosk can really emphasize these relationships. They also want the kiosk to provide information about the different types of wetlands. In addition to being placed in the exhibit at The Aquarium, similar kiosks are also going to be displayed at several regional information centers. Laura suggests that the software should somehow acknowledge each of these regional areas by name and description, because each has provided significant funding and support for the project. Another important theme in the kiosk should be the role wetlands play in Aboriginal culture and heritage. Laura isn't sure how this could be depicted, but Ben thinks there might be some stories included in the materials he provided. Lynn agrees to keep this in mind as she is looking through the materials.

The group stops for a minute and then discusses the options for presenting the information on the screen. Ben enthusiastically describes his idea of showing a bird flying high in the sky, zooming around looking down on the catchment, then quickly flying down into a more detailed billabong setting. Lynn's eyes widen as she throws Janette a sideways glance. Janette has a way of encouraging clients to think big, even if their budgets and timeframes are small. At this point Janette chimes in and reviews the project Statement of Work, which specifies the agreed total content time of 20 minutes at an average interactivity level of "Medium" across the entire kiosk. Medium, unfortunately, does not include things like zooming animated bird life. Lynn is reminded of her frustration with these metrics. What really defines a minute of e-learning? How can she reliably judge the "interactivity" of the ideas they were discussing? This is one thing she's always wanted to improve about the way her company sells and quotes on projects.

The discussion of the 20-minute time limit reminds Ben of another kiosk requirement. They want to be able to measure how much time any learner spends in a particular kiosk section and have a report that indicates the most popular and longest viewed sections. This will allow them to identify areas for improvement and changes for future versions. Janette nods to indicate that this was included in the project scope and mentions to Lynn that Telopea Learning's technical developers shouldn't have an issue with making this happen. Janette then reminds Ben and Laura that although audio narration will be included in the kiosk, the budget did not allow for the hiring of professional voice talent to do the recordings. Instead, the team would use voices from individuals who work at Telopea Learning.

At this stage, Lynn steers the conversation back to how a typical project should run and provides some more detail about next steps. Lynn will return to Telopea Learning's office in Sydney and review all of the content that Ben has provided. She'll decide what topics and activities make the most sense to include in the kiosk and summarize this information in a high-level instructional design document. Laura and Ben are looking forward to seeing this and remind Lynn to call them if any questions come up as she is working. Everyone is happy as the meeting concludes. As they are walking out, Laura quickly mentions to Lynn that she could easily get access to a pilot group of users if needed. There is a senior citizens group that regularly tours The Aquarium and often does small volunteer projects for them. Lynn and Janette say thanks, goodbye, and grab a cab back to the airport. Lynn's stomach begins growling. Why isn't there ever time to eat on these day trips?

## Lynn Reflects on Initial Client Meeting: What Now?

Before takeoff, Janette quickly downloads the day's e-mails onto her phone so she can review them during the flight. Lynn exhales, relaxes into the headrest, and closes her eyes for just a moment. This is often her favorite moment of a day trip—the work is done, and now she just has to fly home. As she begins contemplating how she's going to tackle the design of the kiosk, she is interrupted by a slight nudge and question from Janette.

"So, Lynn, what is your next step with this?"

"Well, it's going to take some time for me to review all of this content. I think Ben gave me three times more than I'll end up using. Once I get some ideas about major themes, I'll start working on the high-level design document."

"Great. So when do you think you might be able to get something back to them? Can you also do the detailed project plan by the end of this week? We'll need to book the development resources."

"Sure, Janette. I have to tell you it seems like Ben has some pretty high expectations about the 'bells and whistles' that might appear in the kiosk. Did you show him some examples of what we could do within their budget?"

"Oh, we looked at a lot of demos together during the web conference we had before they decided to work with us. I know we've got just a medium level of interactivity here, but that's an average, remember, so we might be able to get something short and fancy in there, don't you think? Don't worry, Lynn—if you run into any issues just bring me back into the loop." The flight attendant then announces that the plane has reached its cruising altitude and that electronic devices are now safe to be used, reminding passengers to ensure that their phones are switched to flight mode. Janette begins sorting through her e-mails from the day.

Lynn rests her head again and stretches out her legs. Although the wetlands content is certainly more exciting than insurance product training (her other big project at the moment), she has some concerns. She's never designed for touch-screen devices before. Lynn makes a mental note to do more research on this. Where should the buttons and links go on the screen? Is there an optimal size? She also wonders if Telopea's graphic designer would have any input. How is she going to fit this work into her already fully scheduled week? She contemplates an ideal world where this is her only project and she has unlimited time at her disposal to make it really amazing. Unfortunately, this is not Lynn's reality. She is limited not only by time but also the very tight budget for the project. Lynn hopes she'll be able to keep everyone as happy as they were at the conclusion of today's meeting. She begins to drift off to sleep as the flight to Sydney continues.

# Design Document Review

Two weeks have passed and Lynn is about to participate in a phone conference with Ben and Laura to discuss their review of her design document (Figure 21–2).

Lynn finds a conference room and dials into the conference line. Ben and Laura haven't arrived yet. She drums her fingers in time with the hold music and looks over the printout of their review. They seem to be generally happy with the design, but it sounds like they just want more—of everything. Lynn wishes Janette could have been involved in the call, but she was asked to attend an "important meeting" at the last minute. Salespeople—they always seemed to have important meetings. Although Lynn wishes she could do everything the client wants, she knows she'll also have to ask for a budget increase to make it all happen.

*Beep*. Ben and Laura have just joined the call.

"Hello, there," Lynn says.

"G'day!" Ben sounds in a cheerful mood, which relaxes Lynn a little.

"Thank you for sending through your review comments," Lynn begins. "We'll go through them together in this call so that you can be sure I understand all of your points. I'm sorry that Janette couldn't be here for the call, but I'll get her to follow up on any issues pertaining to the project later today if needed, okay?"

Laura responds, "No worries. We really liked the design, Lynn. It's a great start. Isn't it exciting to imagine what this thing is going to look like? We've never been involved in this sort of project before, and so far we're really enjoying it." She continues to discuss what they liked about the design, including the use of the "Regional Showcase." She mentions that there are now several more regional wetlands they need to include here. She also liked the section about "Types of Wetlands."

Ben then joins in to discuss some of their concerns.

"Lynn, I am not sure where we're going to see anything about the Aboriginal relationship with the wetlands," he begins. "Can we include some of their storytelling here? It would be great if we could get someone to read an Aboriginal Dreamtime story on the kiosk. Hmmm, you probably don't have anyone of Aboriginal descent working at Telopea Learning, do you? I think people might be confused by your American accent!"

"No, we don't," Lynn replies. "But we can look into hiring an actor if you think this is critical—I'll just have Janette provide you with a cost estimate."

"Ah, well—I'm not sure we've got any additional budget for that, but let me see if I can find someone here. We could probably fly them down to you for a recording session, too, or look into getting a recording done here."

**FIGURE 21–2** Lynn's Design Document.

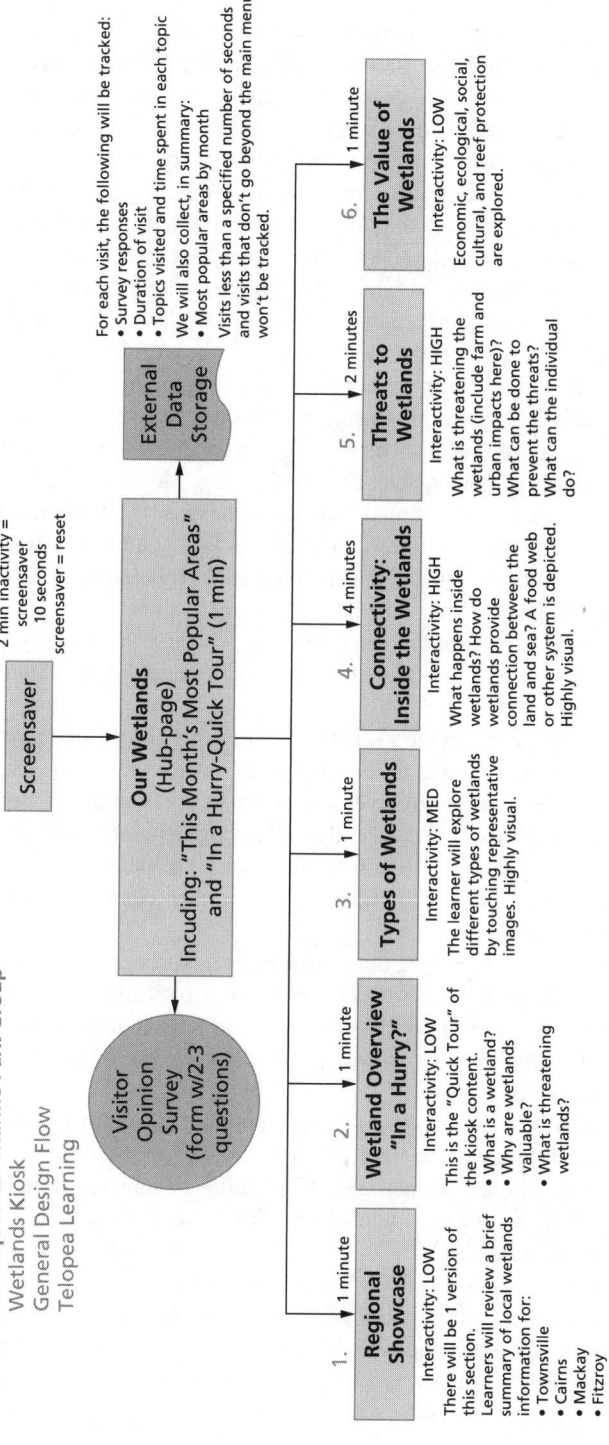

The Aquarium–Marine Park Group
Wetlands Kiosk
General Design Flow
Telopea Learning

**Screensaver**

2 min inactivity = screensaver
10 seconds
screensaver = reset

**Our Wetlands (Hub-page)**
Incuding: "This Month's Most Popular Areas" and "In a Hurry-Quick Tour" (1 min)

Visitor Opinion Survey (form w/2-3 questions)

**External Data Storage**

For each visit, the following will be tracked:
• Survey responses
• Duration of visit
• Topics visited and time spent in each topic
We will also collect, in summary:
• Most popular areas by month
Visits less than a specified number of seconds and visits that don't go beyond the main menu won't be tracked.

1 minute
1. **Regional Showcase**
Interactivity: LOW
There will be 1 version of this section. Learners will review a brief summary of local wetlands information for:
• Townsville
• Cairns
• Mackay
• Fitzroy

1 minute
2. **Wetland Overview "In a Hurry?"**
Interactivity: LOW
This is the "Quick Tour" of the kiosk content.
• What is a wetland?
• Why are wetlands valuable?
• What is threatening wetlands?

1 minute
3. **Types of Wetlands**
Interactivity: MED
The learner will explore different types of wetlands by touching representative images. Highly visual.

4 minutes
4. **Connectivity: Inside the Wetlands**
Interactivity: HIGH
What happens inside wetlands? How do wetlands provide connection between the land and sea? A food web or other system is depicted. Highly visual.

2 minutes
5. **Threats to Wetlands**
Interactivity: HIGH
What is threatening the wetlands (include farm and urban impacts here)? What can be done to prevent the threats? What can the individual do?

1 minute
6. **The Value of Wetlands**
Interactivity: LOW
Economic, ecological, social, cultural, and reef protection are explored.

201

"OK, that sounds promising. I was actually wondering if you had considered involving the local university in the project. They might have access to more content resources, or people of Aboriginal descent to help us out," says Lynn.

"That's a great idea, Lynn," Ben responds. "I'll look into it."

Ben continues to discuss some other issues. "I really was hoping to see some type of game or fancy animation. Could we do something cool in the 'Threats to Wetlands' section? I'd like the users to really understand the impacts that urban development is having on the wetlands, such as pollution, as well as the effects the wildlife population is feeling. I also couldn't tell where the fancy sky-level animation of the catchment area was going to appear. You remember the one I told you about during our meeting?"

Lynn hesitates for a moment, unsure how to respond. She begins by addressing the game request. "I think we could definitely come up with some ideas for a game. It would have to be pretty simple to stay within our current project scope; however, I imagine we could do a type of discovery module where learners investigate the impact of different types of development, such as cane farming. This could be fun!"

"About the animation, I'm going to have to chat with Janette about how much we can do. We are only able to use the graphics that you have provided for us; however, we can manipulate them to some extent. We could probably come up with a nice high-level view of the catchment with some help from you."

"Well, I'd be super-keen to come down for a working session with you and the graphic designers if you like—that shouldn't be an issue!" Ben is always so enthusiastic, it's hard for Lynn to say no.

Laura jumps in with one final point. "Lynn, I'd like to understand more about how you're going to cater to the variety of visitors The Aquarium receives every day. As you've seen, we've got everyone from school-aged children to senior citizens attending the exhibits. There are also some significant world authorities on wetlands who will be interested in viewing it. We also get a lot of international visitors who may only speak a little English. How are you going to ensure that the software will be relevant to everyone?"

Lynn was expecting this question, as it has been something she also wondered herself. "Well, Laura, I think we'll have to get a bit further in the design process before this becomes apparent. I do think that some of the sections will be more relevant to particular audiences than others. However, the combination of all sections should provide a bit of something for everyone."

"OK, that makes sense," Laura replied. "I look forward to the next step, then!"

Lynn breathes an internal sigh of relief that Laura was satisfied with her answer. This is definitely something she's going to have to think through further. And with that, along with the typical discussions about what would be coming next, they conclude the call.

Lynn returns to her desk and reviews her ever-growing to-do list. Various issues of concern are swimming around in her head. In addition to the audience issue that Laura raised, many other questions remain unanswered. She puts her notes aside for a moment and decides to run downstairs for a chicken Caesar wrap and some hot chips.

# Preliminary Analysis Questions

1. Lynn needs to design a solution that works for a variety of learners. How would you design learning experiences that will provide something for everyone?
2. How could a touch-screen kiosk be best used to teach wetlands-related content at The Aquarium? Consider the learning environment, audience characteristics, average time someone will spend, etc.
3. Lynn's initial design document is basic. Choose one section and provide more detailed instructional design strategies that you would use to present the content, using screen sketches and diagrams.
4. Ben is an enthusiastic subject matter expert with a lot of grand ideas. How can Lynn keep him happy while still managing the project within budget?
5. Finding a way to recognize the role the wetlands play in Aboriginal heritage will be difficult for Telopea Learning, especially given that none of the employees, or the clients, are of Aboriginal descent. What are the advantages and limitations of the suggestions made in the case to address this issue?
6. Lynn perceives a disconnect within Telopea Learning between the sales and design teams in regard to what can be achieved within a particular budget for a project. How would you work to improve this situation if you were in Lynn's shoes?

# Implications for Practice

1. What are some visual and instructional design strategies that would be unique to a touch-screen kiosk? What are some instructional design challenges when designing for learning with this technology?
2. Instructional designers often don't have time to perform any type of detailed analysis before beginning a design document. In what ways can designers incorporate an initial analysis "on the fly"?
3. Learning is becoming more and more learner driven, meaning that learners choose what they learn; they control the sequence of information and the amount of time they spend. How can instructional designers adapt instruction to this style of learning, while also ensuring that their learners know how to learn?

# Craig Gregersen

## Balancing a Range of Stakeholder Interests When Designing Instruction

*by Stephen Dundis*

Craig Gregersen was struggling to find his way through what no longer seemed to be a golden opportunity for his budding consulting practice. Five weeks previously, he had been hired by a large international corporation to design an important training program that would be delivered to its employees around the world. The assignment had seemed to be a perfect fit when the Electron Corporation asked him to be the lead designer for a course on product liability. He did, after all, have a law degree and had received his PhD in instructional design a year earlier. However, now it seemed that his name was going to be associated with a course that would satisfy no one and that would almost certainly not accomplish its intended goals.

## Background

When Craig originally spoke with the training project manager and the chair of the Safety Steering Committee at Electron, he had been invigorated by the prospect of using both of his degrees to educate people about an important issue and to increase the company's bottom line. The Electron Corporation was a leader in the design and manufacture of two-way radio systems, cell phones, pagers, and other communication devices, including accompanying software. Stan Neuhaus, one of the senior design engineers for the company and chair of the Safety Steering Committee, described how Electron took the quality and safety of its products seriously. Although product liability suits were not a large problem for the company, Electron was becoming aware of a number of situations that might produce liability—transmission systems interfering with the operation of other electronic equipment in hospitals, defective software causing shutdowns in police communication systems, battery disposal problems, and so on. And, as Electron became more and more involved in the production of consumer-oriented products, it was becoming increasingly concerned about appropriate designs and warnings for consumers.

Both Stan and the training project manager, Louise Masoff, told Craig that the course was intended to provide a proactive approach to product safety—one that would prevent lawsuits from happening. Other than that, however, the content of the course was up to Craig—whatever he thought was needed to make employees more conscious of product liability in their daily behavior. Both Stan and Louise stressed that they wanted a course that would address concerns at every level of the company. In this regard, they presented Craig with a list of initial contacts with line engineers and management at several installations across the country. He was also given free rein to make any other contacts that might prove useful.

Then, of course, the other shoe dropped. Craig was asked to start immediately because there was a lot of pressure to get a course up and running very quickly. Louise believed that two weeks of phone interviews would be enough time to determine what content needed to be included in the course, then another three weeks to develop the course. The course itself could be only a day long, maximum. According to Louise, even though this was considered an important topic, there were just too many other demands on employees' time. And, of course, "legal" (the legal department) would need to be consulted on everything. Louise was sure that legal would have plenty of ideas for him but said that sometimes "they could be pretty unapproachable." Stan added that legal felt rather strongly that it should be carrying out the training in this area but that a prior course it had put together had not gone over especially well.

However, Craig was not discouraged. He was already used to quick turnarounds. Legal might be a problem, but, looking on the bright side, it could be very helpful providing content for the course, including pending cases that might be used as examples. After all, Craig was a lawyer, too. That should eliminate a lot of communication problems. After some initial research, he was ready to start contacting the names he had been given.

## Gathering the Data

It didn't take Craig long to realize that there were more aspects to product liability at Electron than had been discussed in the original meeting. The basic law dealing with product liability was difficult for a layperson to understand, but, given that Electron had plants in 16 countries and conducted business in almost every other country, just understanding the international differences in liability would be a challenge even for a lawyer. In addition, engineering issues were not limited to design considerations. There were also process engineers, who dealt with the manufacturing process and attendant safety concerns, and field engineers, who dealt with the construction and maintenance of large systems, such as transmission antennas and radio relay stations. There was also a multitude of concerns ranging from appropriate procedures for product recalls and risk evaluations to attempts at keeping up with the constant regulatory changes issued by various standards organizations.

The first person Craig interviewed was Richard Mull, the legal contact he had been given. However, if Craig had expected a willing ear for what he saw as the challenges in designing the course, he was mistaken. Although cordial, Richard didn't waste time making it clear that he believed legal should be handling the education on these issues, rather than an outside consultant. When Craig started talking about the various content issues, Richard interjected that, rather than worrying about all the details, engineers needed to develop a general sensitivity to the "legal realities" and that just designing a product to the best of their ability might not be enough. In response to Craig's request for relevant examples, Richard stated that he couldn't discuss ongoing cases and that using any of these as an example in a class would be out of the question. Statements made about these cases could possibly be used against the company. He ended the conversation by suggesting to Craig that he review the four-hour course that Richard and his colleagues had developed several years back—a course that he still thought would be perfectly acceptable with just a few modifications.

Somewhat chastened, Craig started interviewing other people in Electron. He found that his list of suggested contacts blossomed (or maybe "exploded" was a better term) as he spoke with more and more people. Engineering not only broke down into process, product, and field concerns but also included management concerns that often tended to differ considerably from the concerns of engineers on the line. Line engineers wanted to know how to fix specific problems, whereas their managers wanted to know how to make the correct decisions about protecting their areas of responsibility along a number of fronts, often international in scope. Marketing and sales were also making themselves heard. For instance, how far could they go in making claims about various products without these claims coming back to haunt them later? There were also the installation, servicing, and maintenance sectors. How would improper repair or installation affect liability? Who took customer complaints, and how should complaints be processed and documented? How should products be disposed of safely? And there seemed to be no one entity responsible for keeping employees current on all of the manufacturing and design standards that were being promulgated.

## Complications

In a follow-up discussion with Stan Neuhaus, Craig became aware of an even bigger problem. Stan confided that many in engineering had believed for some time that product liability at Electron was much more a communication than a knowledge issue. He argued that, in spite of what legal thought, most engineers were already sensitive to product liability issues. What was lacking, according to these engineers, was a company-wide, systematic approach to these issues that addressed specific questions, such as the following: What was the chain of command for handling product liability issues throughout the company? Should there be a monitoring system for actively searching out potential product defects, and what should be included within it? What was the procedure for taking corrective action, such as a product recall, in a particular instance? How did one document the decision to warn rather than initiate a redesign, or should one do nothing at all? And what were the acceptable timeframes?

Stan produced the draft of a company-wide product safety program that established a comprehensive organizational structure and detailed procedures for a number of the issues he had mentioned. He believed that a course that centered on building an understanding of these procedures would go a long way toward educating people about what they needed to *do,* instead of discussing these issues in a general way. Stan added that the prior course that legal had presented was too mired in such generalities. They had provided few, if any, concrete answers as to what to do in particular situations. Besides, it had been almost all lecture and, after the first hour of hearing about common law principles, "people had found it pretty hard to stay awake."

Although Craig recognized that many engineers had a propensity to see product liability in terms of black and white (which he knew, as a lawyer, was not always possible), he also agreed that providing them with a structured way of dealing with a variety of day-to-day problems made sense. The draft of the company-wide product safety program was extensive. It provided an excellent start for a content outline for what he now considered to be a major part of the training. However, when Craig ran his idea by legal, Richard Mull curtly informed him that the draft had never been approved and that it should never have been passed around, particularly to an outside consultant. Richard argued that the problem with internal standards and procedures, especially when they were more stringent than general regulations and the common law, was that in effect they became a new standard to which the company could be held in a court of law—even if they had been intended only as general guidelines. Providing training on specific procedures and policies could be considered legally equivalent to having a written standard because it evidenced the company's intentions as to those procedures and policies. When Craig countered that the alternative might be even less palatable, Richard replied that this was why Electron had legal to advise it. He reiterated that the course needed to stay away from details, although he did not object to "jazzing it up somewhat" to keep everyone interested.

Craig left the meeting with the growing realization that the project was expanding and moving in several directions. He arranged a meeting with Louise Masoff to brainstorm ways of coping with the scope of the project. But he soon discovered that Louise did not feel that she was in a position to press for any changes to the course's one-day, all-in-one structure. She certainly did not want to get involved in a political tug-of-war with legal about the direction of the course. As he listened to Louise, Craig began to believe that he had been handed what many in Electron had probably already known was an instructional design minefield, with no readily acceptable solutions. In the end, he suspected, the prevailing wisdom had been to let someone from the outside take the fall.

## What to Do Now?

Craig sat in his hotel room, contemplating a project that seemed to be unraveling in front of his eyes. He had more content than he knew what to do with and a rapidly expanding group of target learners with varying interests, all squeezed into a course "box" that seemed way too small. Worse yet, he was being told to go in a design direction that would probably result in little performance change in the company. There would be almost no difference between Craig's course and the older and instructionally ineffective one, except that now the course would have his name on it. His sense of pride, as well as his ethics, would not let him accept this without a struggle. Craig truly wanted to design a course that would make a difference for Electron and its employees, but, with all the conflicting demands that he faced, how could he do this?

# Preliminary Analysis Questions

1. Identify the key issues Craig must consider as he decides what to do next. It might be useful to think in terms of types of issues—for example, needs assessment, organizational development, and instructional content analysis.
2. For each issue that you identify, what solution(s) would you suggest? Then consider the *interaction* of these issues. What effect will these interactions have on your proposed solutions?
3. How would you go about dealing with the impasse between the desire for specifics (engineering) and the desire for generalities (legal)?
4. Do you believe it is possible to accommodate the varying content interests in a day-long course? If so, how would you design the course? If not, what changes would you advise?
5. If you could get no agreement from the various interests and it was decided that you would present essentially a "regurgitated" version of the previous course, how would you react? Provide a rationale for your reaction.

# Implications for ID Practice

1. What organizational issues within a corporate setting can affect the success of an instructional design project?
2. Describe strategies for achieving agreement and buy-in for a training project when stakeholder groups have differing and opposing needs. How might an outside consultant go about making his or her voice heard within a large corporation when decision makers are unable or unwilling to break through an impasse?
3. Describe strategies for dealing with resource and time limitations that interfere with the adequate completion of an instructional design project. How does one make an objective determination of what is "adequate" under a particular set of circumstances?
4. What issues need to be discussed and made part of the consultant/client contract at the beginning of an instructional design project?
5. What are the ethical issues involved for an instructional designer when the client insists on something that the consultant does not believe is in the best interests of the overall project?

# CASE STUDY 23

# Scott Hunter

## Developing Online Assessment in an International Setting

*by David L. Solomon*

Scott Hunter. Vice President, Creative Director. Automotive Performance Improvement Consultants (APIC). There I was—staring at my business card minutes before a tough meeting—and the only insight I could seem to muster was that my title didn't really reflect what I did. I had no idea where I would begin when I approached my supervisor, Ken Young, with the most recent challenge facing the international training team. I remembered being thrilled about my international job assignment—a real opportunity to apply so much of my training in instructional design and technology—but frustration soon replaced enthusiasm.

We had confronted many problems over the past year, and we were now so close to launching the sales consultant certification program that everyone could taste it. One last hurdle remained, and it was gnawing at me. I had to stop myself from saying what I truly felt when Ken asked, "Can you refresh my memory and help me understand what's going on?"

In the first few minutes of my meeting with Ken, I explained the turmoil that seemed to plague this project. First there was Katarina (Kat) Wilder, the abusive training manager at the client organization, Trans-Continental Motors (TCM), who once held the position currently occupied by Antoine Devereux (Figure 23–1).

I couldn't believe it had taken so long for Bob Kelly, the senior manager, to do something about her constant diatribes, but there was an ocean between them and so much red tape. Kat was skilled at generating lengthy e-mail messages and creating a lot of "busy work," but she had no vision of the desired outcomes. We flew overseas for several meetings with TCM and found that "next steps" were always unclear and several disparate projects seemed to appear as each conversation with her unfolded. I remembered wondering if she even knew we were the training supplier or merely considered us to be another department in the advertising agency where we resided. Either way, it was clear to me that we were underused. Unknown to APIC, Kat had been working with Antoine, the training manager from France at that time, to create a certification test for sales consultants. She and Antoine were clandestinely working with a close relative of Antoine's to coordinate a pilot.

"So, Kat was working on a pilot program with Antoine, who hired one of his relatives to develop the certification test, and no one from APIC knew about it?"

**FIGURE 23–1** Client and Consultant Organizational Flowcharts for an International Training Team.

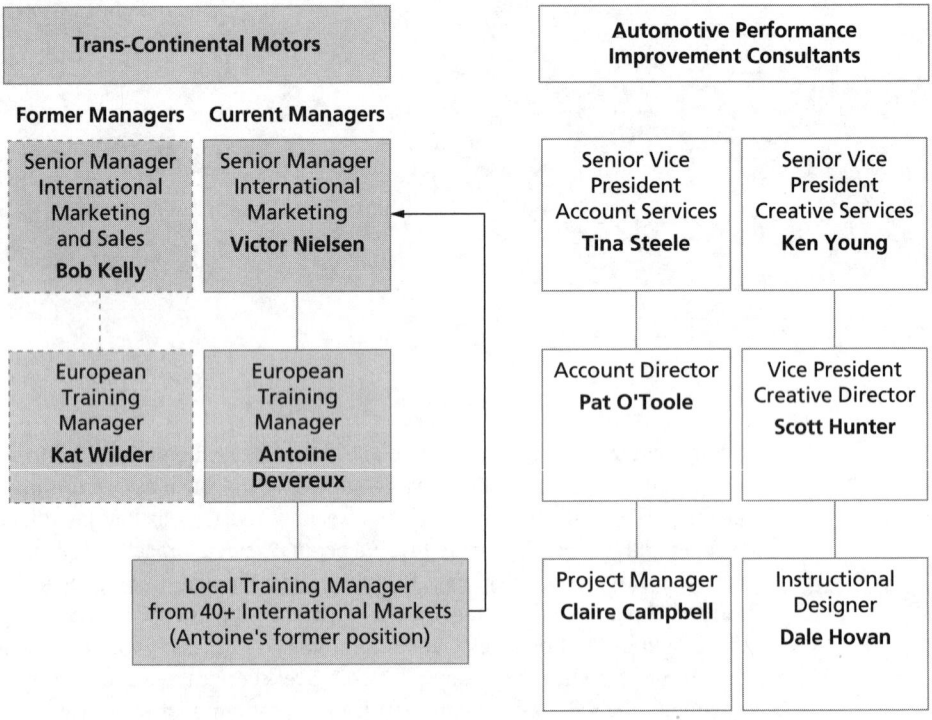

"That's right," I said to Ken, half-surprised that he was following this soap opera. "The certification test was the most critical piece of the certification program, and we had a clearly defined strategy. But, there's more to the story, and a few twists and turns along the way," I said as I continued with the saga.

"We've had our share of headaches, too. We lost about three or four months because of turnover on the account team. Pat O'Toole, the account director, had to move back to the United States from Europe in the middle of all this, and Claire Campbell, the project manager, didn't start working full-time on this project until about six months ago, so we basically put this entire certification program together in less than nine months."

Once the personnel issues were addressed, I explained other concerns that we had confronted. Many of the training managers at TCM had dual responsibilities for the same manufacturer, which included a large European luxury division and our U.S. American brand. The European luxury division had already launched a certification program, and there was pressure to adapt this program for the American brand.

"Makes sense," responded Ken.

"Well, it's true that there is this belief that whatever works for the luxury brand will automatically work for us, but in my experience, this is rarely the case," I explained. "We've got two very different types of cultures operating in this situation, with very different retail environments, product offerings, and customers. Plus, TCM wants everything to be administered online, and the existing program for the luxury brand is mostly paper-based."

"But politically, it looks very good for *everyone* when we can borrow from the luxury brand. Management appreciates when costs can be shared across divisions. Why couldn't we do this?" asked Ken.

At this point, I handed over a copy of my notes from an early meeting of the Block Exemption Regulation (BER) Task Force and offered the following explanation (Figure 23–2).

**FIGURE 23–2**   Scott's Meeting Notes.

**Automotive Performance Improvement Consultants**

**Block Exemption Regulation (BER) Task Force**

**Launch Meeting Summary**

- Global training already has a certification process in place for a luxury brand.

- It has been difficult to adapt this existing program in international markets where the American brand is sold for several reasons:
  - The certification process is complex.
  - The competencies are robust and include more than 250 elements.
  - Behavioral styles and personality characteristics are integrated with the competencies and appear to be culturally specific.
  - The competencies have only been validated locally and may not generalize internationally.
  - The assessment process required a third-party evaluator which can cost up to €2,000 per individual.
  - The curriculum requires a minimum of 18 training days per individual (and does not recognize prior knowledge or experience).
  - The existing program does not include personal development plans, which is a BER requirement.
  - Product knowledge tests are complicated and costly. Multiple correct answer formats increase the cost of translating the number of answers from multiple-choice questions and the computer programming requirements are more complex than for traditional multiple-choice formats. This will also increase costs.

"Well, the existing program was highly complex and required a third-party evaluator to assess each sales consultant, costing about 1,500 euro per day. In addition, in some countries the evaluator had to be an industrial or organizational psychologist. This wasn't an option for the smaller markets, as the costs were prohibitive and the ability to pay varied from one country to the next. In addition, the product knowledge tests were multiple-choice with multiple correct answers that required a sophisticated scoring algorithm. Translation costs, alone, for the product knowledge test would be expensive because of the increased number of answer options needed for the multiple–option format. In addition, complex programming would be needed, requiring more time and money compared to traditional multiple-choice questions where only one correct answer is needed."

Ken's patience seemed to be wearing thin as he asked, "So, what did you do?"

At this point, I pulled out the certification model (Figure 23–3) for the sales consultant certification program and began to summarize some key points.

"We developed this model to explain the certification program to the local training managers. It begins with job descriptions and competencies," I explained. "For this, we *did* use the existing materials from the luxury division's certification program, but we basically edited and simplified the content and their competencies based on our knowledge and expertise in the automotive industry. We later validated these materials, which I can explain in a minute.

**FIGURE 23–3** Certification Model.

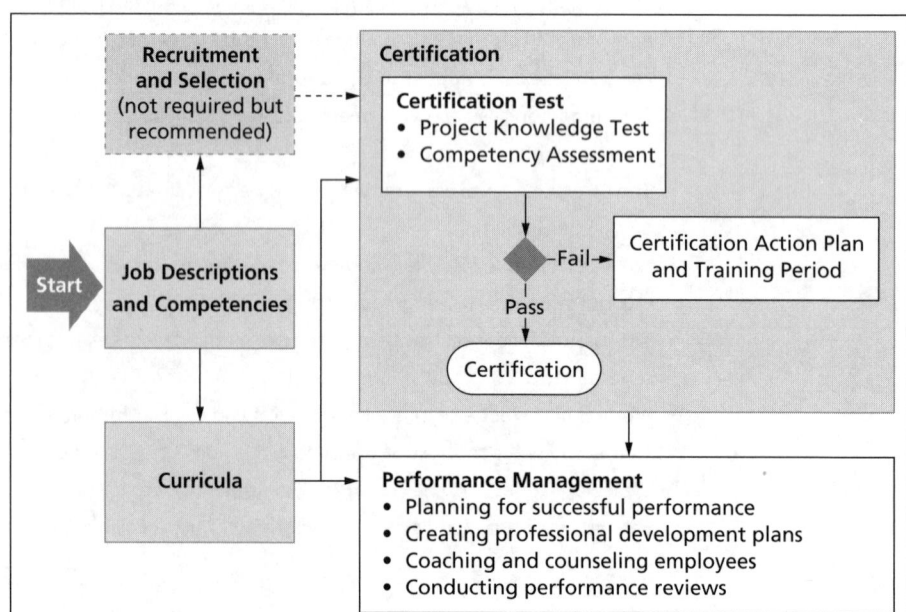

"The next component is recruitment and selection, which is a collection of processes and procedures to ensure that qualified sales consultants are representing the brand. That is mandatory for the European luxury program. The U.S. American brand cannot legally impose recruitment and selection processes for international dealerships because the ability to pay for these activities varies among the different-sized international markets. As a result, in our program it's not required, just recommended.

"The certification component consists of a product knowledge test and a competency assessment. For the product knowledge test, we're writing basic, multiple-choice items that test a sales consultant's factual knowledge of our client's products. Depending on the vehicles sold in a given market and the guidelines we've established, individual tests are generated using randomly selected items from the question pool."

"So how do you handle cheating in the local dealerships?" Ken asked.

"Well, we recommend that the tests are proctored by local training managers or by independent testing facilities, but we've also had to accept that we couldn't prevent cheating from occurring. We'd like to think that people would take the certification process seriously, but those who really want to cheat—or who work collaboratively as a group—will figure out a way to do so. Now, that doesn't mean we make it easy for them! The test items and the response options are generated randomly, and every sales consultant is given a unique ID number and receives a unique test. If people work in groups, they'll have to complete a lot of individual tests, but they'll also learn a lot along the way."

Ken looked skeptical. "So, what's to prevent individuals from answering the test questions with the product reference guides right there in their laps or leaving their computer stations to look up an answer?"

"Well, we can't really prevent that from happening. However, if sales consultants leave their tests for too long, they are automatically timed out of their product knowledge tests. The website will bookmark where they left off, saving everything that had already been answered, but the sales consultants will be required to log in again, and a different test item will then be randomly assigned where they left off. Sales consultants will have to repeat this process over and over again until the test is completed."

"Okay. So, what's up with the competency assessment, then?" Ken asked.

"Well, this was our greatest challenge because we needed an alternative to the on-site evaluator and we had limited resources, both financial and human. We decided to conduct a job analysis with sales consultants in our top five markets using the simplified competencies as a foundation. We removed the parts of the test that assessed behavioral styles and personality characteristics from the luxury program and created operational definitions for eight competencies that would generalize across all of our international markets. For example, we found minimum standards for written and spoken communication and wrote an operational definition for the communication competency. It simply wasn't feasible for us to conduct in-depth evaluations of every sales consultant working in an international market. We decided to conduct the job analysis using the critical incident technique with a small sample of top performers. This allowed us to identify a set of behaviors that were critical to successful job performance. We constructed an online competency assessment using authentic scenarios from the job analysis, and along the way we were able to validate the competency framework and job descriptions."

Ken looked impressed. "That's great! So how does the competency assessment work?"

"We've aligned a series of questions with each of the competencies, and each item has three response options. The best answer is assigned three points and reflects what exemplary performers do in certain situations. There is also an acceptable response, which is assigned two points, and a least acceptable response, which is given one point. This type of scoring procedure was used to discriminate between acceptable performers and those individuals who needed to improve. Once the competency assessment was completed, a score was given for each of the competencies, and the candidate either passed or failed. For those sales consultants who failed, a certification action plan had to be developed by the responsible sales manager to improve on the weaknesses that were identified in the competency assessment. Then, the sales consultants were retested after a probationary period of time."

"So what's to prevent someone from cheating?" Ken wondered.

"The website is programmed in the same way as the product knowledge test, and there is a bank of questions that are scrambled for each candidate. Again, we won't be able to prevent cheating, but we're confident that most sales consultants will recognize the benefit of receiving constructive feedback on their individual performances because it can directly affect their ability to generate sales.

"If they don't pass the required competency assessment, the certification action plan should help them prepare for the retest. Remember, the competency assessment is only designed to discriminate between acceptable and unacceptable performance, and the program is not intended to be punitive. Continuous improvement is the ultimate goal. Once sales consultants become certified, they receive personal development plans when they enter the performance management phase of the program. From here, the only requirement for recertification is successful completion of product knowledge tests. The program can potentially help sales consultants earn more money if they are truly committed to improving their performance."

Ken nodded. "Well, everything sounds great to me. So what's the problem?"

As I took a deep breath, I mentioned that TCM had recently reorganized, and several positions were eliminated or consolidated. Then, I explained that Antoine was now reporting directly to Victor Nielsen in Europe because Bob's position was eliminated.

"And the problem is . . .?"

"The problem is . . . Bob never felt a need to develop a certification test for vehicle delivery specialists. These are customer-facing employees who are only responsible for handing over the vehicles to customers after the actual sales transactions take place. They answer questions and demonstrate how to use certain features such as the radio or air-conditioning system. Bob just didn't think we needed to include them, because there are only about 60 or 70 throughout the entire European Union. But Victor insists that the program must include vehicle delivery specialists, and Antoine is demanding it. However, we've run out of time and money."

Ken probed further. "So, what was discussed at your last meeting with the client?"

"Here's a copy of the Call Report . . . I'm just not sure what to do" (Figure 23–4).

**FIGURE 23–4**    Call Report.

# Call Report

| | |
|---|---|
| **Client:** | Antoine Devereux |
| **Author:** | Pat O'Toole |
| **Participants:** | Claire Campbell |
| | Antoine Devereux (via telephone) |
| | Dale Hovan |
| | Scott Hunter |
| | Pat O'Toole |
| **Purpose:** | Certification Program |
| **Date:** | October 3rd |

**Purpose**

The purpose of this meeting was to discuss the status of the Sales Consultant Certification Program.

**Background**

- All elements of the Sales Consultant Certification Program were reviewed and approved prior to launch, including:
  - Revised job descriptions and competencies
  - Interface design and functionality
  - Product knowledge test items
  - Competency assessment
  - Certification action plan and personal development plan
- TCM inquired about the status of the vehicle delivery specialist (VDS) certification. APIC informed TCM that Bob did not request VDS certification materials because there were less than 70 job incumbents throughout all international markets.

**Discussion**

- TCM informed APIC that VDS certification materials must be prepared by the first of the year so that the manufacturer will be compliant with block exemption regulation (BER) standards.

**FIGURE 23–4**   Call Report, *(cont.)*

- APIC facilitated a brainstorming session to explore various options, which included:
  - Request quotation from competency assessment supplier to conduct critical incident interviews with top-performing VDS job incumbents
  - Check with domestic training team to see if they have any relevant materials to assist with VDS certification
  - Send e-mail message to all relevant training managers to request information on any existing VDS certification materials
- TCM explained that in most markets, sales consultants (SC) handle vehicle delivery and the VDS position is only implemented in very large markets, often in dealerships that sell both the luxury and American brands. The VDS position is often perceived as an entry-level job for the SC position and a VDS should be able to fulfill the basic functions of the SC position.
- TCM informed APIC that certification materials exist in the United Kingdom for the luxury division. A brief training program is delivered in the dealership, followed by a role-playing scenario where the training manager determines if the VDS should be certified.
- TCM also informed APIC that training support must be available for VDS candidates who fail the certification test.

**Next Steps**

- APIC to collect existing assets, which are currently known to include:
  - VDS certification materials from the United Kingdom
  - VDS and SC job descriptions and SC competencies
  - SC competency assessment (including approved items that were not used)
  - Domestic training materials for vehicle delivery including five-point vehicle walkaround positions
  - APIC to prepare request for quotation from competency assessment supplier

"What are your instincts telling you about this one?" Ken asked as he skimmed through the Call Report.

"One thing I know for sure—TCM does not have enough money to hire an outside supplier to conduct the critical incident interviews for vehicle delivery specialists in order to identify key behaviors critical to their successful performance."

"And how complicated do you think this task would be?"

"Generally, my instincts are telling me that vehicle delivery specialists need to be familiar with basic product features, just in case questions arise at delivery. They need to know which product features to present or demonstrate at various interior and exterior positions around the vehicle. Finally, there are some typical situations that might occur during vehicle delivery that require basic common sense, and any customer-facing employee should be able to act accordingly."

"So, what's a typical situation that occurs at delivery?"

"Sometimes the customer is in a hurry and doesn't allow enough time for delivery. Or the vehicle may not be prepped when the customer arrives."

"Do you think Dale Hovan will have any time to work on this?"

"It's a possibility, and he was very involved in the sales consultant certification program, but I guess it depends on whether we can find any existing training programs that can be repurposed for vehicle delivery specialists."

"I see. That makes sense. Well, it looks like we've got about a week to generate some recommendations and submit the report."

At this moment, Ken glanced at his watch and then pointed to a framed quotation on his wall by M. Scott Peck, which stated:

> The truth is that our finest moments are most likely to occur when we are feeling deeply uncomfortable, unhappy, or unfulfilled. For it is only in such moments, propelled by our discomfort, that we are likely to step out of our ruts and start searching for different ways or truer answers.

"I know you're very frustrated with all this, but maybe the certification test for vehicle delivery specialists will be one of *your* finest moments on this project. By the way, whatever happened to Kat?" asked Ken.

"Well, Kat was dismissed, and Antoine was promoted to European Training Manager," I answered matter-of-factly.

Confused, Ken muttered, "But I thought Antoine was—"

"Yes, Antoine established an inappropriate working relationship with his relative," I said. "But he also seemed to get things done, and TCM gave him the promotion with the understanding that his relative could complete the pilot but could not work on any other international business."

"So typical." Ken shook his head and started gathering some papers for his next meeting.

"Thanks for your time," I replied. I found myself thinking that truth is sometimes stranger than fiction. Then I realized that I was the one who would have to fix this mess. One more deliverable, little time, and no budget. "So typical," I echoed as I headed back to my office.

# Preliminary Analysis Questions

1. Given the complexity of the existing certification program, critique APIC's approach to the sales consultant certification program it developed.
2. What are the advantages and disadvantages of using a third-party evaluator compared to an online competency assessment?
3. Scott Hunter states, "If people work in groups . . . they'll also learn a lot along the way." What do you think about this statement, given the strategies used to handle cheating in this case?
4. Evaluate the options that resulted from APIC's brainstorming session (see Figure 23–4). Suggest other approaches to the certification of the vehicle delivery specialists.

# Implications for ID Practice

1. Discuss the design challenges associated with working in volatile client environments where turnover, restructuring, and/or job rotation strategies can significantly impact ID projects.
2. What type(s) of communication strategies would you suggest for global project teams that operate in different countries, especially if English is a second language for many members of the team and/or audiences?
3. Propose a range of strategies for addressing performance improvement needs when the intended audience is very small.
4. Discuss the issues involved in implementing online assessment in real-world settings.

# Margaret Janson

## Developing Learning Objects for Adult Learners

*by Rod Sims and Naomi Waldron*

Simon Wilcowsky reflected on his career at Third Eye Media. Although his original background was in graphic design, he had worked on teams with other professionals on instructional design projects over the past several years and had risen to the position of e-learning production manager. So far, he'd been very successful in managing the needs of his clients while meeting deadlines and making a healthy profit for the company. He had a great team under his supervision: instructional designers, programmers, illustrators, animators, even video producers. Most clients had been happy with the quality of the e-learning materials that the company had produced; Third Eye used high-quality graphics and illustrations that were easy to read and animations that illustrated difficult concepts. The company had won numerous awards for its e-learning products and was one of the most successful companies in the country.

But this latest client was different. The Australian Vocational Network (AVN) had very clear ideas about the development of learning objects that were at odds with what previous clients had requested. Simon wondered again about AVN's request for a Proof-of-Concept that required approximately 40% of the final product—that was some "proof"! But now the client was threatening to pull the project and cancel the contract. Somehow the design practices that had built Third Eye Media's reputation were not working with this very important client. Simon had just spent 20 minutes on the phone with his boss, Caroline Porter, about the memo he'd sent her first thing this morning, trying to explain what went wrong and why he'd almost lost the $100,000 project. She was not at all pleased, but he assured her that he would save the project. But how? Simon knew that other perspectives often helped shed light on difficult issues, so he decided to talk to Margaret Janson, one of Third Eye's more experienced instructional designers, about the problem.

Margaret was sitting at her desk, feeling relaxed because she had just completed a major project and was looking forward to meeting her university friends for tea. She'd just enrolled in a master's program in e-learning, and she loved the challenge. Her instructors had encouraged her to compare the theories she was learning with the practical knowledge she'd gained from working on projects with Third Eye Media. Then Simon poked his head around the door. "Got a minute?" he asked.

"Sure," responded Margaret. "Come on in."

"We have a problem," said Simon. "What do you know about deep-sea oil exploration?"

Margaret shrugged and grinned. As an instructional designer for Third Eye, she was used to unusual projects, and the thought of a new and challenging assignment was exciting. "Nothing," she replied, "but from the look on your face, I think I'm going to find out very soon!"

Simon continued, "You know that $100,000 government contract we won to develop competency-based training in deep-sea oil exploration? The brief required us to develop a set of learning objects for the accreditation of new employees and to re-accredit employees with experience."

He gulped. "The entire project is at risk: we're at the Proof-of-Concept phase, and unless we can figure out what went wrong and fix it—fast—we stand to lose $100,000 of work, not to mention our company's reputation. Our client is the Australian Vocational Network. As you know, AVN is the premier vocational organization in the country. They have a designated project manager as well as an industry-appointed oil exploration expert assigned to this project. So we have a lot of stakeholders to impress here. The AVN and project manager are setting our technical specifications and project requirements but don't know anything about deep-sea oil exploration. On the other hand, Joe Strickler, the oil exploration expert, is very familiar with the needs of the industry, but he doesn't really understand the technical limitations we're working with. So, the design that we created needs to be negotiated to suit both parties, as well as to be achievable within the time and budget we have available."

Simon continued, "They're also very specific about what they mean by a learning object. Have a look at this." He removed a page from the project folder and handed it to Margaret (Figure 24–1).

Simon also handed Margaret the internal memo he had sent his boss earlier (Figure 24–2). "I had to send this to the head office this morning to explain the situation. Maybe you should have a read. I have to go call the AVN project manager now. I'll be back with an update shortly."

Margaret finished reading the specifications and memo and began to speculate on how the project might have gotten to this stage. She began to ponder how Simon's team had missed the requirements for interactivity and active learning that were so clearly specified. She wondered if the main reason were related to the fact that previous clients had requested products that were graphical and fun to use, but rarely had they been so specific about using a preferred learning approach.

When Simon returned, he asked Margaret for her thoughts. "Well," she began a little hesitantly, "you seem to have completely misunderstood the client's requirements. Surely the specifications document you handed me earlier can't be all you were given to work from. How did you go about the instructional design task and sign-off with the client?"

"The first thing that happened," responded Simon, "is that we were invited to a briefing meeting in Sydney. Our lead instructional designer, Janet Smith, went on our behalf. However, she resigned shortly afterward, and we had to put Trevor Adams on the project instead. Trevor's a great guy, but because he missed all the lead-up briefing meetings, we were behind from the start. And although he's fantastic at designing the kind of training

**FIGURE 24–1**    Australian Vocational Network Memorandum.

# AVN

## AUSTRALIAN VOCATIONAL NETWORK
## MEMORANDUM

| | |
|---|---|
| **To:** | LEARNING OBJECT CONTRACTORS |
| **FROM:** | LEARNING MATERIALS DIVISION |
| **SUBJECT:** | LEARNING OBJECT SPECIFICATIONS |
| **DATE:** | 12 JANUARY |
| **CC:** | DIRECTOR, TECHNICAL TRAINING |

**TO ALL DEVELOPERS:**

**THESE SPECIFICATIONS SHOULD BE USED FOR ALL LEARNING OBJECT DEVELOPMENT. PLEASE CONTACT YOUR ASSIGNED PROJECT MANAGER FOR FURTHER INFORMATION.**

**Desired Characteristics of AVN Learning Objects:**

Excerpt from the Tender Guidelines for AVN Learning Objects—Series 3 AVN Project Manager, 5 June

**Learning object structure**

1) Each module is to be designed as a learning object so that it is:
   a) SCORM compliant
   b) Self-contained (i.e., no explicit links between modules)
   c) Deliverable through a learning management system
2) Each module is to contain an associated work-based context that immerses the learner in a realistic, problem-based environment that engages the learner to use the content objects (described in point 3) to solve the problems.
3) Within each module there are to be smaller learning objects that cover single learning objectives. These objects are to be repurposable, content-rich, and include a self-test at the end.

**Teaching and learning approaches**

The modules must exhibit effective teaching and learning approaches as demonstrated by the following features:

- an educational model that recognizes an active, constructive role for learners
- learning activities that engage the learner in active processing rather than mere knowledge acquisition
- resources that are visually attractive, motivating to use, and organized logically
- representations of authentic, real-life settings in preference to textual descriptions

**FIGURE 24–2**  Simon's Memorandum to Caroline Porter.

**Third Eye Media**
Suite 65, 100 Spotty Gum Lane
Eucalyptus Business Park
Gooneellabah NSW 2480
AUSTRALIA
P: 61-2-6623-4567
E: support@3im.com.au

**CONFIDENTIAL**

TO:        CAROLINE PORTER, CEO
FROM:      SIMON WILCOWSKY
SUBJECT:   AVN E-LEARNING PROJECT
DATE:      23 JULY

BACKGROUND

The Australian Vocational Network (AVN), through its funding body the Australian Education Committee, commissioned Third Eye Media to develop a suite of web-based learning objects for deep-sea oil exploration and underwater drilling.

During initial consultations it was emphasized that a critical element and measure of functionality for the learning objects would be active learning contextualized in a problem-based environment. The AVN specifications required the materials to integrate interactivity for engagement and learning, although there was no definition or examples of these terms.

The key personnel identified for the project were the project manager (appointed by AVN), the subject matter expert (appointed by the Oil Exploration Industry Committee), and the instructional designer and multimedia software developers employed by Third Eye Media.

Based on our understanding of the requirements, and following our development of what we considered a Proof-of-Concept, the AVN has recommended the contract be terminated.

KEY FACTORS

The following represent the key factors and issues that have impacted delivery of the desired outcomes and placed the overall project in jeopardy.

- The project start date was delayed due to disagreements between the AVN Project Manager and the Industry Committee on the selection of content.

- We encountered initial delays to the commencement of the instructional design phase due to the resignation of our instructional designer.

- We experienced difficulties in obtaining and identifying content resources. One reason for this was that the units had previously only been taught in a face-to-face apprenticeship model, with no written content available, apart from advanced textbooks material.

- The specifications for the Proof-of-Concept appeared consistent with our prior experience with the production of a sample product, and we used this knowledge as the basis for the initial deliverable.

This combination of factors meant we were challenged to meet the requirements of the initial Proof-of-Concept.

CURRENT STATUS

Our initial instructional design for a sample learning object and the accompanying Proof-of-Concept was not completed to the satisfaction of the AVN Project Manager. Two reasons were provided in their feedback report: First, the Proof-of-Concept did not demonstrate what they considered to be the key components of problem-based and exploratory learning; secondly, the Proof-of-Concept was not consistent with their expectations for style and layout. With respect to the overall design, the initial determination from the AVN Project Manager was that the content was poorly structured, there were no clear pathways through the content, and that the interface design was rudimentary.

In retrospect there was a conflict between our understanding of the Proof-of-Concept and that of the client's; our expectations were that it represented a rough work in progress, while their expectations, determined only recently, were that 40% of the learning objects would be complete. This was certainly well beyond the Proof-of-Concept requirements for previous projects.

I propose redoing the Proof-of-Concept at no cost to AVN, and within the agreed timeframe. I have since spoken with our primary contact at AVN and they have agreed to speak with us later this morning.

The income from this project is $100,000 with the expectation of further work next year if the project is successful. It is my opinion that given the influence of the Australian Vocational Network, any concerns about loss of profit from redoing the Proof-of-Concept should be weighed against the potential loss of reputation from the project's failure.

Yours sincerely,

*Simon Wilcowsky*

materials we've done before, he was a bit lost when faced with issues related to authentic learning contexts. As you know, Trevor's been trained on the job and doesn't have a background in education. I didn't pick up on that gap until recently, and this Proof-of-Concept is the first sign-off point we've had with the client."

Margaret skimmed Simon's memo to Caroline again. "Forty percent completion for a Proof-of-Concept! That's a bit much isn't it?"

"Sure is," agreed Simon. "Based on our previous experiences, we assumed a Proof-of-Concept wouldn't need to be so complete, and with the change of staff and Trevor's inexperience with this level of development, we somehow didn't pick up that the AVN expectation for Proof-of-Concept meant we had to complete nearly half the work! We haven't worked for AVN before, but apparently that's just what they expect."

Margaret was silent for a while, then carefully added her own perspective. "You know, this project is quite different from most of the others we've completed. That would explain why you overlooked some of the requirements. Most of our clients just want an "electronic textbook" solution—they want classy-looking information presentation. For this project, though, we were clearly asked to work at a much more sophisticated level, and to engage the learner with the content through structured interactive activities."

She paused. "Let me see if I understand the situation correctly. We won this project and, after some initial staffing issues, in our effort to meet the submission requirements, we just did what has worked for us in the past."

Simon shuffled in his seat looking uncomfortable. "That's one way of looking at it. Margaret, I just got off the phone with AVN, and they have agreed to continue with the contract. However, we must identify and assign a new instructional designer to the work. Because Trevor doesn't have an education degree, I'd like you to take on the project. We have exactly three weeks to develop a completely new Proof-of-Concept at our own cost. If it's successful, then we'll be paid for the whole project. If not, we'll be out of pocket for the extra work."

Margaret laughed nervously. "Three weeks! That's ridiculous. A project like this should take months. Can't you talk them into giving us a few more months?"

Simon looked at Margaret gravely. "You don't know how hard it was for me to convince them to give us another chance. They were adamant that we couldn't have any more time. The only reason they're giving us three weeks is because I convinced them that we had the production capacity to pull it off."

Margaret took a deep breath. "So who else is on the project, then?"

Simon was quick to answer. "You can have anyone you need—the whole team, if necessary. Just don't let me down."

*Wow. This is going to be some project*, thought Margaret. She asked Simon, "Where are the learning outcomes and content?"

Simon replied, "There are some industry-based underwater exploration competencies, but because it's such a specialized field and very skills-oriented, there is no written training material at all. Until now, training has all been apprenticeship based. There is one expert, Martin Howe, who's been training people for years. However, because he lives in Tasmania and was off-shore on an oil rig for a lengthy period of time, Trevor could only contact him briefly by phone and by e-mail. I believe he is back now, and if you want, I will approve a flight for him up here and have him spend dedicated time with the team. Anyway, think about what you'd like to do, and come back to me with a plan of attack first thing in the morning."

Contemplating three weeks of hard work and little sleep, Margaret returned to her desk and reviewed the client's feedback from the initial Proof-of-Concept (Figure 24–3) that Simon had left with her.

Even at first glance she could see there were some serious problems—the score on the Teaching and Learning Approach was 6/25, Product Functionality scored 10/20, and

**FIGURE 24–3**   AVN Assessment and Feedback Report.

# AVN AUSTRALIAN VOCATIONAL NETWORK MEMORANDUM

| | |
|---|---|
| **To:** | SIMON WILCOWSKY, THIRD EYE MEDIA |
| **FROM:** | L.J. SMITH, DIRECTOR, LEARNING MATERIALS DIVISION |
| **SUBJECT:** | PROOF-OF-CONCEPT FEEDBACK |
| **DATE:** | 20 JULY |
| **CC:** | DIRECTOR, TECHNICAL TRAINING |

Dear Simon,

We have received and reviewed the Proof-of-Concept for the Deep-Sea Oil Rig learning object.

Attached please find the formal assessment and feedback.

As you can see, we have serious reservations about the ability of Third Eye Media to complete the project.

We advise that you contact your AVN project manager to discuss the status of the project.

Yours sincerely,

*L J Smith*

L.J. Smith
Director, Learning Materials Division

Enclosures:          Assessment and Feedback Report

**FIGURE 24–3**  *Continued*

### Third Eye Proof-of-Concept: Assessment and Feedback Report

| Teaching and Learning Approach | Rating (1–5) | Comment |
|---|---|---|
| The learning object is based on an educational model that recognises an active, constructive role for learners. | 1 | The product does not appear to be based on any known educational model. |
| Learning activities require learners to process the subject matter, rather than mere knowledge acquisition. | 1 | The activities do not engage the learner, and use of interactivity is at a low level. |
| The learning setting and tasks encourage meaningful communication (among learners as well as between teachers and learners). | 2 | There is no direct reference to communication among learners or between teachers and learners. |
| The learning setting represents real life in preference to textual descriptions. | 1 | The learning environment is very plain, and does not suggest the environment of deep-sea oil exploration. |
| The product is visually attractive, motivating to use, and organised logically for ease of navigation. | 1 | Navigation is very confusing; there is no logical pathway through the product and the appearance of the product is poor. |
| **Product Functionality** | **Rating** | **Comment** |
| The product uses non-proprietary development software. | 3 | The product is developed in HTML and Flash, but is very unappealing. |
| Content that is likely to be changed is represented in HTML or Word. | 4 | Most of the content is represented in HTML text or is in a Word document. |
| The product allows for multiple pathways through the material, although a suggested learning sequence may be appropriate. | 1 | Navigation is confusing, and there are no directions for learners on different pathways. |
| The product can be easily split into a series of reusable, independent learning objects. | 2 | Although the technology supports it, there do not seem to be any sections that would lend themselves to being separate learning objects. |
| **Compliance with Standards** | **Rating** | **Comment** |
| The product complies with W3C Priority-1 Web Content Accessibility Guidelines. | 5 | Most content is represented in plain HTML. |
| Conforming to the above guidelines should not result in any loss of desirable qualities in the features of the product. | 2 | The product needs to be made more engaging. |
| The product is SCORM compliant. | 3 | The product is technically SCORM compliant, but the separate learning objects have not been defined. |

**FIGURE 24–4**   Course Opening Screen.

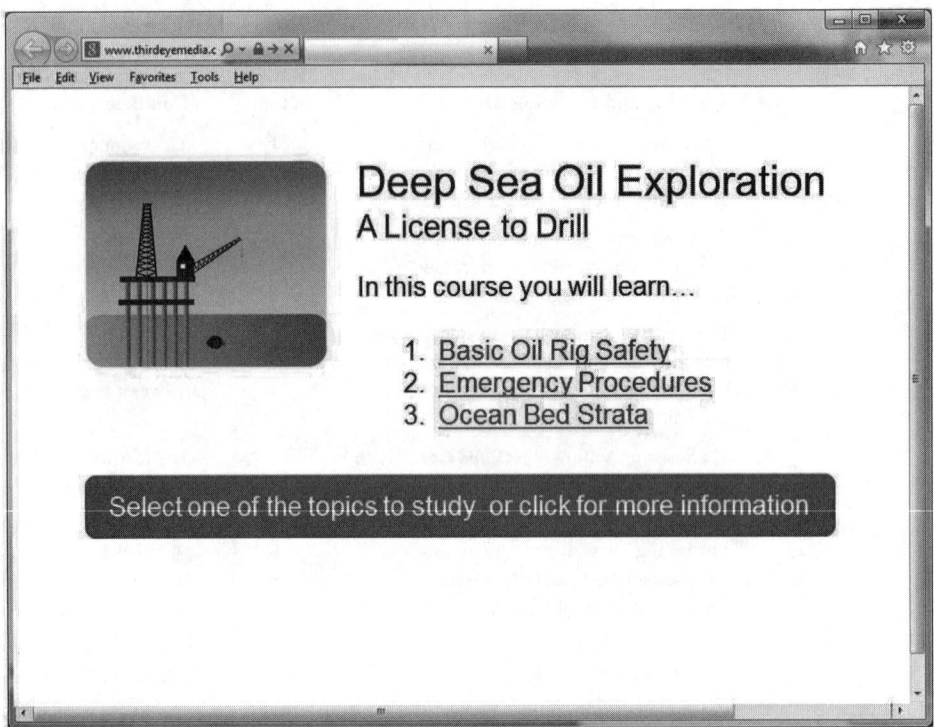

Compliance to Standards scored 10/15. It was clearly very fortunate that Simon had managed to negotiate a resubmission of the Proof-of-Concept. Looking at the review scores and comments more closely, Margaret reflected on why the Teaching and Learning Approach component had scored so much lower than the other criteria.

"What went wrong?" she wondered. "Hadn't the team seen the rubrics before they started development?" She reviewed two of the screenshots (Figures 24–4 and 24–5) and the flowchart (Figure 24–6) for the design submitted to AVN for the Proof-of-Concept.

As Margaret proceeded through the modules, her suspicions were confirmed—the team had not really integrated the types of interactivity and authenticity that AVN had requested. Was this the missing link that had nearly caused the project to be lost? Were there some aspects of instructional design for e-learning that Third Eye was not integrating into its applications? It was then that Margaret remembered listening to a presentation by a visiting professor who had talked about the importance of designing engaging interactions and authentic learning experiences. Perhaps he would have some additional ideas that would help them while completing the project.

The next day Margaret found the professor's business card. Geoff Charles was an e-learning consultant who had written widely on interactivity. When he spoke to Margaret's class, he was very clear about the importance of developing effective interactive learning

**FIGURE 24–5**   Module 1 Opening Screen.

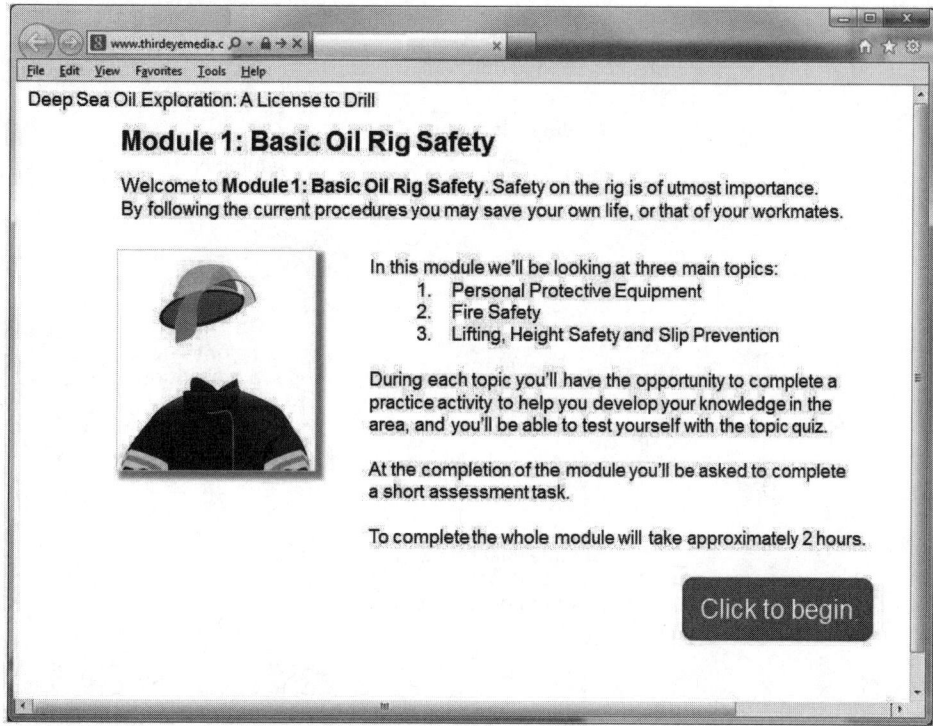

experiences. Margaret picked up the phone and called Geoff. Luckily, he was free for a coffee that afternoon.

"Tell me, Dr. Charles," Margaret asked, "how can we create an e-learning object that integrates interactivity for authentic engagement? We've got a project for training deep-sea oil explorers, and I need some new ideas fast! I learned a lot from your presentation, but I would really appreciate some further input."

Geoff thought for a moment and then replied carefully, "It seems you may have a context issue here." He then went on to explain, in some detail, several projects he had worked on, describing different interactive strategies that had proven successful for different types of learners in a broad range of contexts.

After an hour of talking with Dr. Charles, Margaret's suspicions about the reasons for the rejected Proof-of-Concept seemed confirmed. For most of Third Eye's previous projects, the emphasis had been on translating some very dreary content into a more accessible and presentable format. The clients had been happy with what they called their new "interactive" e-learning products. But this client had quite different expectations for interactivity—ones that were much more aligned with Dr. Charles's ideas. It was not just about presenting attractive content, but also about engaging students in the learning material through their participation in authentic activities. As Margaret started back to the office, she felt she had the basis for re-creating a Proof-of-Concept that would meet the needs of AVN.

**FIGURE 24–6**    Course Flowchart.

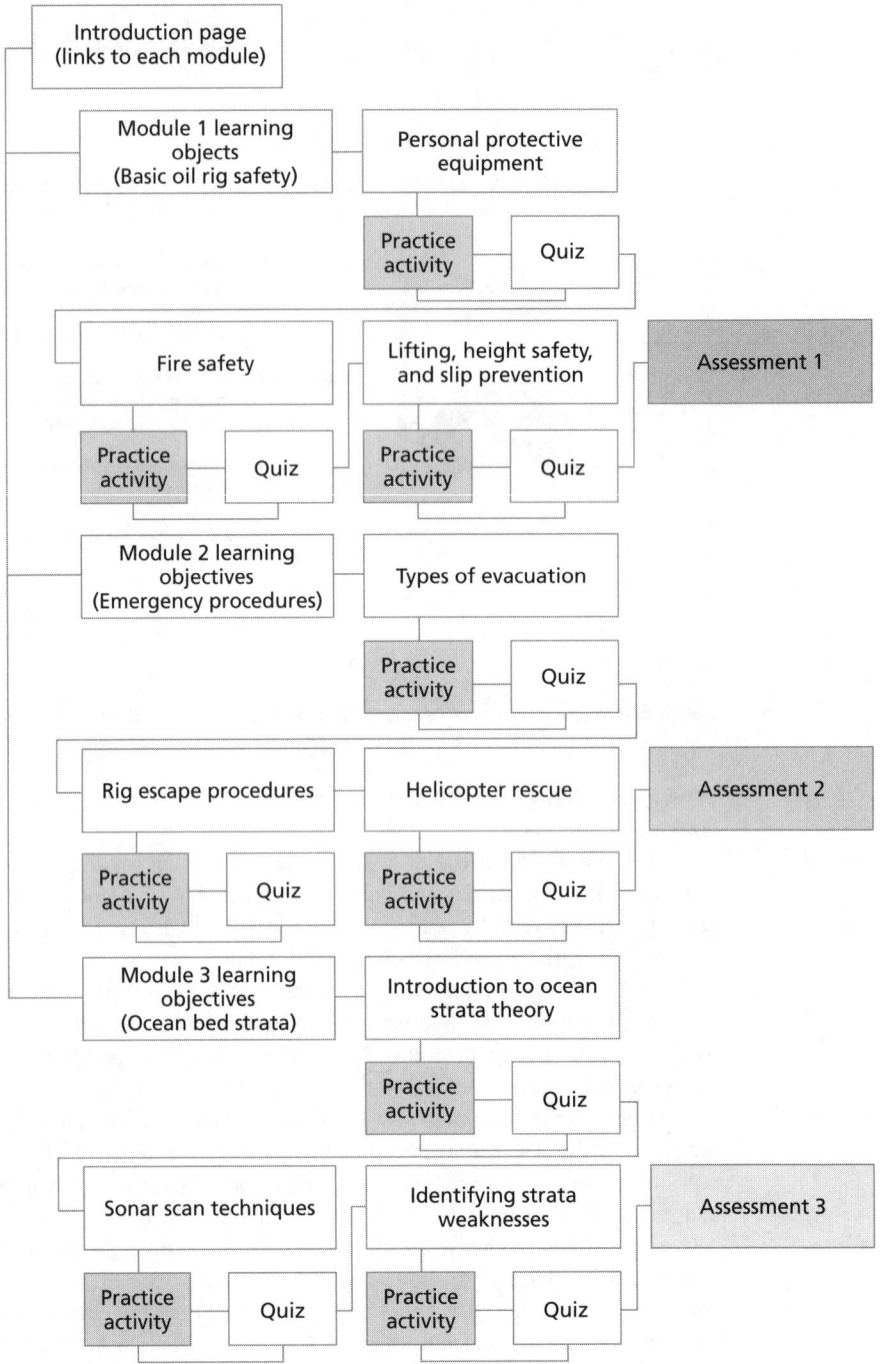

# Preliminary Analysis Questions

1. Describe the differences between the learning objects required in the memorandum presented by AVN and the Proof-of-Concept delivered by Third Eye.
2. There were a number of misunderstandings and false assumptions made in this case. Suggest strategies for improving communication between AVN and Third Eye.
3. Develop an action plan for Margaret to present to Simon. Draw up a three-week calendar, with project briefing on day 1 and project submission on day 21.

# Implications for ID Practice

1. Instructional design project managers have been compared to jugglers—they have to manage the often-conflicting requirements of different stakeholders within the constraints of time, money, and resources to design a quality product. What strategies might be employed to ensure that the client, the manager, and the developers are satisfied with the design?
2. Learning objects are intended to allow for maximum reusability; however, a common criticism is that they may lack a context to make learning meaningful and authentic. How would you respond to this criticism? What design considerations might you take into account to counter these criticisms?
3. Compare the approaches to achieving interactivity (student-student, instructor-student, student-content) in face-to-face and online learning environments.

# CASE STUDY 25

# David Jimenez

## Performance Improvement of Engineers

*by Martha Mann, Valerie A. Larsen, and Mable B. Kinzie*

Carillon Productions is an instructional design firm that grew from a small team of instructional designers in the mid-2000s to well over 50 employees in only a few years. Carillon became well known among its clients—educational publishers—for its development of multimedia-based supplemental textbook materials. David Jimenez was an instructional designer at Carillon who had been specializing in the design of science and mathematics instruction for the past four years. His innovative and award-winning designs covered a wide range of applications from interactive problem-solving physics modules to 3-D calculus tutorials. David credited the successful design of his products to his skills as an instructional designer, to his programming skills, and to his 10 years as a secondary science teacher. His teaching experience provided him with insight into learners' needs and enabled him to serve as both content expert and instructional developer. In this way, he was able to work on his own as he designed and developed products for Carillon's clients. David had to modify his formula for success, however, when he was promoted to project manager and assigned to head up a project for Dragone Drilling Technologies, a leading manufacturer of petroleum analysis tools and extraction equipment. Due for market release in 90 days, Dragone Drilling's Odysseus System was being promoted as a cost-effective technology that had the potential to revolutionize natural gas hydrate exploration. The firm wanted a training module that would encourage the use of this new analysis, archiving, and forecasting system.

The Odysseus System project would be David's first experience as a manager and his first as a designer dependent on others for their content expertise. However, David was enthusiastic about these new challenges and saw this as an opportunity to expand his leadership and instructional design (ID) skills. Dragone had conducted a field test with the beta version of the Odysseus System, and they cited results that they interpreted as a need for training among users. According to executives at Dragone, the engineers resisted using the product, a problem they thought was generally common to organizations introducing new technologies. In their report, they noted specifically that 17 engineers had been asked to use the technology for a period of two months in the field. By the end of the second month, the engineers had abandoned the new technology and had returned to their standard data-collection tools.

# David's Team

After Carillon won the Dragone contract, its Department of Human Resources allocated one graphic designer, three software/interface programmers, and two entry-level instructional designers for the Odysseus System project, all working under David's direction. David thought it was important to introduce the client to his team and arranged for the graphics designer and lead interface programmer to participate in their first face-to-face meeting with the client. David had each of them describe the variety of products they had produced as he pointed to the numerous awards their educational materials had received. A manager from Human Resources at Dragone Drilling and the marketing director for the Odysseus System represented the client.

After introductions, the marketing director for Dragone presented the promotions packet for the Odysseus System and described its functionality. He explained that standard methods for data collection were laborious, necessitating hours of manual gauge calibration, along with the manual recording of each data probe in the field, followed by lengthy analysis in an off-site lab. The Odysseus System streamlined this process, with automated calibration and on-site analysis. The system involved a three-stage, on-site digital system that collected data on compositional gradients and hydrate gases from potential drill sites. Complex analyses of the reservoir fluid properties were automated and integrated with satellite-networked databases, equipped with algorithms for forecasting site productivity.

According to the marketing director, the petroleum industry was facing a combination of finite, diminishing petroleum resources and increased competition. Those firms with access to new technologies for natural gas hydrate exploration, such as the Odysseus System, had the potential to maintain or increase their market share.

Representatives from Dragone Drilling explained what they were looking for from Carillon Productions: an interactive, self-study training module that would be ready for distribution with the final release of Odysseus in three months. Dragone wanted the engineers to experience the benefits of the Odysseus technology and recognize its ease of use. The goal was to ease the learning curve for the use of the Odysseus System in the field. Their thinking was that an effective training solution would lead to widespread adoption of the Odysseus System.

David shifted into high gear at this point in the meeting and segued into a discussion of the design process. He believed it was important to secure approval for a needs assessment, and, using examples from prior projects, he enthusiastically described how the process could pinpoint the needs of the field engineers and help match the training module to those needs. The Dragone Drilling representatives agreed that a needs assessment seemed to be a practical way to ensure that the training module resolved the problem of technology adoption. They emphasized that time was critical, however, and were reluctant to postpone development of the training module until the needs assessment was completed. As an alternative, Dragone Drilling suggested that David obtain any information he needed from the project manager of the programming team that was contracted to design and develop the Odysseus System.

After some discussion, David and his client agreed to a compromise: They brainstormed some initial ideas for the interface design and for the structure of the instructional module, including options for software or web-based materials. After the latter option was selected, David's team agreed to start development right away. To ensure that appropriate content was included in the module, however, David convinced his clients to approve an initial two-week time period for the collection and analysis of needs data from the Odysseus developers and potential users of the product.

Under David's supervision, his team members began to storyboard the instructional sequence, and he was pleased with his team's progress. He was impressed with the competence of his lead developers. Recognizing that he himself worked best when given wide latitude within general guidelines, he instructed them to proceed with the development of the interface components they'd discussed, designing the best interface they could for the anticipated content.

# The Lompoc Technology Team

David made arrangements to begin the needs assessment with a visit to the software development company, Lompoc Technology Group (LTG), located in a Southern California beach community. There he met Bill Peters, the project manager of the Odysseus development team, who would serve as his content expert for the instructional module.

Bill greeted David with a coffee mug and a company tour, where he met everyone from the chief information officer (CIO) to the company's interns. The LTG facility provided a friendly work environment, with music playing throughout the "house," a large, open workspace for the programmers, and a conference/game room stocked with food and crash pads for those all-too-frequent times when programmers worked through the night. The programmers appeared absorbed in their work as they hammered away at their keyboards and stared intently at their monitors. David observed a small group of programmers congregated around a dry-erase board as they engaged in an active discussion about a glitch with the login form for the Odysseus intranet.

The tour of LTG concluded in the company's conference room with an overview of the intranet communications system that drove the Odysseus System and a striking visual display of the project's milestones. The first item on the display was a description of the guidelines that Dragone Drilling had presented to the Lompoc team in the form of a flowchart, which listed each of the required functions that the Odysseus System would perform. The last item was a chart displaying the final stage of revisions that began during the beta test of the product. Bill then led a discussion with David and the Odysseus software team about the product and its projected implementation. They walked David through the product demo on a laptop computer similar to those distributed with the Odysseus System. The software team, mostly young men and women averaging two to five years of experience in the software design industry, believed that Odysseus was vastly superior to the current manually driven analysis tools because it handled all of the data-collection and analysis tasks within a single product.

The programmers explained that Odysseus was a simple application to use once the user understood each of the screens and its functions. Also, given a user's guide that was accessible from within the program and a smart tool that defined functions when pointed to, they believed that a separate training module for the engineers would be superfluous. One of the lead programmers noted, "The field engineers who don't 'get' Odysseus are the ones too set in their ways to adopt new technologies at this point in their careers." Another programmer suggested that it might take a new generation of engineers to break a tool such as this into the market.

David left LTG with an Odysseus System laptop and a copy of the beta software. The project manager provided contact information for the engineers who had participated in the Odysseus System beta test and phone numbers for overseas field engineers who they thought were representative of the potential Odysseus System user population.

## Reservoir Fluid Property Analysis

Over the next four days, David was able to contact seven potential users of the Odysseus System. Six of the seven engineers David interviewed spoke English as a second language and practiced their profession in their home countries. They had earned their degrees from prominent U.S. schools of engineering, such as Texas A&M and Purdue University. They described their practice as 60% technical and 40% "a feeling of the gut." They had developed their skills under the guidance of experienced field engineers; although the standard equipment they used was old, they were comfortable with the process and found it to perform reliably under a variety of conditions. They claimed that they would embrace a tool that expedited the analysis and forecasting of hydrocarbon reserves, but it would have to perform the reservoir fluid property analysis efficiently and accurately. Four of the engineers were wary of using new technologies promoted by their superiors. They described previous tools that were supposed to "deliver the world," according to management—but when the equipment failed, it was always the engineers' performance that came into question, rather than the tools that management had adopted.

David spent his second week meeting at various sites around the Houston area with eight of the beta test engineers for the Odysseus System. Four were recent university graduates who planned to return to their native countries in the near future. David was able to observe the new data-collection methods and discuss the engineers' beta test experiences with them. According to the engineers, the first month of the beta test had focused on programming glitches. The intent was to resolve minor bugs and ensure functionality. The majority of the bugs identified involved intranet access (login problems) and problems with user input that caused the system to crash because it was not supported by the analysis algorithms. The engineers were then left to use the new technology in the field for a period of four weeks. During this time, David spent considerable time observing the engineers using Odysseus in the field.

After taking Odysseus through its paces, the engineers reported that they had experienced some drawbacks, which one engineer described as "shining a new light on our old equipment, making the old methods seem like a model of modern perfection." They had found the Odysseus software difficult to navigate and described the multitude of screens that had to be set up for each drill site, with parameters specific to that site. The engineers explained that they often became lost in the system, which required them to start over with their data entry. Consequently, they did not feel confident using Odysseus and had elected to return to their standard tools to ensure accuracy. The beta test engineers remained reluctant to use the final release of the tool, explaining concerns about the functionality and the accuracy of their data entry.

# Attitudes, Performance, and Beta Test Data

David returned to the Carillon office and spent the next few days compiling data from the interviews. David also reflected on his own usability observation notes from the field, which contributed to his understanding of Odysseus's basic functions, as well as its limitations.

Meanwhile, David supervised his designers as they moved forward with a highly sophisticated and attractive interface for the learning module. When the needs assessment data were ready for a final analysis, David asked his instructional designers to take a break and help him review the findings. They found a complex series of concerns (Table 25–1 and Table 25–2), which seemed unlikely to be solved by attempts at "attitude adjustment" (suggested by Lompoc) or "performance training" (requested by Dragone).

**TABLE 25–1  Hardware Concerns Highlighted During Field Beta Tests of the Odysseus System.**

**Contrast/Lighting**

- Laptop screen presents significant lighting and contrast problems in direct sunlight. The earth tone colors are attractive but are too similar to differentiate between objects on the screen, especially in varying lighting conditions.

**Pulley System**

- Data probes must drop up to 20,000 feet underground. A pulley controls the probe cables and organizes the different probes for each type of sample. The device also reduces the tension placed on the laptop connections. The pulley occasionally crimps the wires, resulting in a negative reading.

**Setup of the Data Probes**

- Setup takes approximately three hours (the same as the standard system). The engineers are accustomed to calibrating their tools prior to each data-collection session and are not comfortable with the "self-correcting" calibration in the new system.

**TABLE 25–2    Software Concerns Highlighted During Field Beta Tests of the Odysseus System.**

### Navigation

- There are between 8 and 14 windows among which a user must navigate for data entry and analysis.

- The only way to determine if data are missing is to run the analysis, which takes several minutes. After the analysis, a screen prompts the user for missing information.

### Online Help

- The three engineers who spoke English as a second language found the help screens inadequate. The screens did not define the steps needed to complete the task in question, and the engineers didn't know what terms to input when searching for navigation tips.

- The two engineers for whom English was the primary language thought the help screens were too simplistic and were cumbersome to access.

- The search engine did not cover all of the system terminology and provided simplified definitions of functions.

- The user guidelines often referred to links or buttons without directing the user to their location.

### Functionality

- Several of the software functions were assigned names unique to the software, rather than names reflecting their physical counterparts.

# Next Steps

As he reviewed these data, David wondered how he could move forward with a training module when it seemed the product itself needed to be revised. David needed his colleagues' input and a resolution for this dilemma. He had known all along that he could be compromising the effectiveness of the instructional design process when he had the team move directly into interface design before the needs were articulated. And, although he was aware of the potential problems that could result from beginning product development before the completion of a needs analysis, he was surprised to uncover so many concerns that were not instructional.

In less than 24 hours, David and his team would present their findings and their progress on the development of the instructional module interface. David and his team members needed to determine how they should address the discrepancies between the needs analysis data and the module that was now under development. As he leafed through the data tables, he thought, "If only Dragone Drilling would allow me to close myself in a room for the next year, I could redesign the Odysseus software and make it the innovative solution that they envision."

# Preliminary Analysis Questions

1. What information led the client to conclude that there was an instructional need? How might David have explored this topic in greater depth at the initial meeting?
2. How can David encourage the client's consideration of problems in its own product, instead of just problems with the users' knowledge, skills, and attitudes?
3. Considering the time constraints placed on this project, what other options might David have pursued concerning the immediate development of a training module?
4. Given the situation at the end of the case, how might David and his team proceed with Dragone Drilling?

# Implications for ID Practice

1. How do you direct a client to consider all stakeholder perspectives when the client has predetermined an instructional need?
2. List and explain project management skills an instructional designer needs to have to lead a design and development team.

# Davey Jones

## Designing an Electronic Performance Support System

*by Gary Elsbernd and Donald A. Stepich*

Davey Jones had worked for WidgetMart for 10 years. He had begun as a technical writer, documenting procedures for the company's point-of-sale system, but had taken on a number of other responsibilities over the years. Because of his increasing knowledge of store operations and personnel, and the lack of formally trained instructional designers, Davey had been thrust into the roles of both instructional designer and stand-up trainer, responsible for teaching everything from new procedures to interpersonal skills.

WidgetMart was making a transition to an integrated electronic performance support system (EPSS) to replace its existing training and performance support materials. Existing materials were being repurposed and new information developed for online presentation. Davey's expertise in computer interface design made him a natural for the project, and he had been given the task of heading up the project team. It was a high-profile project, the kind of assignment that could be a real feather in Davey's cap. But it wasn't going to be easy.

## Background

WidgetMart had grown steadily, from 1 store in 1971, to 800 stores in 1994, to 4,000 stores in 2006. At the time of this project, it was the nation's largest discount widget retailer, with 5,000 stores throughout the United States, Puerto Rico, the U.S. Virgin Islands, and Canada. Each year, the company sold more than 250 million widgets to nearly 150 million customers, with sales of approximately $4 billion. The company was actually made up of three related stores:

- WidgetMart—selling high-quality widgets at affordable prices in self-service stores
- Universal Widgets—catering to the upscale widget market
- BuyMore—a leased sales operation with department space in large retail stores

Throughout the company's history, an effort had been made to teach the associates and managers working in the stores the best practices of day-to-day operations. During the old days (before 1994), most of this took the form of "sit with Fred" training, in which new trainee managers spent 6 to 18 months with experienced managers and district supervisors, who carried best practices from store to store.

However, there were several problems with this kind of training. One was that the procedures varied from region to region and sometimes from store to store. The six regional management offices could rarely agree on the most efficient procedure for anything from processing an incoming shipment to handling customer returns to setting displays. This resulted in six different sets of best practices and difficulties in transferring associates from region to region. Another problem was that the information degenerated as it passed from person to person, much like a photocopy of a photocopy. The first trainer might understand the procedures and the rationale behind the procedures, but the next trainer might understand only the mechanics of the procedures. By the time the information had passed to the associates in the stores, the compelling business reasons were often lost and the procedures themselves were often changed, similar to the telephone game played by kids at camp. It's fine for the message to degrade in a game, but in business it leads to inefficient and ineffective performance.

These problems became more noticeable during the company's explosive growth in the 1990s and early 2000s. As a result, management had decided to make the information more formal and consistent. Company-wide standards were adopted, and a team of technical writers collected best practices throughout the stores and compiled them into an operations manual ("ops manual"). As an example, before 1994, merchandise displays were left to the individual store. Some managers displayed the best-selling widgets, hoping to extend the sales of those units. Others displayed the widgets with the biggest inventory to increase product turnover and free up shelf space. Still others chose seasonal widgets to match their concepts of fashion. To make displays more consistent, the ops manual included a standard for product displays, based on projected sales throughout the company and designed to present a consistent image to customers. Similar standards were developed for other store operations.

The ops manual became the foundation for a set of structured workshops and paper-based, self-paced training materials, which were made available to all store managers and associates. However, the ops manual and the training materials were organized differently. The ops manual was organized by functional area within the corporate office: leadership, human resources, store administration, merchandise administration, marketing, loss prevention, and store maintenance. The training materials were organized by position responsibilities for store associates: orientation, merchandise, customer satisfaction, sales transactions, store administration, supervisory skills, and management skills. Over the years, the ops manual and the training materials were updated, but more effort went into adding new information than into deleting old, obsolete information.

In 1998, a text-based online reference tool was added, consisting of more than 1,100 topics presented as ASCII text files in an indexed and searchable browser. This opened up the possibility of reusable, hyperlinked information. But the technology available at the time limited the online reference tool to 1 megabyte of information within a DOS environment, and the system was, at best, rudimentary. However, the company now has much more current technologies. This has opened up the prospect of overhauling the training and performance support of the associates.

# The EPSS Design Plan

The plan was to use the new, more sophisticated computer technology to update and replace the existing materials with a system that was entirely online. The online materials needed to be accessed easily and just as easily revised. They also had to include best practices related to all aspects of store operations—loss prevention, retail operations, merchandising, human resources, and so on. The goal was to embed the knowledge in the software as field edits, prompts, and error messages that provided the necessary knowledge or tools to perform the task on demand or in the background. This would radically redefine the work in the stores and would allow managers and associates to focus on tasks that required human intervention, rather than tasks that were more easily completed by the computer, such as looking up information or calculating numbers. One example was the scheduling system. Previously, the manager created work schedules manually, based on his or her knowledge of the workload, labor laws, and associates' requests. Under the new system, an EPSS scheduling function would take the current best knowledge of these factors and create a draft schedule for the manager to review and edit or approve, optimizing the scheduled work to the projected workload. As the manager made changes to the schedule, the software reviewed the change against workload, labor laws, and associates' requests and preferences, providing warnings or recommendations as necessary.

In tasks completed away from the computer, such as rack allocation, the EPSS software would present the necessary data (e.g., number of racks, inventory), the decision criteria (e.g., current and projected sales, seasonal promotions), and the recommended process (each rack charted by size and style) in an easy-to-use job aid accessible with handheld devices. The challenge was to create a system in which knowledge and best practices of every process were embedded in the EPSS software and support systems.

Some steps had already been taken. A thorough analysis of the performance environment had been performed to determine where and how information was used in the stores. Because WidgetMart was a self-service store, associates were rarely on or near the computer. They spent most of their time processing shipments in the back room or stocking displays on the sales floor. Store managers spent only about 15% of their time on the computer, completing tasks such as scheduling and inventory tracking. Still, all managers and associates had access to the computer and used it for timing in and out. Based on this analysis, the EPSS would be made up of four functions:

- Applications with embedded knowledge—software applications for computer-mediated tasks in which data, best practices, and business rules would be embedded, negating the need to learn or even review the knowledge. For example, the use of an inventory finder with embedded suggestions for cross-selling would support customer satisfaction.
- A reference function—a repository of knowledge, which could be accessed whenever needed. For example, if a manager needed to determine how many days off had been provided to an associate whose grandfather had died, he or she would be able to access this information.

- A job aid function—a database of records and documents, which would be accessed on handheld devices to support performance away from the computer. For example, the rack allocation guidelines would dynamically generate the optimal display guidelines and outline the process for changing the racks for new associates.
- A computer-based instruction function—structured information and guidelines designed to help associates internalize the information. For example, when an irate customer walked in the door, the associate needed to be able to react properly in the absence of any external support. Therefore, associates must learn how to deal with difficult customers.

With these functions in mind, the project team decided to meet to work on the design of the EPSS. The first meeting was arranged for a Monday morning.

# The Project Team Meeting

After coffee and rolls, everyone settled down so that Davey could explain the next stage of the project. Looking around the table, Davey thought about the knowledge represented by the team. No one had formal training in instructional design, but each member of the team was an expert in different aspects of store operations. Ellen Tyson understood merchandising processes and had designed many of the business applications that would be incorporated into the EPSS. She would also take on some of the project's administrative responsibilities, allowing Davey to continue to build sponsor support and advocacy and to determine a long-range strategy for the system. Josie Bednarksi worked on the acquisition team for Universal Widget and was instrumental in defining the training system for BuyMore. She understood better than anyone else the variations in the information required for WidgetMart, Universal Widgets, and BuyMore. Tim Hosch was the translation expert. He understood the variations needed in the information from country to country to account for customs, language, and governmental requirements. Barry Murphy, the newest member of the team, had been brought in for his experience in management development and interpersonal skills. His focus would be on the internal marketing and change management aspects of the system, rather than the technical implementation. The team had a wide range of talents and the knowledge necessary to complete the project.

"You know the background," Davey began. "We're creating an online performance support system with four functions—applications with embedded knowledge, a reference function, a job aid function, and a computer-based instruction function. The problem is that there is a massive amount of information. Information has been accumulating in the ops manual and training programs over the years, and not much has been done to combine or weed out the outdated information. The information sometimes overlaps. Sometimes it's downright contradictory. And, sometimes, different employees get different information at different times in their careers, which confuses things even more. To make matters worse, there is a whole collection of new information that comes with the change we're making to a new system and new processes.

"In order to create the new online system, this information will have to be collected, sifted, and assigned to one of the four functions. The goal is to have a completely integrated system that presents accurate information in the most concise, reusable form possible. In other words, we have a big pile of information and four buckets—five, if you count the trash bucket. Our job is to figure out how to break down the information into the smallest usable bit, catalog it, and sort it. We'll have to come up with a way to decide what information to keep and a way to decide where each piece of information goes. We'll also have to figure out how to make sure that the functions support one another, without any inconsistencies.

"The challenge is to create a single, seamless package that includes everyone from entry-level shipment processors to district managers with responsibility for 20 to 30 stores, and it has to include variations of the information for our 3 stores—WidgetMart, Universal Widgets, and BuyMore—and the unique requirements for the various countries we're in.

"How should we start?"

## Preliminary Analysis Questions

1. Outline a method (or methods) that can be used to gather all of the information. Describe how this information can be broken down into the smallest chunks that would be appropriate for the knowledge inventory.
2. Suggest a method that can be used to catalog the information into the five buckets mentioned in the project team meeting. That is, how can the team make consistent decisions about what information should be converted (vs. discarded) and about what information should be placed into each of the four established functions of the EPSS—maintaining the consistency of the information without making it unnecessarily redundant?
3. Describe a method that can be used to make sure the inventory is complete—that it includes all of the relevant information. Suggest a method or methods that can be used to maintain the inventory once it has been completed.
4. Describe a method that can be used to make sure the inventory is accurate.
5. Outline a plan for adapting the inventory for all the variations within WidgetMart (stores, countries, and languages).

## Implications for ID Practice

1. Describe the purpose of task/content analysis in instructional design and the particular importance of doing a careful task/content analysis when developing an EPSS.
2. Outline a plan for the task/content analysis for a proposed EPSS – including strategies for gathering relevant content, breaking that content down into a consistent "chunk" size, and sorting it into the different functions of the EPSS.
3. Describe ways to validate the accuracy and completeness of a completed task/content analysis for a proposed EPSS.

# Diane King

## Rapid Design Approach to Designing Instruction

*by Ronni Hendel-Giller and Donald A. Stepich*

Diane King, a seasoned instructional designer with IDEAL Performance Solutions, hung up the phone. Stan Smith, her client from the automotive insurance division of Delta Financial Group, had called to tell her that he would like her to design and develop training for team leaders ("leads") in the collections departments of Delta's branch offices.

## Background

About a month earlier, Diane had completed a course for Delta's phone representatives ("reps"), which covered issues associated with customer handling. The audience for this course had been reps who were new to Delta and had limited experience with collections work. These new reps needed to develop an approach to customers that was assertive without being aggressive and alienating. Most new reps had difficulty finding the right balance. This balance was needed to help customers find ways to bring their accounts current and to show them the importance of doing this.

Diane and her team developed a model for handling calls and designed a three-day course that helped participants achieve the desired balance in their calls through the use of this model. The "soft" skills required to support the model (listening skills, negotiation skills) were developed and practiced, using very specific role plays and case studies. Diane had been excited about the work she'd done—she had a great team of designers and knew the course was well designed. She had received great support from her subject matter experts (SMEs), and she knew that the course was built from a deep understanding of Delta's business challenges and priorities.

Early on in the project, however, Diane and Stan began to realize that the ultimate impact of the course would be limited. Although new and recent hires were being trained to be appropriately assertive when handling calls, their colleagues and managers were not aware of what was included in the training. And, to make matters worse, most of the current supervisors and team leads had learned their jobs by trial and error. According to

Diane's SMEs, the team leads and the more veteran reps were generally too aggressive or too passive with customers, which was one reason that Delta had a problem with delinquency. It was clear that the new reps would not be supported in implementing what they had learned in the course.

To complicate matters further, the team lead job was relatively new. Recently, the entire collections function had been redesigned and the team lead role established. The team leads had been promoted from the ranks of advanced reps. Now, instead of being responsible for handling the difficult calls themselves, their job was to coach and monitor a team of reps. A new system had been installed that tracked measures, such as call time. Until now, no tracking devices had been used. In addition, a call monitoring system was put in place that allowed team leads to record and listen to calls and provide feedback to reps. When the new systems were rolled out, Delta provided about two hours of systems training for the team leads, but no training was provided on how to use the data that the systems generated to give feedback to the reps.

Diane and Stan had asked to develop team lead training concurrently with the development of training for the reps. At the time, however, Stan had been unable to convince members of the operations group to make this investment. The rep training had already been budgeted, and the team lead training didn't fit into anyone's budget. The restructuring and new systems had been expensive, and there just wasn't any money left.

## The Present Problem

When Stan called to ask Diane to design a team lead course, they both almost had to laugh. Finally, the organization had realized that it had to start with the team leads. It was apparent, in every Delta branch, that the team leads were not performing their jobs as they had been defined. They were reluctant to give feedback to people who had only recently been their peers, they weren't sure how to use the data they received, and they didn't necessarily handle the calls in the most effective ways themselves. Most team leads had slipped back to their previous behaviors and were spending the majority of their time taking the hard calls and ignoring their leadership and management roles. Their supervisors were at a loss—they really weren't much better than the team leads at managing the new processes and tools. Most supervisors had minimal guidance, support, and training in their own roles as coaches and leaders.

Stan and Diane, although frustrated that it had taken this long, were excited that they finally had the opportunity to "do it right." They even hoped to include supervisors in the training process and start from the top down. At the same time, there were a number of challenges that would make this project difficult. Delta was now concerned about what was happening in its branches and had determined that this training was a high priority, meaning the timeline would be very aggressive. It needed to be deployed as soon as possible. Also, Delta had a minimal budget for this effort.

Stan understood that this meant that they'd need to find ways to speed up the ID process. IDEAL Performance Solutions had previously prepared materials for Delta that were robust—participant guides that were graphically impressive and facilitator guides that were highly detailed. Diane knew that Stan would have trouble with any materials that were less than polished and with any approach that appeared to short-circuit the design process. IDEAL Performance Solutions was known for the quality of its process and its deliverables. "Fast and cheap" was *not* its motto.

Nevertheless, Diane was not discouraged. She knew the work environment at Delta, had met with several team leads during the design of the customer rep training, and thought that she understood the organization's culture. She also knew that a quicker, less labor-intensive design process was something that IDEAL needed to develop. More and more clients were emphasizing speed, and more and more vendors were developing training to support organizational change initiatives that were being implemented at a rapid pace. If Diane could succeed with this project, she'd be helping IDEAL become more competitive in the marketplace, as well as helping her client meet its goals.

# The Existing ID Process at IDEAL Performance Solutions

Diane decided to try to figure out ways to speed up the existing ID process at IDEAL and to reduce labor costs. The existing process consisted of the following steps:

1. A commitment to a thorough needs analysis: IDEAL told its clients that analysis was key to training effectiveness and that a thorough analysis was critical. Typically, IDEAL spent three to four weeks conducting research, including interviews, focus groups, and surveys of the training audience. An assessment report was generated and discussed with clients before proceeding to the design phase.

2. Development of a detailed design plan with clear and well-defined performance objectives was a must. The timeline for design plan development was usually about two weeks (for a two-day workshop), with a week for client review and a full-day client review meeting. Another week was allotted for revision to the design plan and final sign-off on the design.

3. First-draft development was allotted about a month, with a full-time designer assigned to the project; Diane served as primary client contact and occasionally did some development herself. This included the development of participant and facilitator guides. Role plays and case studies were very detailed, incorporating specific work situations to ensure better transfer to the job. When necessary, the designer talked with SMEs to gather additional data.

4. The first draft review and pilot draft development usually took about three to four weeks and included walkthroughs of activities to gain formative feedback from SMEs, accuracy checks by SMEs, and the involvement of a desktop publishing team to develop a polished product for the pilot.

5. A pilot was held with a representative sample of end users. Following the pilot, a month was allotted for pilot revisions and production of the final materials.

Based on this process, a two- to three-day course, such as the team lead course, would take about 20 weeks, or five months, from start to finish. In some cases, IDEAL could speed up the process by increasing manpower—which reduced the timeline but did not affect the cost of the project.

# Rapid ID Strategies

Diane had heard about rapid design and decided to do some research. She wanted to develop some strategies for reducing the time and cost of the design and development process while continuing to deliver training that would meet the needs of the learners and would achieve the desired organizational results. From her research, she learned that there were several key assumptions underlying traditional design and that many of these assumptions were being challenged by those suggesting rapid design strategies. Key assumptions included the following:

- All components of the design process are required to deliver a robust product.
- Design is a linear process, in which each component of the design model appears once and is not reconsidered unless revision is required.
- Effective design requires a commitment to the full execution of each component of the design process.
- Failure to complete a component of the design process will reduce the effectiveness of instruction.

Diane recognized that these assumptions were at the heart of IDEAL's design process and were assumptions that she herself had made in her work as an instructional designer. She also knew that these assumptions were often hard to live by. There had been times when she had tried to short-circuit the traditional design process and had often felt as though she were "cheating." She discovered that proponents of rapid design methods were challenging these traditional assumptions and suggesting new approaches and strategies. Some of the rapid design principles that Diane discovered included the following:

- A belief that instructional design is a nonlinear process and that there is no one right way to design. Different stages can be completed in tandem and then revisited in an iterative manner. Initial budget constraints can result in an initial set of lean materials, which can, if necessary or desired, be enhanced at a later stage.
- Analysis and design are considered a collaborative process. Designers work with key stakeholders to quickly complete the analysis and design work. The end user is often a key player in the design process, both contributing to the development of materials and testing prototype materials as they are developed and refined.
- Analysis is completed rapidly by making full use of extant data and by limiting the quantity of data collected with a condensed, targeted analysis.
- Budget and time constraints are addressed by focusing on content and instructional strategy, rather than on level of production. Minimalist facilitator and participant

materials can be developed—especially for an initial pilot. If necessary, these can be expanded and enriched at a later stage in the project.

■ The use of participant input in the actual training session can eliminate some of the need to develop extensive role-play and case-study scenarios. Eliciting real issues and concerns from the course participants can reduce design time and increase value and relevance.

Using these strategies, Diane set out to define a project plan that would allow her to conduct the first training of the team leads within two months of the start of the project and then be able to train the rest of the team leads within two weeks after that.

# Preliminary Analysis Questions

1. Review each step of IDEAL's instructional design process in light of the rapid design principles described in the case study. What suggestions can you make to speed up the process and reduce labor costs?
2. How receptive do you think Delta might be to these suggestions? What concerns or objections might be raised by the client? What might you do to sell your rapid design strategies to the client?
3. How can Diane ensure that the training she develops using a rapid design methodology is consistent with the quality for which IDEAL Performance Solutions is known?

# Implications for ID Practice

1. In this case, the use of rapid design is important because of a request to speed up the process used to design and develop instructional products. What other factors might push instructional designers either toward or away from the use of rapid design?
2. What are the risks and benefits of a rapid design approach? In what kinds of situations would rapid design be most useful? Are there situations in which rapid design should be avoided?
3. How does using a rapid design approach change the knowledge and skills required of the designer?

# Natalie Morales

## Managing Training in a Manufacturing Setting

*by Krista D. Glazewski and Shanna M. Hicks*

Natalie Morales started her new position at Chipex Manufacturing by wondering what the project would entail. It was her first consulting job after having recently earned a master's degree in instructional technology (IT). When one of her former professors alerted her to this opportunity, Natalie jumped at the chance. Natalie had previously worked for this professor on a number of IT jobs in manufacturing settings and felt this would be right up her alley—in a large, semiconductor organization that manufactures electronic microchips used in everything from computers to traffic lights to cell phones. Although this particular factory was in the Southwest, Chipex was a large manufacturer with factories all over the United States and the world.

Natalie arrived promptly to her 8:00 A.M. meeting with Rich Davis, a human resources representative, who gave her more information about the task at hand. "We have a training problem," Rich explained. "I'll give you the basics, and you'll meet shortly with Michelle Griego for the details. We're hoping you can identify some solutions. We've noticed a problem in the factory with our technician certification process. The technicians are the people who actually work on the floor moving the wafers through the line. They are responsible for obtaining and maintaining their own certifications, but it's come to our attention that the supervisors have been prioritizing the certifications differently and there's not a standard process."

Natalie was writing as quickly as she could, but the look on her face must have betrayed her confusion. Rich stopped himself. "OK, let me back up a bit and give you some more information. The training culture at Chipex can be summed up in one phrase, 'You own your own development.' In other words, employees are expected to plan their own training and development. In particular, technicians are responsible for obtaining and maintaining various certifications. Some certifications are required for every technician, such as compliance with safety procedures. Others are area-specific or job-specific. The more certifications a technician holds, the more highly his or her skills are valued, which is a strong factor in promotion and yearly raises."

Natalie nodded, continuing to write while Rich went on. "It was Michelle who brought to our attention a persistent problem with certifications. She's a supervisor of one of the process areas in the factory and manages a team of technicians. You'll be meeting with her later today, and she'll oversee your work. The basic problem is that we don't have a standard process in place for managing and prioritizing certifications. Every supervisor prioritizes differently; so, for example, some technicians hold numerous certifications, but these may not be the most strategic ones based on shift or area needs. On another shift, the technicians might not hold as many, but they are the strategic ones for the area. At any rate, Michelle will explain all this to you in more detail. You'll meet with her at 7:00."

Natalie looked at her watch—8:15 A.M. "Seven o'clock?" she asked.

Rich clarified, "This is a 24/7 factory and Michelle is on the night shift. You'll meet with her at 7:00 P.M. In the meantime, I'll have you meet with my administrator, who can get you set up with the paperwork, an ID badge, and a temporary e-mail account. I'm looking forward to your final report and recommendations in a few weeks."

Natalie left a short time later feeling challenged by the complexity of the task facing her. She decided to organize her notes and make a list of questions for Michelle. Everyone here seemed to be in such a hurry, and she wanted to make the most of her time.

After organizing her notes, she came up with a list of questions for Michelle:

- What is a "process area"?
- How many technicians are in an area? How many areas are there?
- How exactly are certifications obtained?
- How long does it take to obtain a certification?
- How do technicians maintain their certifications?
- Whom else should I speak with?
- When can I speak to some of the technicians?

Natalie also used the time before her meeting with Michelle to learn more about Chipex. She went online to learn about the electronic microchip manufacturing process and found out that the chip starts off as a silicon wafer. It goes through layering phases, called process steps; at each step, something is applied to the wafer, such as a chemical, metal, or etching. The wafer goes through numerous processes and is built, literally, from the bottom up. At the end of the fabrication, it is cut into hundreds of microchips.

Natalie connected the information to some statements Rich had made earlier and concluded that when he referred to a "process area," he was talking about one of the areas that applied a chemical, metal, or etching process to the wafer. She noted that each process area must, therefore, consist of a supervisor and a team of technicians. She was happy to cross the first question off her list.

Before she knew it, Natalie's research had taken most of the day. Remembering Rich's statement about the 24/7 factory, she expected that it might be a late night. Natalie took a short nap and then grabbed dinner before heading off to her meeting with Michelle, who smiled warmly as she welcomed Natalie. "Thanks for coming on board to work on this project. It's something important to me because I think a lot of shift frustrations can be addressed by tackling this issue."

Natalie smiled in return, relieved that Michelle didn't seem as frantic as Rich. "I'm glad to be here, and I'm anticipating a productive experience. I made a list of questions based on my meeting with Rich. I'm familiar with what is meant by a process area, but can you start by telling me more about the process areas and certifications? How many people are in an area, and how does someone become certified?"

"OK, that's a good place to start. Each process area consists of about 20 to 30 technicians and one supervisor per shift, but numbers can fluctuate. There are about 17 areas for my shift. Technicians are responsible for earning certifications, meaning they have gone through official training and can perform the skill. Factory-wide certifications, such as those related to compliance with safety procedures, are required of every technician. These are usually obtained by taking a class, though there are exceptions. Those that are job-specific or area-specific involve demonstrating skills with a tool that applies a process to the wafer. Do you know what I mean when I refer to the wafer process?"

Natalie nodded, pleased that she did know.

"Good. As I was saying, there are large tools that actually apply the process to the wafer. When I say 'tool,' keep in mind these aren't small tools like you'd find in your garage. In fact, some tools are so large they couldn't fit in your garage! So, becoming certified on a tool is a two-step process: first, taking a class or working one-on-one with a peer trainer, and second, obtaining a sign-off from the trainer after demonstrating skill proficiency. Depending on the complexity of the tool, a certification can take up to 18 months to complete, but most only take a few months and some can take only a few weeks. When a new tech is hired, he or she shadows a trainer until the certification has been earned and the technician can work independently. In effect, the longer someone has been an employee, the more certifications they should have. Are you with me so far?"

Natalie nodded and continued to write as Michelle proceeded with the explanation. "For a given skill, there are also 'levels' of proficiency: 1, which represents basic operational skill, through 4, which represents an expert level. A Level 4 could perform complex preventative maintenance on a tool or repair it if something goes wrong. Trainers for the various tool certifications are technicians who hold at least a Level 3 certification and a 'peer trainer' designation. Finally, if someone needs a certification but no one on the shift can train, the technician has to schedule training with someone on another shift.

"So," Michelle continued, "now that you have the background on this, let's move on to some of the problems. For one thing, this is currently self-monitored by the technicians and the trainers, though supervisors like myself are expected to manage technicians' certifications and make sure shift needs are met. For example, it doesn't make a lot of sense for me to have a bunch of Level 1 certifications among my technicians without balancing this with higher levels. Similarly, it's a waste of time to have a bunch of Level 4s—that level of skill takes so long to master but is rarely needed. But it's not as if there's a magic ratio of lower to higher levels, because every process area is different. The supervisor just has to know the needs of the area intimately and work with technicians accordingly. Unfortunately, this can be difficult, especially because some technicians and supervisors are short-sighted. They take a 'more-the-merrier,' shotgun approach and try to rack up as many Level 1s as possible. Some technicians are awarded with raises in this manner. Plus, it's difficult to obtain higher levels, which involves longer-term goal-setting."

Natalie took a moment to think, realizing she would need to speak with some of the technicians as soon as possible, and probably some other supervisors as well. "That helps me understand more about the problem," said Natalie. "I'd like to speak with some of the technicians, if possible. How can I go about getting their perspectives?"

"Yeah, I figured you'd want to speak with them, and I've got to go to another meeting. I don't really know the best process for setting up interviews because they're working in the factory. The best I can do is set you up in a conference room and send some technicians your way during the next few shifts. It might involve some late nights, and the interviews might be short and intermittent. Can you handle that?"

"Sure—let's get started tonight, if possible."

"Great. I've got two people in mind that I'll send to you shortly—Hector Madrid and Tran Nguyen. They've both got a wide range of certifications, they're both peer trainers, and they've been here for a number of years. They'll probably be able to give you some key information. Anything else I can help you with?"

Natalie looked over her notes for a moment. "I'm not sure I understand the difference between a job certification and an area certification."

"Well, that's a good question. A job-specific certification deals with operations; in other words, operating the tool that moves the wafer through the line. An area certification means the technician has to understand the process of the wafer in the area. It's an advanced skill, and technicians with area certifications understand more about the priority of the product and how to most efficiently move the product through based on where the wafer is coming from and where it will go next.

"Oh, and that reminds me . . . I made a simplified matrix for you that should help you understand the certifications on my shift (Figure 28–1). I've only been supervising this team for a few weeks, so I wanted to see the current status myself. It includes the names and length of employment in descending order down the left. There's a list of certifications across the top, but I simplified this because you wouldn't really understand our codes and it's not important anyway. Skills and their related proficiency levels are listed below. The numbers 1 to 4 indicate the level of certification, but you'll notice that safety is required of everyone and there aren't levels. In addition, process skills are only two levels. Finally, a 'P' means that the technician is in the process of getting that certification. Also, keep in mind that this matrix is only a sample of a few tools and a few process certs. I'm still working on making a complete representation for all the tools and processes, but this will get you started."

Natalie studied the matrix briefly and then filed it among her materials for later reference. She knew she would need to study this more deeply.

A short time later, Natalie was sitting with Tran and Hector at one end of a big conference table. She asked them about their perspectives on the certification process.

"Well," began Hector, "the certifications are an interesting approach to training. I like being in the role of trainer, but I hated when I was the new guy trying to get the Level 1s. For one thing, it involves trying to schedule time with someone. If they're in a hurry, you won't get quality instruction. That's why it can take so long—the training can be intermittent, and you might forget things in between the sessions. I try to be really sensitive to this fact. If I know someone needs certification, I really try to work with that person."

"Yeah," Tran remarked, "but things are a lot easier for them now. Back when we were getting our first certifications, there were *external* certifiers who would actually watch you

**FIGURE 28–1**    Status of Employees' Training Certifications.

| Name | Length of Emp. | Safety A.1 | Safety A.2 | Operations: Tool A | | | | Operations: Tool B | | | | Operations: Tool C | | | | Operations: Tool E | | | | Operations: Tool F | | | | Process: PCMT | | Process: Ops | |
|---|---|---|---|---|---|---|---|---|---|---|---|---|---|---|---|---|---|---|---|---|---|---|---|---|---|---|---|
| | | | | Level 1 | Level 2 | Level 3 | Level 4 | Level 1 | Level 2 | Level 3 | Level 4 | Level 1 | Level 2 | Level 3 | Level 4 | Level 1 | Level 2 | Level 3 | Level 4 | Level 1 | Level 2 | Level 3 | Level 4 | Level 1 | Level 2 | Level 1 | Level 2 |
| Hector* | >6 yr. | X | X | X | X | X | X | | | | | X | X | X | | | | | | | | | | X | X | X | X |
| Tran* | >6 yr. | X | X | | | | | X | X | X | | | | | | X | X | X | X | X | | | | | | | | |
| Rod* | 5 yr. | X | X | X | X | | | | | | | | | | | | | | | X | X | X | | | | | | |
| Phuoc | 4 yr. | X | X | | | | | X | P | | | | | | | X | X | P | | | | | | | | | | |
| James | 4 yr. | X | X | X | X | X | | | | | | X | X | X | X | | | | | | | | | | | | | |
| Tinh | 4 yr. | X | X | | | | | | | | | | | | | X | X | X | P | | | | | | | | | |
| Mario | 4 yr. | X | X | X | X | X | | | | | | | | | | | | | | X | | | | | | | X | |
| Angela | 3 yr. | X | X | X | P | | | X | | | | X | P | | | X | | | | X | P | | | | | | | |
| Carlos | 3 yr. | X | X | X | X | X | | | | | | X | P | | | | | | | | | | | X | P | | | |
| Carmen | 3 yr. | X | X | X | P | | | | | | | X | X | X | | | | | | | | | | | | | | |
| Phuong | 3 yr. | X | X | | | | | X | P | | | | | | | X | P | | | | | | | | | | | |
| Gregg | 3 yr. | X | X | X | X | | | | | | | | | | | | | | | | | | | | | | | |
| Pete | 3 yr. | X | X | X | P | | | X | | | | X | | | | X | | | | P | | | | | | | P | |
| Tong | 2 yr. | X | X | | | | | X | P | | | | | | | X | | | | | | | | | | | | |
| Amato | 2 yr. | X | X | X | | | | | | | | X | P | | | | | | | | | | | | | | | |
| Rachael | 2 yr. | X | X | X | | | | X | | | | | | | | | | | | X | | | | | | | | |

*Indicates peer trainer designation

perform the skills and sign off. Now, because they've cut back on staff, it's the trainers like us that certify a person. You can imagine that it's easier to get signatures now. Even if the person can't perform it right then and there, I can think, 'Well, I know I taught that skill, and I saw the person perform it at that time.'"

That didn't seem appropriate to Natalie, but she nodded anyway. "Wait a second," exclaimed Hector, "you mean to tell me you're signing off on techs who you haven't seen actually *perform* the entire skill?"

"Well, I didn't say that," replied Tran. "I just meant that if techs skip a step or two but I know that I saw them do it previously, I'm going to let it go. I'm saying it's better that we do the sign-offs, because we know what we taught them. Besides, the more people I can certify, the more highly I'm rated in my effectiveness as a trainer."

"Are you serious?" Hector appeared furious. "Here I am being painfully thorough, only to find out you're handing out certifications like Halloween candy so you can get higher ratings for yourself."

"Not like Halloween candy—"

"OK," Natalie interrupted. She knew she had to do something before this went further. "This brings me to another question. How do you decide who to train?"

She could tell Hector was still angry, but Tran jumped right in. "Usually they come to us. But hopefully the supervisor is working on a plan with the techs, and helping them to know which Level 1s to get, and when to start getting the Level 2s and up. We just figure if people are asking, they know what they need."

"Well, what Tran's saying is not entirely accurate," added Hector. "Sometimes, it can depend on other factors. For example, I speak Spanish and Tran speaks Vietnamese. When we get techs in here who can't speak English very well and they're from Vietnam, they go to Tran and get training. Now we've got a number of Vietnamese techs, and their skill sets are limited only to what Tran can train them on. Over time, their English will get better, but until then. . . ." Hector shook his head, then added, "It's the same with me and those who speak Spanish but not much English."

Natalie nodded, making a note to refer to the matrix at a later time to see if there was a pattern there.

"What does a typical supervisor do to address all of these issues?" Natalie directed the question to Hector.

"Well," began Hector, "it can really depend on the supervisor. Some supervisors want to look like their technicians are really productive, so they've got them obtaining all these certifications left and right. The problem is, when are these technicians doing their actual *jobs*? If they're spending time accumulating all these certs, they aren't doing their jobs. Or it can backfire, and the managers will think there are too many staff members on the shift. But then again, it's also a problem if a shift has too few certs."

"Well," added Tran, "I'm not sure I agree with Hector about too many certifications being a problem. Is there a problem with 'too many skills' on the team? For me, there is a bigger issue. Supervisors tend to get shifted around on a yearly or bi-yearly basis. What one supervisor said was important may not be what the new supervisor prioritizes. It's hard to know, and we're sometimes stuck in the middle. I mean, techs like Hector or myself aren't in jeopardy, but the newer techs aren't always able to set goals and make a plan, so it really throws them when supervisors change."

"For once, I can say Tran and I are in agreement," said Hector, "but I don't have time to go into all that. It's time to get back to the factory."

That left Natalie not quite knowing *what* to think herself. She recognized that the project incorporated numerous issues, each of which seemed equally important. Though she was exhausted, Natalie decided to take another hour to study the matrix, make a list of what she had learned so far, and develop a plan of work.

# Preliminary Analysis Questions

1. Identify the factors that are affecting the training certification process at Chipex. What other information do you think Natalie needs to help her address these factors?
2. List the ways in which language impacts workers' performance and ability to get ahead in the situation described in this case. What are some potential strategies for addressing this issue?
3. Hector and Tran have different motivations and approaches to training technicians. What problems do these cause for Chipex?

# Implications for ID Practice

1. How can contextual factors affect how trainers manage the implementation of training in an organization? How can instructional designers account for these factors when providing guidelines for the implementation of training?
2. List and discuss the legal and ethical issues involved when employees don't have equal opportunities for training.
3. Discuss the benefits and challenges of one-on-one peer training. Suggest a set of guidelines for implementing and managing one-on-one peer training in an organization.

# Andrew Stewart

## Managing Consulting Activities in an Evaluation Context

*by Steven M. Ross and Gary R. Morrison*

Dr. Andrew Stewart looked forward to his meeting on Tuesday with Dr. Lois Lakewood and her staff at Rainbow Design. Aside from wanting to see Albuquerque again (it had been about 10 years since he had last visited), he believed that he was well prepared to handle his assigned role as program evaluator in Rainbow's design project and would enjoy it as well. Andrew was a professor of instructional design (ID) at a large university in Boston. He was knowledgeable about many aspects of design theory and practice and was considered a national expert in educational evaluation.

## The BTB Global Transport Contract

For Andrew, the professional challenge and opportunity seemed tremendous. Rainbow Design had been awarded a $1 million contract from BTB Global Transport (a large and profitable shipping firm) to develop a user support system for a new computer system, called Galaxy, being developed for BTB. The new system would support nearly all business functions, such as inventory management, accounting, billing, and ordering, and would require substantial changes in employee job functions and specific tasks.

On Tuesday, Andrew arrived early at Logan Airport in an effort to escape some of the office distractions and to gain additional time to review Rainbow Design's plan of work. By the time the airplane boarded, he had become thoroughly reacquainted with the essentials of the plan. Rainbow Design would need to develop varied types of user supports, using a learner-control–type format. Specifically, for each job task (e.g., accessing a customer's order number), the employee would be able to select online support when needed from a menu of options, including, for example, cue cards (brief definitions, reminders, or directives), web-based instruction (WBI), wizards (intelligent demonstration/application functions), and coaches (response-sensitive correction/feedback). Andrew's main responsibility would be to conduct a formative evaluation—first of the overall design approach and later of the individual support tools as they were developed.

Engrossed in his reading, Andrew barely noticed the smooth takeoff as the plane left Boston behind and cruised toward the West and Albuquerque. The effects of his early rising made him drowsy, but, before allowing himself to drift off, he wanted to study one additional part of the plan—the staffing section.

It looked good. Rainbow Design had a project manager, Cecilia Sullivan, who would perform necessary administrative functions but remain removed from ID decisions. Lois Lakewood, a talented and experienced designer with a doctorate from a nationally recognized graduate program, would head a diverse team of seven designers, including experts in text instruction, computer programming, WBI, and technical graphic design. In a vague, semiconscious way (especially in his sleepy state), Andrew experienced some discomfort with the role of a second, external design team housed in St. Louis. Because BTB Global Transport had a large satellite division in St. Louis, Cecilia thought it wise to hire local designers who could interface with the computer programmers in St. Louis to acquire a better understanding of how the Galaxy computer system would work when completed. A formidable challenge in this project was that user support prototypes would need to be developed based solely on impressions and draft models of Galaxy, because the real system wouldn't exist for an indeterminate time. The St. Louis team consisted of three young designers, all having master's degrees in instructional design from Davis University in St. Louis. Their leader, Alicia Rosenthal, was in her early thirties and was completing her doctoral dissertation there.

# The Planning Meeting

After arriving in Albuquerque, Andrew immediately took a taxi to the Rainbow Design office, which was located in a suburban strip mall about 10 miles from the airport. The meeting started as scheduled at 1:00 P.M. All the major participants were there, including the Rainbow team, the St. Louis team, and the BTB project manager, Carlton Grove. Lois did an excellent job briefing the group on the purposes of the project. Carlton described his expectations and, despite having little formal ID training (his background was human factors), displayed an excellent intuitive grasp of how user support should be employed and how to increase attractiveness and utility.

Several times during the discussions, Andrew observed that the St. Louis team, through facial gestures and side comments, was inattentive and disapproving of the orientations being proposed. The team had prepared a set of detailed flow diagrams, which, according to their brief description, established a support selection model based on the works of Gagné, Mager, and other theorists. However, there was little time to study the selection model sufficiently. Also, as Andrew noticed, the St. Louis team members themselves had little interest in it—they appeared to be primarily a practitioner-oriented group. Lois, he noted, frowned in response to the antics of the St. Louis team, and, when speaking, seemed somewhat tense and guarded.

Andrew closed the day with a clear and forceful overview of his formative evaluation plan. He described it as involving progressive stages of increasing focus and comprehensiveness, as the support prototypes evolved from early drafts to near-final products. In all phases, the evaluation would include multiple data sources (different instruments from different participant groups) to provide triangulation and increase the amount of feedback regarding the quality of the design and its products.

## Project Progress

Over the next two months, the Rainbow staff generated several user support prototypes for various employee job functions. Disappointingly, the St. Louis group, given the same assignment, was slow to produce any materials and still seemed constrained by their strict adherence to textbook models they had studied in their ID courses.

In several conference calls among Andrew, Lois (Rainbow), Alicia (St. Louis), and Carlton (BTB), there was obvious strain in the discussions. Provoked largely by Alicia's frequent resistance to the directions proposed, each stakeholder increasingly pursued an individual agenda for his or her team's work. Andrew's agenda, however, was already clearly defined by the current status of the project. With the first series of user supports developed and substantive costs already incurred (as Carlton frequently reminded the group), it was time to initiate the formative evaluation. Carlton wanted it done "yesterday," but "next week would be OK." Andrew mused that this was exactly the type of real-world situation he had recently warned his graduate students to expect.

## Developing an Evaluation Plan

Over the next few days, Andrew drafted questions and rough instrument plans and faxed them to Lois, who turned them—almost magically, it seemed—into a professional, polished set of materials. The final product was an "evaluation manual," consisting of a complete set of instructions, prompts, and instruments for guiding the evaluation step by step. In brief, the basic orientation, as designed by Andrew, was one-on-one trials, in which each interviewee would (1) describe his or her background and job activities; (2) walk through a simulation of a computer-based job function in the transportation industry (specifically, scheduling rail shipments); (3) examine sample user support tools made available for specific tasks; (4) rate each tool on various utility, user-interface, and aesthetic dimensions; (5) "reflect aloud" on its possible application; and (6) make recommendations. The manual was directly coordinated with the computer simulation and provided (so Andrew and Lois believed) tight control over the data-collection process, as well as an efficient data-recording system.

The final steps before launching the evaluation were to arrange for interviews and to train the evaluators. Interviewees would be approximately 10 employees at each of six national BTB sites. The evaluators would consist of designers from Rainbow Design and would include, to a more limited extent, Andrew (given time and travel constraints) and St. Louis staff (given Lois's concerns about their commitment and orientation).

Three days before the first set of interviews were to take place in the Minneapolis division, Lois received a call from Alicia, who said, "Given that we've been kind of impeded in our work with the BTB tech types here, I am very interested in taking a lead role in collecting evaluation data from the users. This would give me and my staff a really good feel for who's out there in BTB. User analysis is really our strength." Lois felt a tinge of anxiety about this proposal, but the idea did have some merit. It would occupy the St. Louis group (finally!); it would be good politics with her boss, Cecilia, who had hired the St. Louis team; and it would free the Rainbow staff, who now wouldn't have to travel as much, to work on the design task with their increasing demands. An agreement was reached whereby Alicia and staff would do the bulk of the user interviews (about 40 of 60). They flew into Albuquerque, met with Andrew and Lois, and, along with the Rainbow crew, received training on the evaluation procedure.

## Implementing the Evaluation

Data collection began. Over the next few weeks (through the end of March), Andrew and Lois each administered a few interviews and felt good about the procedures and materials they had designed. Alicia called Lois intermittently to give status reports from the field (they were always positive). Carlton from BTB called Andrew on April 2 to request that an evaluation report be submitted as a "deliverable" on April 15. "This can be done," Andrew thought, but he'd need Alicia to wrap things up in a week or so and get the data to him. Alicia, in a call to Lois, agreed.

On April 10, a large package with a St. Louis return address arrived at Andrew's Boston office. He opened it with anticipation. He would now need to contact his graduate student assistants, who would code and analyze the data. Pulling up the flaps of the box, he immediately saw a cover memo from Alicia ("Here are all of our data forms—42 interviews!!"). He then removed a stack of about 10 evaluation manuals from the top. All seemed to have the top page correctly filled out—interview name, employee name, time, date, and so on. When he turned to the second page, he noticed that it wasn't filled out. There were no user ratings of the first support tool, only the evaluator's handwritten notes. The same was true for the rest of the manuals—no ratings, only brief, often illegible comments. "Perhaps this one just didn't go right," he thought. "Really, can't use it." Looking at the next manual, his pulse increased, and then at the next manual and then two more, while his heart raced even faster. He dug into the middle of the box and grabbed a stack of three manuals—same thing. All were filled out in the same informal way that completely omitted the ratings.

## Truth and Consequences

It was the next day by the time his call to Lois produced the call to Alicia that brought Lois's call back to him—with the bad news. Alicia's group had decided on their own that the evaluation manual was really just a "heuristic" (general guide) and that the rating scales and specific comments weren't actually needed. "For doing user analysis," Alicia explained, "my designers favored a more holistic and qualitative orientation." Thus, they formed global opinions that they were certainly willing to share. (Andrew, too, had some opinions, but "share" would be too gentle a way to present them.)

The aftermath in the next few days was that Alicia and her group were severely reprimanded by Cecilia and put on probation in the project. But Andrew had a report to submit. Carlton, from BTB with his scientific orientation in human factors research, would be expecting at least some quantitative results (bar charts and the like), and Andrew had only about 13 correctly completed evaluation manuals—the ones from him and Rainbow Design. The report was due in three days.

# Preliminary Analysis Questions

1. Discuss each issue in the case from the perspective of the four key roles featured: evaluator, design manager, external design team, and client project manager.
2. Evaluate the actions taken in the four key roles in terms of making the final product (the evaluation study) successful.
3. Discuss what actions you might have taken in each of the four roles to avoid the problems that occurred.
4. Create a scenario in which the evaluation study is successful and the four key stakeholders are satisfied with the results.

# Implications for ID Practice

1. Describe the role of formative evaluation in the instructional design process.
2. Describe how instructional design practices can be affected by unexpected variables and events in real-life contexts.
3. Differentiate among the roles of a project business manager, a project design manager, an instructional designer, an evaluator, and a client project manager.
4. Describe the importance of a good management system for coordinating the activities of various consultant groups on a design project.

# CASE STUDY 30

# Jack Waterkamp
## Managing Scope Change in an Instructional Design Project

*by Shahron Williams van Rooij*

## Early February

Jack Waterkamp, Director of the Curriculum Development Group at Complex Data Systems, Inc., was feeling upbeat as he walked to the conference room for the Human Resources (HR) division's monthly meeting. Elizabeth Henderson, his boss and HR VP, had e-mailed a last-minute agenda item, and Jack was certain that it meant a new project for him and his team. He had recently celebrated his two-year anniversary with Complex Data Systems, a $960 million software development company that provided business software systems, classroom-based training, technical support, and annual maintenance agreements to small and medium-sized companies. He smiled as he passed the full-color organizational chart hanging on the corridor wall (Figure 30–1), envisioning his name among the other executives reporting directly to the company president.

Jack had arrived at Complex Data Systems with seven years of experience at an e-learning courseware vendor plus a bachelor's degree in computer science and a master's degree in instructional design. His career had been progressing well. The previous year, he had successfully introduced a small selection of self-paced refresher courses for employees and for client technical staff using Complex Data System's homegrown Learning Management System (LMS), although classroom-based training remained the standard for new products.

Yesterday Jack learned that the instructional design document he had written for the training curriculum for the new customer relationship management (CRM) software product was approved and ready to move into development. Now, this new project, whatever it was, would give him another opportunity to demonstrate his leadership skills and put him on senior management's radar for future executive team candidacy.

## The HR Division Meeting

Elizabeth Henderson switched on the LED data display system. "Good morning, everyone. Last night I e-mailed a new agenda item, so I'd like to start with that. The item is called *New Training Directions*. It's the result of an executive team meeting earlier this week,

**FIGURE 30–1** Complex Data Systems, Inc., Organizational Chart.

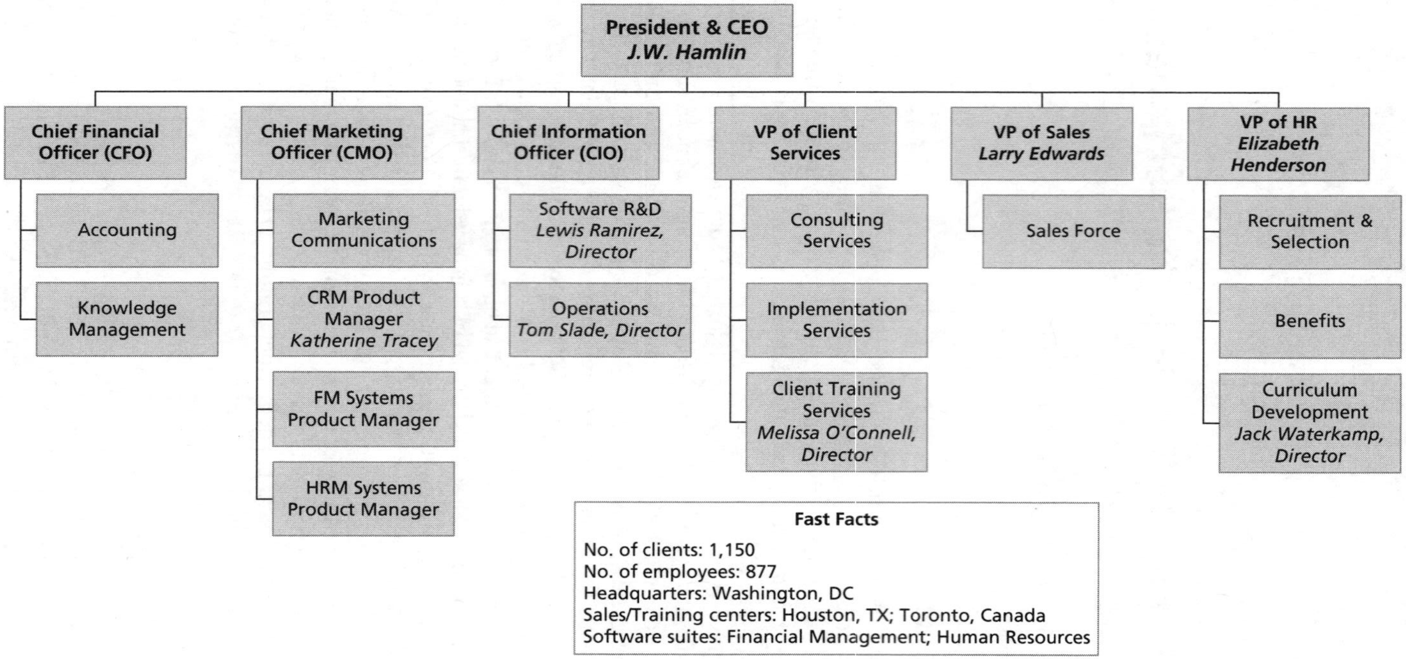

President & CEO
*J.W. Hamlin*

Chief Financial Officer (CFO)
- Accounting
- Knowledge Management

Chief Marketing Officer (CMO)
- Marketing Communications
- CRM Product Manager *Katherine Tracey*
- FM Systems Product Manager
- HRM Systems Product Manager

Chief Information Officer (CIO)
- Software R&D *Lewis Ramirez, Director*
- Operations *Tom Slade, Director*

VP of Client Services
- Consulting Services
- Implementation Services
- Client Training Services *Melissa O'Connell, Director*

VP of Sales
*Larry Edwards*
- Sales Force

VP of HR
*Elizabeth Henderson*
- Recruitment & Selection
- Benefits
- Curriculum Development *Jack Waterkamp, Director*

**Fast Facts**

No. of clients: 1,150
No. of employees: 877
Headquarters: Washington, DC
Sales/Training centers: Houston, TX; Toronto, Canada
Software suites: Financial Management; Human Resources

and I thought it would be best if the entire division heard the news at the same time." She reviewed the 3-year downward trend in revenues from both classroom-based training offered at Complex Data Systems and classroom-based training offered at individual client sites. "So," she concluded, "J.W. has decided that the training curriculum for the new CRM product and for our other training offerings should include both web-based and classroom-based training."

Jack immediately asked about timelines and resources. Although his current plan called for sales-ready, classroom-based CRM curriculum for the November product launch, he had not made provisions for scheduling and resourcing any web-based CRM training, or for any modifications to the curriculum of Complex Data Systems' other software products.

"I have good news and bad news," Elizabeth replied. "The good news is that the executive team did not mandate a timeframe for developing web-based training for our existing product line. The bad news is that the November delivery date for the CRM software product and training curriculum is not negotiable, nor is your budget and staffing."

When the meeting ended, Jack walked out of the meeting with two action items: revise the CRM Curriculum Development Project Charter to reflect the scope change resulting from the executive mandate and send it to Elizabeth for executive sign-off, and have a revised instructional design document with a project plan for completing the work ready for Elizabeth's approval at the end of the month. Using previous instructor-led classroom training development projects as a guideline, Jack had originally budgeted this project at $280,000, using his own staff, which consisted of one graphic artist, one audiovisual specialist, and one programmer. If what he had learned at industry conferences and from industry networking sites was accurate, he would need three to four times his current resource levels to add web-based training to the new CRM curriculum.

## The Following Week

Jack requested a meeting with three key individuals: Katherine Tracey, the CRM product manager; Lewis Ramirez, the software development R & D director; and Melissa O'Connell, the client training services director. He needed to get their feedback on his idea of confining the web-based CRM training to system administrators (SAs) responsible for deploying and maintaining the new software system. He began the meeting by explaining that the SAs are the group that is most critical to CRM product success. "So, what do you think?" Jack asked.

"I've got some serious concerns," Melissa began. "First of all, I've got 130 trainers, none of whom possesses experience with online training. I'm certainly not going to have them give up billable days in the field for them to learn how to train online and perhaps ruin a great record of high client satisfaction ratings. Besides," she declared, "I'm not convinced that the self-paced approach you used for the online refresher courses would work for new product training, even with SAs."

"SAs are tech savvy," Lewis countered, "and aren't as scared of online training as some of the functional users who are subject matter experts as far as what product features do, but know little about what's under the technology hood, so to speak. Besides, we've seen how well this works with SAs from the high satisfaction ratings for those online refresher courses."

"I don't see a problem, either," said Katherine. "Your trainers need to keep up with the times, and anyway, this is what our CEO wants."

Jack reminded the group that the executive mandate had two components—one short-term, related to the new CRM product launch, and the other long-term, related to adding web-based training to the total inventory of training offerings. He also reminded them that the immediate concern was the CRM launch. He noted that Complex Data Systems' semi-annual Train-the-Trainer Week would take place in May, providing an excellent opportunity for Melissa's trainers to learn about online facilitation.

Jack concluded the meeting by proposing next steps. "Let's have a two-week virtual work session on our company intranet," he said. "I'll post a revised instructional design document based on the SA target audience, then the three of us can work collaboratively to finalize it and flesh out a plan for completing the work. Lewis, would it be possible to host the new training modules on the password-protected Clients Only section of the company website? Our LMS hasn't been a hit with our clients."

"Work with Tom Slade in Operations on that," Lewis replied. "He's been hoping we'd replace that clunker of a system with something that's easy to maintain and doesn't add to his budget."

The next day, Jack e-mailed a summary of the previous day's meeting to Katherine, Melissa, and Lewis and included a link to the intranet workspace where he had posted a revised CRM Curriculum Development Project Charter. He also requested their electronic signatures on the charter if they agreed with his revisions.

"Before I sign," Melissa responded, "please highlight or bold the concerns that I expressed at the meeting."

Jack revised the Project Charter to include a bulleted list of all of Melissa's concerns (see Appendix 30–A) and uploaded the document to the intranet. Katherine and Lewis submitted their electronic signatures as requested. Two days later, Jack phoned Melissa and left her a voice mail asking for her electronic signature. In her e-mail reply, Melissa acknowledged receipt of his voice mail and of the link to the intranet workspace. Although Melissa had not "signed," Jack felt that her last e-mail was sufficient evidence that she was aware of what was discussed and agreed.

# Late February

The revised instructional design document and project plan were taking shape with a great deal of input from Katherine and a few tweaks from Lewis regarding the software's new technical specifications. Jack had just e-mailed Elizabeth his weekly project status report (Figure 30–2) when the phone rang.

"OK, Jack," Elizabeth began, "I can't wait to hear your explanation as to why Melissa thinks you're trying to eliminate classroom-based training."

**FIGURE 30–2**    CRM Curriculum Project Status Report.

**Project Status Report**

**Project name:** CRM Curriculum Training

**Team:** Curriculum Development Group

**Date:** February 27

**Design/Development Summary**

The CRM curriculum consists of two tracks:

1. System Administrator's (SA) Track
   a. Installation Foundations (web-based)
      i.   Pre-instructional video with audio
      ii.  Seven self-paced instructional modules based on slides created for classroom-based training
      iii. Practice tests after each module
      iv.  Posttest using data on client's CRM testing servers
      v.   Memory aids in the Tech Doc section of the Clients Only section of Complex Data Systems website
   b. Advanced topics (classroom-based)
      i.   Implementation
      ii.  Maintenance

2. Application End-User Track (classroom-based)
   Three segments per application × 22 applications = 66 segments
   a. Segment 1: System overview (2 days)
   b. Segment 2: Data entry and retrieval (4 days)
   c. Segment 3: Reporting (2 days)

**Posted to Our Intranet Workspace**

1. Revised Project Charter

2. Communications matrix describing the purpose/description of each communication needed for the project, the document or medium used, the audience, and frequency.

**Overall Project Status:** On schedule

"Perhaps she hasn't had a chance to review the minutes of our last meeting," Jack offered, "and is misremembering our goal of developing web-based training only for the system administrators to learn the product basics. All of our application end users will take our normal classroom-based training."

"Well, I suggest you get moving with the communications plan. The last thing we need is a misunderstanding that leads to panic among clients and employees."

"Already started," Jack assured her. "Katherine Tracey has been working with our Marketing Communications folks on a series of information briefings to our clients over the next couple of months. That should nip any potential misinformation in the bud."

Jack also noted that he would include the schedule of client briefings in his project status reports and in the project plan. With this assurance, Elizabeth signed off on the revised CRM Curriculum project plan.

# Early March to Mid-April

Jack's team was on time and on budget for both the web-based and the classroom-based components of the CRM curriculum. The Marketing team had launched a series of webinars announcing Complex Data Systems' plan to include web-based training opportunities for system administrators. Anecdotal information indicated a strong interest in the web-based training, and Jack was certain that he had neutralized the misinformation threat successfully. The next step was to figure out a way to incorporate online facilitation training into May's Train-the-Trainer Week schedule. He was about to send Melissa an e-mail about this, when he heard a sharp voice behind him.

"Where's the pricing, Waterkamp?" The tall man in the business suit walking toward him was Larry Edwards, the VP of Sales. "Look, I'm on board with this web-based training thing, but my folks don't have any pricing information or whether the clients get to choose their favorite trainers."

"As always, it is the product manager who submits a pricing proposal for executive approval six months before product launch," Jack replied. "My understanding is that Katherine won't have the CRM pricing ready until next month."

"I need it now," Larry pressed. "We've fired up the clients with those webinars and you know that our competitors have been offering training online for as little as $150 a pop."

"I'll e-mail Katherine and see if we can get some preliminary pricing by the end of April," Jack replied. "I'll copy you on the e-mail so you can follow up with her."

"Okay, but I hope the new pricing won't be a show stopper for new CRM sales," Larry added as he strode away. "If nobody buys, you've got nobody to train, online or otherwise."

"I'm on it, Larry," Jack called out.

After sending the pricing request to Katherine, Jack turned his attention back to online facilitation for the field trainers. He and Melissa had not yet agreed on how to include online facilitation into the May Train-the-Trainer Week program, particularly since she was not ready to delete anything from the standard program sessions. Jack picked up the phone and called Melissa.

"What if," he began, "we deliver the online facilitation training as an online workshop for a small group of trainers? Let's start with 10 trainers that you select to participate, and I'll develop and conduct the workshop myself, just as I did at my previous company. I'll even post the materials on the intranet in advance, making it easier for your road warriors," he concluded.

"You're the expert," Melissa replied. "Send me your workshop program, and I'll look it over."

"Great. Feel free to add comments or modifications, since you know your trainers better than I do."

The next day, Jack sent Melissa his workshop program. No sooner had he hit the "send" key than he received a brief reply agreeing to the program if it would contribute to the overall success of the project. She also promised to send out a call for volunteers to her trainers asking them to e-mail Jack if they would like to sign up for his online facilitation workshop.

## Two Weeks Later

Three days before the start of Train-the-Trainer Week, Jack still did not have a list of trainers for the online facilitation workshop. He sent out a broadcast e-mail to the Client Services division announcing the online facilitation workshop, its purpose, and its benefit to Client Services employees as well as to clients. Participation would be limited to the first 10 trainers who responded. Other trainers would be placed on a follow-up list for training at a later date. As a hook, he added that the workshop would be offered totally online, enabling participants to "practice what they are going to preach," and that all participants would receive a 16-GB USB flash drive as a token of thanks for participating. Jack knew he was taking a risk. Flash drives cost about $25, each and if he got a large response, it would certainly cut into his project budget. Nevertheless, he was determined to keep his project on track.

At the conclusion of Train-the-Trainer Week, Melissa sent Jack a brief e-mail. "I hear you not only reached your 10-person maximum, but pulled in an additional 47 trainers and 11 field consultants interested in your next online workshop," she wrote. "Congrats. You're a hero."

Jack smiled. Although he had to figure out a way to schedule more online workshops for the remaining 58 people on the follow-up list, as well as absorb the $1,700 hit to his project budget for the flash drives for all 68 participants, the enthusiastic responses were certainly worth it.

## Mid-June to Mid-September

Pilot testing of the SA track modules was going well, and Melissa's field trainers were reporting that they were becoming more comfortable with online facilitation. There had been several issues with the classroom-based offerings in both the SA and the end-user Applications tracks, but Jack was confident that his team would be able to make their usual last minute adjustments as needed.

As he monitored the software R & D area on the company intranet, Jack clicked on the link to the CRM GANTT chart, a bar chart that shows the project schedule, listing target start and finish dates for all project tasks (see Appendix 30–B). His heart sank as he compared the beta testing target completion dates with the graphic showing the percentage of work completed. Software testing of Module 1a should have been completed on June 22, but as of today, only 39% of the work had been completed. There was no indication on the graphic as to if and when that remaining work would be done. Upcoming test dates also appeared to be in question, with software testing of Module 1b scheduled to be completed next week, yet only 43% of the testing had been completed. Jack was sure that these delays would cascade into the software testing of the remaining modules.

Lewis had not posted any status changes to their collaborative work area, so Jack was puzzled by the apparent delays in the software beta testing. Jack phoned Lewis and left a detailed voice mail requesting project status clarification.

"I missed your reply to my voice mail," Jack said when he walked into Lewis' office the following afternoon. "Perhaps I'm not reading your GANTT chart correctly, but it looks like we've got some delays."

Lewis stood up and said, "I'm on my way to put out a fire, Jack. I'll get back to you as soon as I can."

As soon as Jack got back to his office, he saw the instant message alert at the bottom of his laptop screen with a request from Katherine to call him ASAP.

"Tiny glitch," she said. "It looks like a few critical pieces of functionality failed to be programmed into the software. We've got no automated direct mail, no database merge-purge of duplicate entries, and only one entry field for e-mail addresses. Your application end-user classroom sessions covering that functionality will have to be skipped during field testing."

"What about—" Jack began.

"There's more," she went on. "Several of the technical procedures required for system implementation have been altered, making three of the seven online modules in the SA track inaccurate. I'm working on getting the missing functionality restored and field tested in time for general delivery, but the technical procedures are another matter. Sorry, Jack," she said and hung up.

The next morning, Melissa burst into Jack's office.

"What's this about errors in the web-based modules?" she snapped. "This is going to blow my client satisfaction and trainer satisfaction ratings out of the water."

"Take it easy, Melissa," Jack said. "Katherine has already contacted our beta test clients about the software changes and—"

"This debacle is proof that web-based training doesn't work for new products," she declared as she stormed out.

As the beta testing process continued, Jack learned that Katherine had been successful in restoring some, but not all, of the missing functionality. However, the three web-based modules would still have to be reworked to accommodate changes to the software. In their weekly team meeting that Friday, Jack's staff balked at the idea of having to redo three of the web-based modules. Jerry Burns, the programmer, was the most vocal.

"We've already scheduled the updates to other workshops in our training inventory," Jerry said. "Do you want us to cancel those?"

When Jack nodded, Jerry added, "I've been here 11 years and can't remember when software beta testing has gone off without a hitch. I'll bet there will be a few more unpleasant surprises that are going to land in our laps."

Jack acknowledged that it was still unclear as to what the final software product would contain, because Katherine was still working on restoring the remaining pieces of functionality. He also reminded them that the CRM software would be delivered in November, with or without that functionality, and that it was his team's responsibility to deliver a sales-ready curriculum at the same time as the general delivery of the software. He was at the wheel, but how was he going to drive this curriculum project to successful completion?

# Preliminary Analysis Questions

1. To address the change in scope of the CRM curriculum project, announced in the February HR division meeting, Jack decided to focus on a subset of Complex Data's target audience, namely the system administrators. What other alternatives could Jack have considered to address the change in project scope? Discuss the pros and cons of each alternative.
2. One of the challenges of instructional design project management is knowing what the project manager should/should not be doing, particularly if a task or activity is deemed to be the responsibility of other project stakeholders. Review Jack's handling of the pricing issue with Lewis and the online facilitation workshop issue with Melissa. Explain whether or not Jack's actions were consistent with his role as CRM curriculum project manager.
3. Given the status of the software beta testing at the end of the case, how might Jack proceed to successfully complete the CRM curriculum by November? Keep in mind the budget and staffing constraints presented in the case as you explain and justify your recommendations.

# Implications for ID Practice

1. Develop a set of guidelines for formulating a communications plan to help manage the impact of changes to the scope of an instructional design project.
2. What role does a project charter play in managing changes to the scope of an instructional design project?
3. How can instructional designers develop instruction in the use of a product while the product is still being developed? Identify some potential "red flags" that indicate that product *training* development and product development are moving out of sync.

# APPENDIX 30–A

# Revised Project Charter

---

**Customer Relationship Management (CRM) Software System**

**Product Training Curriculum**

**Curriculum Development Group, Complex Data Systems, Inc.**

Version: 1.5                                         Revision Date: February 12

Approval of the Project Charter indicates an understanding of the purpose and content described in this document. By signing this document, each individual agrees work should be initiated on this project and necessary resources should be committed as described herein.

| Approver Name | Title | E-signature Received On: |
|---|---|---|
| Katherine Tracey | Product Manager, CRM | 02/13 |
| Lewis Ramirez | Director, Software R & D | 02/15 |
| Melissa O'Connell | Director, Client Training Services | E-mail acknowledgment of link to intranet workspace received on 02/18 |
| E. Henderson | VP, HR | 02/21 |

1. **Problem Statement**

   Revenues from classroom-based training as well as from on-site training at client offices have been declining. Anecdotal information from field consultants suggests that in addition to the problem of tight budgets, clients are dealing with smaller numbers of staff unable to take time out from busy schedules to attend training. At the same time, new, more complex software products, as well as updates to older products, demand a well-trained user for successful implementation.

2. **Project Description**

This project will enhance Complex Data Systems' training revenue potential by providing CRM clients with web-based learning opportunities alongside classroom-based training events.

3. **Project Approach**

This project will be undertaken as an add-on to the current CRM Curriculum Training development Project Charter (version 1.0). The current classroom-based CRM Curriculum targets technical System Administrators (SAs) and functional users. The add-on web-based training will target SAs only.

4. **Project Scope**

Project includes:

- Review of current CRM training topics to determine which can be parsed to include web-based as well as classroom-based components
- Small group evaluation and field testing of online and classroom-based components concurrent with the 90-day software beta testing cycle
- Standard pre-launch orientation and training of Complex Data Systems field trainers/consultants
- Standard pre-launch orientation of Complex Data Systems sales force

Project excludes the creation by the Curriculum Development Group of web-based training for Complex Data Systems products other than the new CRM software system.

5. **Critical Success Factors**

- A written communications plan that indicates the following:
  - Who needs what information
  - When information is needed
  - How information will be given
  - Who will provide the information

6. **Assumptions/Constraints**

- There is strong corporate commitment to offering web-based training to both clients and employees
- Any web-based training offerings must not replicate, and thus not cannibalize, the classroom-based offerings
- Pilot testing of the web-based training components will include an assessment of client satisfaction with/attitudes toward online versus classroom training
- The expansion of project scope to include web-based training components must be accomplished within the current budget of $280,000 and with the current four-person Curriculum Development group staff

7. **Potential Risks for Client Training Services (per M. O'Connell)**

- Client Services field trainers have no experience with online training facilitation
- Client Services field trainers need to be trained in online facilitation without sacrificing either billable days or client satisfaction
- Effectiveness of online format for new product training is unproven

### 8. Major Milestones

| Milestones/Deliverables | Target Completion Date |
| --- | --- |
| Development of web-based components for SAs | March |
| Announcement of web-based opportunities to clients | April |
| Online facilitation training for Client Services field trainers | May |
| Curriculum pilot testing | September |
| Sales-ready curriculum launch | November |

### 9. Project Stakeholders

| Role | Name/Title/Organization | E-mail |
| --- | --- | --- |
| Project Manager | Jack Waterkamp, Director, Curriculum Development | jwaterkamp@complexdata.com |
| Executive Sponsor | Elizabeth Henderson, HR VP | ehenderson@complexdata.com |
| Subject Matter Expert (SME) | Katherine Tracey, CRM Product Manager | ktracey@complexdata.com |
| Implementation | Melissa O'Connell, Client Training Services Director | moconnell@complexdata.com |
| Software Product Development | Lewis Ramirez, Director, R & D | lramirez@complexdata.com |
| Training Module Hosting | Tom Slade, Operations Director | tslade1@complexdata.com |
| Product and Training Sales | Larry Edwards, VP Sales | ledwards@complexdata.com |

### 10. Revision History

| Version | Date | Name | Description |
| --- | --- | --- | --- |
| 1.0 | 02/04 | J. Waterkamp | Version approved by E. Henderson |
| 1.5 | 02/18 | J. Waterkamp | Scope changed to include web-based offerings as add-on |

# CRM Software Development GANTT Chart

Report generated on: 07/06

CRM Software Suite:
Beta Test Phase

| Project Lead: | Division: | | | Workday | Th | F | M | T | W | Th | F |
|---|---|---|---|---|---|---|---|---|---|---|---|
| Lewis Ramirez (Product) | Software R & D | | | | 6/30 | 7/1 | 7/4 | 7/5 | 7/6 | 7/7 | 7/8 |
| Jack Waterkamp (Training) | Curriculum Development | | | | | | Holiday | | | | |
| Tasks | Target Start | Target End | % Complete | | | | | | | | |
| Beta Setup | 5/30 | 6/3 | 100% | | | | | | | | |
| Package beta software bundle | 5/30 | 5/31 | 100% | | | | | | | | |
| Installation Foundations training beta (Web-based) | 5/30 | 6/3 | 100% | | | | | | | | |
| Ship to beta software clients | 6/1 | 6/1 | 100% | | | | | | | | |
| Technical systems check | 6/2 | 6/2 | 100% | | | | | | | | |
| Documentation check | 6/3 | 6/3 | 100% | | | | | | | | |
| Beta Test | 6/6 | 9/28 | | | | | | | | | |
| Module 1a (All Apps) | 6/6 | 6/22 | 39% | | | | | | | | |
| Classroom training | 6/6 | 6/15 | 100% | | | | | | | | |
| Software testing | 6/6 | 6/22 | 39% | | | | | | | | |
| Module 1b (All Apps) | 6/23 | 7/13 | 43% | | | | | | | | |
| Classroom training | 6/23 | 7/6 | 100% | | | | | | | | |
| Software testing | 6/23 | 7/13 | 43% | | | | | | | | |
| Module 2 (All Apps) | 7/14 | 8/21 | 0% | | | | | | | | |
| On-site classroom training | 7/14 | 7/27 | 0% | | | | | | | | |
| Software testing | 7/14 | 8/21 | 0% | | | | | | | | |
| Module 3 (All Apps) | 8/24 | 9/28 | 0% | | | | | | | | |
| On-site classroom training | 8/24 | 9/2 | 0% | | | | | | | | |
| Software testing | 8/22 | 9/28 | 0% | | | | | | | | |
| Legend | | | | | | | | | | | |
| | Work completed | | | | | | | | | | |
| | Work remaining | | | | | | | | | | |
| | Work not started | | | | | | | | | | |